100 Careers in the

Music Business

2nd Edition

100 Careers in the

Music Business

2nd Edition

Tanja L. Crouch

BARRON'S

Published in 2008, 2001 by Barron's Educational Series, Inc.
Text © Copyright 2008, 2001 by Tanja L. Crouch
Text design and cover © Copyright 2008, 2001 by Barron's Educational Series, Inc.

All inquiries should be addressed to:
Barron's Educational Series, Inc.
250 Wireless Blvd.
Hauppauge, NY 11788
www.barronseduc.com

ISBN-13: 978-0-7641-3914-7
ISBN-10: 0-7641-3914-2

Library of Congress Catalog Card No.: 2008005034

Library of Congress Cataloging-in-Publication Data

Crouch, Tanja.
    100 careers in the music business / Tanja L. Crouch.—2nd ed.
        p. cm.
    Includes bibliographical references.
    ISBN-13: 978-0-7641-3914-7
    ISBN-10: 0-7641-3914-2
    1. Music—Vocational guidance. 2. Music trade—Vocational guidance.   I. Title.
II. Title: One hundred careers in the music business.

    ML3795.C74   2008
    780.23—dc22

                                                                              2008005034

Printed in the United States of America
9 8 7 6 5 4 3 2 1

CONTENTS

APPENDICES

INTRODUCTION

I grew up in a small Eastern Oregon town where the only people I knew in the music business were my high school band and choir teachers and my piano and voice instructors. Although music filled my life—my father played guitar and sang in barbershop quartets, he and my mother sang in church choir, my brother had a garage rock and roll band, and I was instructed in piano, saxophone, clarinet, and voice—it never occurred to me that if I didn't pursue a career as a performer, I could still combine my love of music with a job and work in the business side of music. Job titles like song plugger, engineer, promotion director, A&R, and road manager were not only foreign to my ear, but completely out of my realm of understanding. Never did I dream I would one day become an agent, working on tours for artists like Vince Gill, George Michael, Roy Orbison, Tina Turner, Randy Travis, and others, nor that I would one day manage an artist, run a publishing company whose writers wrote number one songs for Brooks & Dunn, Martina McBride, Reba, and George Strait, place music in film and television programs such as *In Dreams, For the Love of the Game, Love Letter, You've Got Mail, Ally McBeal, Beverly Hills, 90210,* and *Felicity,* travel around the world representing the Roy Orbison estate song catalog and masters, or write and produce music documentaries and books.

I did not discover the business side of music until I was 26 and took a temporary job at the Triad Artists, Inc. talent agency. Within a week, I was hired as assistant to agent Rick Shipp and my career was launched. It took me a few more years to discover the depth of possibilities for talented people to express their creative skills in the music business. Today I am still discovering new avenues and am often impressed by those who saw a need and carved out their own careers, making something new, indispensable.

This book is meant as an inspiration and catalyst for those who want to pursue a career in the business side of the music industry. The book presents over 100 jobs with descriptions and explanations of duties and functions, and profiles individuals working in those capacities, sharing their personal journeys of how they got where they are today and offering invaluable advice on how to break into the business and become successful.

Each person profiled was specifically interviewed for this book. Their comments are not excerpts from other interviews. In talking with each person, there are four recurring themes that emerged:

1. **THE IMPORTANCE OF EDUCATION.** While some in this book do not have a college degree, many of them agreed that in today's marketplace it is an advantage, and in some cases has become a prerequisite for admission into company training programs. Of equal importance is self-education. Read every book and magazine you can find about the industry, educate yourself about

the business and trends, and become familiar with names of important individuals.

2. **NETWORKING IS VITAL.** The adage "It's who you know" is true. Success in the music business is a team effort and when building your team, you pick the players you know you can work with. There are many organizations in need of volunteers to work on a broad range of events. Find a place where you can serve the music community. In return, you will meet people and they will have a chance to see your talents and work ethic shine.

3. **INTERNSHIPS.** Internships are invaluable for providing you with a look inside the industry and allowing others to evaluate your skills and work ethic for potential employment. Several of those profiled in this book expound on the importance of gaining practical experience through an internship program and many describe individuals who were hired as a result.

4. **FIND A MENTOR.** Some colleges will link students with an industry mentor while still in school. Many find their mentor early in their career. Find someone who you respect and admire and make a connection with that person. A mentor can offer advice and help you navigate your career through the industry to minimize stumbles and maximize successes. Everyone can use a role model and champion in their life.

Working in the music business is exciting. Thus there are thousands of people competing for the job you want. Someone has to fill the job and that someone can be you. Prepare yourself by studying the industry, arm yourself with skills, and be prepared to start at the bottom. Work hard and passionately, and you will succeed.

CHAPTER 1

COMPOSING— SONGWRITING

"It all begins with a song" is a phrase often heard within the music community. Songs are the foundation of the music business. Without a songwriter to pen words and compose a melody, the most remarkable voice would never be heard.

Many songwriters and composers drift between writing songs for artists and having their songs used in film, television, and advertising. The songwriters profiled in this chapter have been categorized by primary role and are divided into three categories: Songwriter for Recording Artists, Composer/Songwriter for Film and Television, and Composer/Songwriter for Advertising.

SONGWRITER FOR RECORDING ARTISTS

COMPOSER • LYRICIST • SONGWRITER • WRITER

JOB OVERVIEW

Songwriters compose music, write lyrics, or both. Individual songwriters approach the business of writing in many different ways. Some schedule daily time to write alone or with a co-writer. Others wait until inspiration strikes and then they write until that song is finished. Most are comfortable writing both words and melody, but some may only compose music or write the lyrics. Artist/writers and producer/writers generally focus on writing songs for their upcoming album, while many songwriters compose their best song, and then choose which artists to submit it to.

FUNDAMENTAL SKILLS

While playing an instrument is not a requirement, it is an asset. Most songwriters can play guitar or piano. "Having an ear for harmonies and the basic knowledge of chords," adds Jennifer Kimball. "Having an ear for the cadence of words."

A DAY IN THE LIFE

Many publishers provide a writing room for their staff songwriters. This is particularly true in Nashville, where most writers keep regimented schedules, booking co-writing appointments at 10 A.M. and 2 P.M. daily. Other writers, particularly those with home recording studios or music rooms, will begin work on an idea and continue until they have completed the song, or reached total exhaustion. Often, they will lay down tracks or record work in process.

AFTER THE SONG IS WRITTEN

If a writer is signed to a publishing company, he turns in work tapes and lyric sheets for his publisher to approve a demo recording session. Very successful writers may skip the approval process and schedule a session whenever they feel they have enough songs to record. Writers who own their own studios may complete the demo before playing it for their publisher. Typically, once the demo is complete, it becomes the publisher's job to get the song recorded. Many writers have their own connections and will also pitch the song. The ultimate goals of songwriters are to have their songs recorded and have them become hits or standards.

CAREER TIPS

Keep a notebook with hook lines and ideas for songs jotted inside. This may be the same book used to record lyrics and music notes as you write. It is a good idea to carry pen and paper or a portable cassette player with you at all times so you can write down or record ideas as they come.

Always carry a portable cassette recorder to writing sessions so you have a record of the work in progress and to ensure ideas are not forgotten. At the end of the session, record a rough copy of the completed work.

"Songwriting is mind discipline. Always be working on something."—WJ

"The best songwriters have good people skills. Other people want to write with them and they can present themselves well when they're pitching songs."—JK

POINTERS FOR THE JOB SEARCH

In most cases, if you are just beginning and want to become a successful songwriter (one whose songs are recorded and earn money) you need to live where the core of the business is—Los Angeles, New York, or Nashville. Once you become an established writer, or have a publisher pitching your songs, you can live virtually anywhere you want. Until you have established a track record, you must be where you can network with other songwriters, publishers, artists, producers, and people in the business who can help you. Many writers begin by making regular trips to one or all of these cities to develop contacts before making a permanent move.

Before making the trip to one of these cities, contact a writer relations representative at one of the performing rights societies: ASCAP, BMI, SESAC (see Appendix). Explain that you are a songwriter who is planning an eventual move and that you are coming to check out the area first. Inquire about upcoming writer showcases, workshops, or other events that might be of interest to you and plan your trip around them. Ask about clubs in the city that feature writers and consider their suggestions for networking opportunities with other writers.

Make a friend with someone at one of the societies and this person might be the very one who will champion your cause to become a successful songwriter. Never underestimate the power of relationships. Next, ask this person to spare a few minutes to meet with you, listen to a couple of your songs, and give you feedback. Try to meet with a representative from each of the societies, but do not sign with one until you feel you have made a connection with a representative who will be there for moral support. Since the society is there to collect your performance money, you do not need to sign with one until you actually have a song cut and there is money to collect.

PREPARING FOR YOUR FIRST TRIP

Select two to three of your very best songs and make a guitar or piano and vocal demo of them. If you have access to a studio, you may want to do a more elaborate demo, particularly if you are a programmer or you need it to display the particular sound of the song. Do not spend money you don't have. Most publishers are able to hear the song from a simple guitar or piano and vocal demo, and many prefer it. Print lyric sheets for each of the song samples you plan to take. You should have several copies of the songs with lyrics that you can give to people without expecting them to be returned to you. Make sure your name, address, and telephone number, as well as the title of each song and writer credit (your name and all co-writers) are on the cassette and the lyric sheets.

POINTERS FOR THE JOB SEARCH

Without being overly pushy, try to get your songs heard by other writers and publishers. Remember though, while you might have great potential, it is more likely you still need to hone your craft. There are many writers who have success in getting songs recorded who are without publishing deals. Signing an unproven writer is a big risk. Be humble and grateful for any meeting, criticism, or help you receive. These are people you potentially want to work with. Ask writers you admire if they would like to co-write with you. This is a great way to get to know people in the business and improve your writing skills. Do not be discouraged if you are turned down, because it may simply mean the writer has his schedule filled, or that he doesn't want to start with a new writer. Find someone else to ask until you get a "yes."

CASE STUDY:

WILL JENNINGS, SONGWRITER, COMPOSER

East Texas native Will Jennings' lifelong love of music began in his childhood through the traditional musical forms of the South: blues, country, and gospel. His first instrument was the trombone, but after being exposed to jazz in his teen years, he switched to the guitar. The guitar meshed naturally with Jennings' gift for writing poetry, forming the beginning of his songwriting career. Eventually, he earned a

VOICES OF EXPERIENCE

THE LEAST FAVORITE THING ABOUT THIS JOB:

"You never know what's going to happen."—WJ

"Rejection—we get many more songs not cut, than cut. Many of them are as dear to us as the ones that do get cut, so it's hard to stay positive and excited. The gap between the creation and your reward; you have to take your pleasure in the creation because it may be years and years and years before the song gets recorded—it may never get recorded."—JK

THE BEST THING ABOUT THIS JOB:

"You never know what's going to happen."—WJ

"The joy of creation is definitely the best part of this job. It's a great job that allows you an incredible lifestyle to work when you want to."—JK

Masters degree in music, teaching for three years at a junior college in Tyler, Texas, and three years at the University of Wisconsin at Eau Claire.

In 1971, Jennings made a leap into the unknown, moving to Nashville to try his hand as a professional songwriter. "I became a songwriter because I couldn't make a living as a teacher. It was something that I had to do for self-preservation. I had to give it a shot." Arriving in town with a tiny bankroll, he began making the rounds of local clubs, where he met fellow songwriter, Troy Seals. They wrote together without pay for a fledgling publishing company, scraping by for several months until some of their songs were recorded. The break came when Dobie Gray ("Drift Away") recorded several of Jennings' tunes on his *Shift to White* album. Following that, Jennings' work began to attract attention.

After signing with Almo Irving Music Publishing in 1974 and moving to Los Angeles, Jennings commuted between the West Coast and Nashville for several years. His first sound track writing was in the film *Casey's Shadow*, but it was two more years before he got another chance. While sound track work eventually brought him the greatest publicity, Jennings views it as being a separate, but parallel, career to his songwriting. Signed to Warner Chappell Music in 1981, his second film was *An Officer and A Gentleman*, for which he co-wrote the theme "Up Where We Belong," and won an Academy Award for Best Original Song.

More film work followed, and in between, Jennings wrote such hits as "Didn't We Almost Have It All" (Whitney Houston); "Looks Like We Made It" and "Somewhere In The Night" (Barry Manilow); "Finer Things," "Higher Love," and "Roll With It" (Steve Winwood); and "Tears in Heaven" (Eric Clapton). He won a Golden Globe, an Academy Award, and a Grammy Award for "My Heart Will Go On" (Celine Dion), the theme from the film *Titanic*. His songs continue to provide the perfect mood for film and television, including *Moulin Rouge!, A Beautiful Mind; How to Lose a Guy in 10 Days; Yours, Mine and Ours;* and *Freedom Writers*.

CASE STUDY:

JENNIFER KIMBALL, SONGWRITER

"I didn't really think I would be in the music business. I thought I was going to be an actress when I was in high school," says Jennifer Kimball, who grew up all over the world, wherever the Army stationed her father. At the University of Alabama, Kimball focused on a career as a college professor, but in her senior year she met a budding singer/songwriter named Tom Kimmel and her path was changed forever. She became a background singer for Tom and an editor of his songs. Along the way they fell in love—"that's how I got in the music business." A year later they married and moved to New England, "where we thought we'd make our fame and fortune." Notoriety and wealth eluded them and after a year, they moved back to Alabama to regroup. Tom had jobs at two different factories while Jennifer worked in an office.

After a year, Jennifer yearned to give music another shot and drove to Nashville one weekend with demo tapes in hand.

"People saw me," she muses, "God knows why they did." Troy Seals was one who liked what he heard and arranged for Almo Irving Publishing to fly the Kimmels back to Nashville to work with him. "He did it on my voice. He was producing me as a singer." Seals also signed a deal to acquire some of Tom's songs and co-wrote with him. Later that year, they moved to Nashville and Tom took a job cleaning studios "as a janitor, like Kris Kristofferson." Through a relative they got a meeting with producer/songwriter Alan Reynolds.

Reynolds recommended them to Roger Cook and Charles Cochran, who hired Jennifer as a demo singer. "Charles got me an audition with Crystal Gayle and within six months I was singing backgrounds on the road with her." Not long after, the couple separated and divorced. In the wake, Jennifer took up songwriting. Building on what she had learned about the craft from Tom, she experienced quick success. "One of my first songs, 'Fool, Fool Heart,' was cut by Don Williams."

Gayle band mate, saxophonist Jay Patton, introduced Jennifer to his publisher at Sony Tree (now Sony/ATV Music). "They published my first songs for 100 percent of the publishing and no draw," Kimball laughs. "But I still love those people, especially Donna Hilley. It was a family atmosphere and very inspirational to be around all those greats—Sunny Throckmorton, Bobby Braddock, Curly Putman. It was an incredible place, as a beginning songwriter, to be a small part of it. They gave me free studio time in those days—24 track and great players."

Kimball built on the Williams success with smaller cuts and eventually landed a publishing deal with an advance. Her first pop hit came in 1984. Co-written with fellow background singer Cindy Walker, "Almost Over You" was a smash for Sheena Easton. ("We wrote it in the dressing room at Caesar's Palace, between shows.") The following year, Kimball was awarded Country Music Association's 1985 Single of the Year for her song "Bop," recorded by Dan Seals.

Kimball has gone on to score several number ones including the mega-hit "I Can Love You Like That," which All-4-One took to the top of the Billboard AC single charts for three weeks, and hit number three on Billboard Hot 100. Their version of the song was nominated for two Grammys and won ASCAP Pop Awards in 1996, 1997, and 1998, BMI Pop Awards in 1996 and 1997, and was featured in the Disney film *First Kid*. John Michael Montgomery's recording of the song landed the number one slot on the country charts for three weeks and was also nominated for two Grammy Awards. It was named 1996 ASCAP Country Song of the Year and received BMI's 1996 Most Performed Country Song Award. Her co-written Brooks & Dunn/Reba duet "If You See Him/If You See Her" earned another Grammy nomination. Others who have recorded songs penned by Kimball include America, Johnny Cash, Faith Hill, Bette Midler, and The Trio: Emmylou Harris, Dolly Parton, and Linda Ronstadt.

COMPOSER/SONGWRITER FOR FILM AND TELEVISION

COMPOSER • LYRICIST • SONGWRITER • WRITER (FILM AND TELEVISION)

JOB OVERVIEW

Composers/songwriters for film and television compose music, write lyrics, or both, and often produce the music recording.

SPECIAL SKILLS

Many composers are adept at playing piano, sequencer, synthesizer, or a combination of the three, and most have the ability to produce the music they write. Success requires the ability to compose memorable melodies and lyrics.

"Writing a score is a different skill than songwriting, where you come up with a melody and you either write a lyric yourself, or you collaborate with another person, and you write a song," says Steve Dorff. "Writing a score for a film is an integral part

CAREER TIPS

"There are a lot of people that have a gift, but that don't have the innate common sense and the innate tenacity that it takes to be successful over a long period of time. Anybody can have a hit, but to succeed over and over and over again, over a 20- to 25-year period, requires that intangible thing that allows you to pick yourself up and dust yourself off when you have bitter disappointments."

"Stay grounded when you're having a tremendous cycle of success. Always have a couple of balls in the air at the same time. It's hard when you've only got one thing that you're doing, you finish it, and you have to get something else going. It's easier to always try and have something in the wings waiting to segue to."

"I've spent a lot of time learning all facets of the business side of music. Take the time to read contracts and learn about what publishing and subpublishing is. You should know what you're getting into. Become a well-rounded, intelligent person about the business side of any field you're entering into."

THE LEAST FAVORITE THING ABOUT THIS JOB:

"Having time on my hands, when I'm not busy. That's frustrating for me."

THE BEST THING ABOUT THIS JOB:

"I love being busy. I love the actual going into the studio and recording with an orchestra. Hearing for the first time those things that I only heard in my head. When it works, that's my favorite part."

of the post production process, where you're musicalizing every moment of the movie with orchestral or some kind of music, generally without lyrics, that underscores the action, whether it is romantic, action-adventure, scary, or exciting. The creative process is the same with television as it is with film. The only difference being, there is a much smaller budget for television than for film."

A DAY IN THE LIFE

Steve Dorff is usually in his studio by ten each morning. "I generally co-write, so I'll usually set up an appointment once or twice a week with a co-writer." When not booked with a co-writer, he works on his own ideas or may demo out a song. "When I'm working on a film or television series, my time is much more scheduled. I'm usually writing and/or orchestrating, looking at the film, from nine in the morning until two or three in the afternoon, everyday. It generally takes six to eight weeks to complete a film score. I'll work four to five days a week, five to six hours a day, looking at the film and creating motifs for the different elements, orchestrating, or putting thematic ideas down on tape."

POINTERS FOR THE JOB SEARCH

To gain some experience composing songs or scoring for film, contact film schools and make yourself available to student filmmakers.

"Really try to understand the business. When you read books and manuals, know what the games are and know what the pitfalls are. Know that just writing a song is only half of it. Knowing what to do with a song after you've written it is maybe even more than half of it. You need to know how to demo it, how to pitch it, how to present it. I'm not going to open the hood of a car and try to fix a carburetor without knowing what I'm doing."

The transition from songwriter to film composer for Will Jennings came through a request from his publisher to write a song for a movie. It took another two years and a change of publisher before he got another film opportunity. In the interim, he continued to write songs for various recording artists.

CASE STUDY:

STEVE DORFF, SONGWRITER—COMPOSER

"I always wanted to do music for movies," says Steve Dorff. He started playing the piano at age four and was composing little tunes soon after. He began writing songs in junior high school and formed a rock and roll band, emulating the Beatles. To appease his parents, he enrolled at the University of Georgia, getting a degree in journalism, but his real interest remained songwriting. After graduation, he traveled between Atlanta and Nashville trying to break into the music business, finally landing his first songwriting contract with Lowry Music in Atlanta. While he dreamed of writing music for films, it took about four and a half years before he made the move to California.

Arriving in Los Angeles in 1974 without any contacts, and just enough money to last for two weeks, Dorff began making the rounds. "I just knocked on doors." A demo tape he left for producer Snuff Garrett resulted in an audition and a contract for $250 per week. Dorff cut his musical teeth writing for five of Clint Eastwood's movies (among them, *Every Which Way But Loose* and *Bronco Billy*), producing seven number one hits in a row.

In 1984, Dorff signed a co-publishing deal with Warner Chappell Music, scoring music for television shows that included *Growing Pains, My Sister Sam, Murphy Brown,* and *Reba.* With production partner and lyricist John Bettis, Dorff wrote the Broadway musical *Say Goodnight,* which is based on the life of George Burns and Gracie Allen. He continues to write for films (*Blast from the Past, Michael, Tin Cup, Jake's Corner, Small Town Saturday Night,* and many more), as well as write hit songs for artists such as Barbra Streisand, Whitney Houston, and George Strait. Dorff and lyricist Marty Panzer are recipients of an 8 million performance award from BMI for the Kenny Rogers hit "Through the Years."

COMPOSER/SONGWRITER FOR ADVERTISING

JINGLE WRITER/PRODUCER • COMMERCIAL MUSIC PRODUCER • ADVERTISING COMPOSER • SONGWRITER/PRODUCER

JOB OVERVIEW

Composers/songwriters for advertising write, arrange, produce, and record music for commercial advertising.

SPECIAL SKILLS

To succeed, you must be creative, have the ability to compose music and lyrics, and be able to produce recordings of your ideas.

A DAY IN THE LIFE

Being the owner, as well as the creative force at Hummingbird, Bob Farnsworth's day is filled with both business and artistic tasks. "Today I came in and had to deal with tax issues with our bookkeeper. Then I had three clients that each called about projects we're working on. Often I'll have calls that have to do with some marketing aspect of the company. Typically I spend some time planning various projects. By afternoon I may be taking instructions on a specific account and then determining budgets for demos. I might call up four or five outside writers and ask them to present me with demo'd ideas. I would provide them with an assignment sheet with pertinent information such as demographics of the target audience, whether there should be lyrics, if it is for radio or television, style of music, if it's a national or regional campaign, and so forth. While they each write a pitch, I'm writing my idea as well." After sketching out some rough ideas, Farnsworth may call his agency contact and present them, getting feedback about which ones he should develop. He then takes the new information and filters it back to the team of writers that is working on additional ideas. On any given day Farnsworth may spend time in the recording studio laying down tracks, or mixing a project, until 7:30 or 8 P.M.

POINTERS FOR THE JOB SEARCH

Record a demo reel with campaigns you would propose for a specific product if you had the account. Approach small, regional companies to gain experience. Talk

VOICES OF EXPERIENCE

THE LEAST FAVORITE THING ABOUT THIS JOB:

"*There is no loyalty and you have to constantly prove yourself over and over again.*"

THE BEST THING ABOUT THIS JOB:

"*The moments I love the most are when you have musicians in the studio and they like what you're doing, and you can see they are having fun playing what you've written. You've got your headphones on and it starts to come together, and you realize your idea is much better than you thought it was going to be. It really feels like a great piece of music.*"

with radio stations and seek opportunities to handle some of their advertising spots. "My advice would be to consider the pros and cons of the area you want to be involved in. Pro: the advertising industry can be a more financially stable source of income than the record industry. Con: it is incredibly competitive and there is not a great amount of loyalty; you have to constantly prove yourself over again. Perhaps the biggest pro is that you have an opportunity to write, perform, and produce all kinds of music."

CASE STUDY:

BOB FARNSWORTH, CEO, HUMMINGBIRD PRODUCTIONS

Bob Farnsworth came to Nashville in 1974 with a simple plan: make a quick million or two as a recording artist to finance his dream of being a missionary along the Amazon River. Amazingly, he and partner Mike Hudson landed a recording contract with ABC Records within weeks of their arrival. Although critically acclaimed as the heirs to Simon and Garfunkel, the duo's album was scorched in the first wave of disco inferno.

With his recording career in flames and faced with the prospect of returning to South Carolina to sell life insurance, Farnsworth sought another way to use his musical abilities. He opened Hummingbird Productions and built a reputation for award winning, but off-the-wall, jingles and advertising campaigns. Beginning with regional advertising, his first job was for a Knoxville company. "I told them, 'Look, I'm a recording artist. I can assure you I can do a jingle. Just give me a shot.'" Told to deliver "something really different," Farnsworth returned with a commercial that featured a granny killing her husband and chopping him up for sausage. He was thrown out of the office. Undaunted, he continued to pursue regional work and soon progressed to national campaigns for customers such as Kellogg's, McDonald's, and Walt Disney.

On the strength of these successes, Farnsworth opened Hummingbird offices in New York and Chicago, continuing to gain an industry reputation for the diversity of his product. As the needs of the advertising business changed, these branch offices were eventually phased out, but Farnsworth's ability to give advertisers something new and different kept increasing. His Budweiser Frogs campaign is now an industry legend and earned him a Clio Hall of Fame Award. The Hummingbird library contains over 7000 works, including Farnsworth compositions for Coke, Pepsi, and McDonald's. Farnsworth has also composed music for numerous IMAX Signature films. *www.hummingbirdproductions.com*

CHAPTER

2

MUSIC PUBLISHING

Publishers are song salesmen. They are in the business of obtaining copyrights by signing staff writers or purchasing existing catalog and exploiting their use. They do this by licensing song rights to artists, record companies, film and television studios, and advertisers. The publisher negotiates and issues licenses for songs, collects earnings, and ensures that proper royalties are paid. Publishers also act as managers of the songwriter's career. They critique newly written songs and give creative input, publicize the writer's achievements, and set career goals. An essential role of the publisher is to introduce the writer to other songwriters, artists, and producers with whom they may co-write or pitch songs to. Publishers also may try to secure recording contracts for artist/writers or production jobs for producer/writers.

This chapter focuses on five areas of music publishing: Executive Office; Creative Services; Film, Television and Advertising Licensing; Business Affairs; and International. Similar names are often used to define departments within large publishing firms, while smaller companies may only divide the responsibilities into Creative Services and Business Affairs or Administration.

EXECUTIVE OFFICE

**CHIEF EXECUTIVE OFFICER • PRESIDENT • VICE PRESIDENT/
GENERAL MANAGER (MAJOR MUSIC PUBLISHER)**

JOB OVERVIEW

These chief executives chart the direction of a company, manage daily operations, and ultimately are responsible for all business decisions, including selling or acquiring catalogs and signing new writers. At Windswept Pacific, Jonathan Stone oversees all aspects of the day-to-day operations and provides motivation and direction for the staff of 60. His primary focus is to discover and sign songwriters, whether they are artists, writers, or producers, and to acquire existing song catalogs. He is also heavily involved in the area of film and television music and works closely with the firm's in-house music supervisors.

PREREQUISITES

To be successful, you must have the ability to recognize good songs and talented songwriters. It is important to have a broad knowledge of how the music

"Patience is important. It takes a long time to see the fruits of our labor in the music publishing business. From the time you find a writer, sign him, and get a song cut, it's another two or three years before you see any money from your investment."

industry works and solid personal contacts within it. To achieve an executive position, you must have an understanding of publishing contracts and copyright law in the United States and around the world. The capacity to motivate and work closely with a diverse group of people is also helpful.

A DAY IN THE LIFE

A large part of Stone's day is spent on the telephone with lawyers negotiating contracts, discussing pending deals, and exchanging information with music industry contacts about potential acquisitions. "I'm constantly working the phones trying to find new catalogs to acquire. I have an open door policy. My staff is in almost every ten minutes with news that they've heard, and we're constantly sifting through all the information that comes into our company on a daily basis, picking and choosing. I listen constantly to music and analyze new deals." Scattered throughout the day, Stone has meetings inside and outside the company with songwriters and artists, often going out to see them perform at showcases or concerts. Part of his day is spent talking with staff songwriters about upcoming projects or renegotiating contracts, and attempting to interact with all 60 employees on a daily basis. "It's not uncommon to have 10- or 11-hour days."

Listen to what songwriters say. Listen between the lines when talking with Artist & Repertoire (A&R) people and producers to discover what they are really looking for. Listen for information that can help you be successful.

No job is too small when you are trying to get your foot in the door. Be the best tape copy or lyric typist there is and use the opportunity to listen and learn.

POINTERS FOR THE JOB SEARCH

Apply for an internship or an entry level position as a receptionist, in the mail room, or tape copy, and discover if publishing is for you. "At our company, we've promoted almost every intern that stayed with us," says Stone. "People that started with us in the mail room have been promoted. Secretaries and receptionists—one of our former receptionists is now our director of creative services."

"Music publishing is the less talked about, or less known part of the business, but it's also the most solid. Friends of mine have been in music publishing for years and years. Once you get a little bit of that fever, working with writers in the very infancy of their careers and developing them, it can be very rewarding."

VOICES OF EXPERIENCE

THE LEAST FAVORITE THING ABOUT THIS JOB:

"When you have built relationships and helped develop the careers of writers, producers, and artists and then you come to the end of their first publishing agreement, and have to go about the process of renegotiating a new deal, it can be a challenging and sensitive process because you've developed friendships. Nine times out of ten we manage to keep people. It's not real pleasant when something you've worked on and developed is walking out the door and going to see every other publisher in town. That's a challenge."

THE BEST THING ABOUT THIS JOB:

"I love the very first time that I hear something. Somebody sends me a song by a writer, a band, or a writer/producer and I hear something new that I think is just fantastic. I love bringing the person in and showing them the genuine enthusiasm I have for their music. I get a little star struck. When somebody really puts together a fine piece of work—whether it's country, or rap, or R&B, or pop, or rock, no matter what it is—I get very excited about that. The next step is to meet the person and spend time with them; to relay the enthusiasm I have and to see their eyes kind of light up because there is someone that is excited about what they are doing. That is still the most exciting part for me."

CASE STUDY:

JONATHAN STONE, PRESIDENT, WINDSWEPT PACIFIC ENTERTAINMENT COMPANY

As the son of Country Music Hall of Fame recording artist/music publisher Cliffie Stone, you might think that Jonathon Stone had his career handed to him on a silver platter, but you would be wrong. At age seventeen, Stone spent his summer break from high school hanging out at his father's music publishing office, getting his first taste of the business. "That's when I started understanding what a music publisher was." After a year attending Los Angeles' College of the Canyons in the mornings, and working for an independent record promoter in the afternoons, Stone was offered a part-time mail room job at ATV Music (who handled the Beatles catalog) in 1974. Seeing it as an avenue into music publishing, he took the job. Several months later, when ATV opened a Nashville office, the 20-year-old Stone transferred to take a tape copy/song plugger job. Over the next four years, he worked hard to learn the publishing business from the ground up, and eventually was promoted to professional manager.

Stone returned to Los Angeles in 1979 and worked as a professional manager at a small publishing company for several months before taking a position at MCA Music Publishing's recently expanded southern California office. As manager of creative services, he spent the next four years building, what was essentially a small studio holding company, into a major contender in the music publishing world. When Stone's wife became pregnant with twins and decided to quit her job, he needed a larger increase in income than MCA was able to provide.

"At that point I made what proved to be a pivotal move in my career. I heard that Quincy Jones was looking for someone to run his publishing company and I went over and met with him and his lawyer." Stone left MCA in 1985 and went to work for Jones, running his music publishing company, doing A&R work for his production company, and screening material for Michael Jackson's records.

Jones restructured in 1987, hiring Warner/Chappell Music to administer his holdings, and Stone briefly went out on his own as an independent song plugger, doing consulting work for MCA and Gene Autry Music Publishing, as well as brokering publishing and recording deals for independent songwriters. When Chuck Kaye and Joel Sill formed Windswept Pacific in 1988, they hired Stone as general manager. Promoted through the ranks, Stone was named president of U.S. operations in 2000. *www.windsweptpacific.com*

PRESIDENT • VICE PRESIDENT • GENERAL MANAGER (INDEPENDENT OR SMALLER MUSIC PUBLISHER)

JOB OVERVIEW

The executive officer oversees the day-to-day operations of the company by managing the creative and administrative personnel, staff songwriters, and the acquisition and exploitation of catalog. Major Bob president, Lana Thrasher, supervises the administrative and creative staff (which includes songwriters), the exploitation of catalog, and is also heavily involved in the production of song and artist demo recordings. Thrasher interfaces with subpublishers around the globe as well as her independent song pluggers. She looks for artist/writers, producer/writers, and songwriters to sign, and also negotiates contracts. She also oversees Major Bob Productions, a company set up to develop, produce, and secure recording deals for artists.

CAREER TIPS

Watch and learn from those around you. Be patient, work hard, and be willing to do whatever task is given to you with a good attitude.

"Don't be afraid to start at the bottom and work your way up." Too many people think they are going to see success overnight, and, when they don't, they give up. It takes time to make contacts and build your reputation.

PREREQUISITES

To succeed on the executive level, you should have an understanding of both copyright administration and the creative affairs side of music publishing. You should have solid contacts within the music industry and the ability to recognize great songs. Studio production experience and strong people skills are necessary. You should be self-motivated and have a willingness to perform whatever tasks are needed to get a job done.

A DAY IN THE LIFE

A typical day for Thrasher begins with appointments to play songs for artists, producers, and A&R people; to meet with her staff, or to listen to new songs by one of her writers, or a writer looking for a deal. Then, she may run over to a recording studio to hear and approve the mix of demos from the previous day. Throughout the day there are phone calls to take and return, budgets and bills to sign off on, and pending deals to negotiate or approve.

CASE STUDY:

LANA THRASHER, PRESIDENT, MAJOR BOB MUSIC CO., INC.

"I have always loved music," states Lana Thrasher. A southern California native, she grew up going to clubs with her parents, where her mother pursued the dream of being a singer. Thrasher majored in business and minored in music at University of California at Los Angeles (UCLA), with the intent of becoming an attorney. While in school, she took a part-time job at Kenny Rogers Productions' Lion Share Publishing Company, but it was the recording studio upstairs that changed the direction of Thrasher's life.

During the two years that she swept floors, photocopied, typed, and did whatever was needed, she got to peek into the studio and watch Quincy Jones produce. "I was attracted to the studio and I started ditching school to be there. I worked and learned and just watched Quincy Jones and absorbed everything that was going on. That is when I decided this is what I'm going to do when I grow up." Through meeting Jones, Thrasher earned an opportunity to work as a runner at A&M Studios during the making of the "We Are The World" project.

At the invitation of a friend, she traveled to Nashville in 1988, fell in love with the city, and decided to relocate. The following summer, she arrived with a Volkswagen Bug and $68. "That was all I had. I was pitiful." Soon after her arrival in Music City, Charlie Monk offered Thrasher an internship at Opryland Music Group. To supplement her income, she worked as a roving musician at Opryland and performed aboard the General Jackson Showboat, where she was able to eat for free. When Monk's friend Bob Doyle was about to open a new publishing company, he recognized Thrasher would have more opportunity to grow with the new firm and recommended her for a job. "They were this little company that had just signed Garth Brooks, but he didn't even have a record deal yet. Bob said, 'I can't pay you anything, but I'll give you a key.' I was so excited—I had my own key! They bought my lunch

THE LEAST FAVORITE THING ABOUT THIS JOB:

"When you sign a truly good writer or truly great artist, you put time and money into working with them and you become like family. When it doesn't work, when you don't know how to make money with them (can't get their songs cut or secure a record deal) and you have to let them go, that's hard."

THE BEST THING ABOUT THIS JOB:

"I love taking somebody's lyrics and music into the recording studio and producing the song—hearing it come alive. That is very exciting. Working in the recording studio is my favorite part of my job."

VOICES OF EXPERIENCE

and I started making tape copies and typing lyrics." At times, Thrasher was so broke she bummed quarters from friends and co-workers and used them for gas money.

As the publishing company grew and achieved some success, Thrasher was given a paid position. She learned the business of publishing from the ground up, from intern to secretarial and administrative duties, to all aspects of the creative process. In 1995, Thrasher was promoted to president of Major Bob Music and later assumed management of Major Bob Productions. Honing her production skills on song demo recordings and working with developing artists, Thrasher has added record producer to her resume. She has produced albums for Curb Records and has two other projects in the wings. *www.majorbob.com*

CREATIVE SERVICES

VICE PRESIDENT/GENERAL MANAGER OF CREATIVE SERVICES • GENERAL MANAGER OF MUSIC PUBLISHING (MAJOR MUSIC PUBLISHER)

JOB OVERVIEW

This area of music publishing directs the creative affairs of the company with regard to the exploitation of songs, acquisition of catalog, and signing of new writers.

At Sony/ATV Music, Woody Bomar's chief responsibilities are to manage and motivate the creative department and staff songwriters, and to exploit the song catalog by securing recordings and licensing use to film, television, advertising, and other forms of performance. He is involved in acquiring existing catalog and scouting new writers to sign with the company. The recording of demos and cataloging of songs also fall under his direction, as does interfacing with personnel at joint venture publishing companies.

PREREQUISITES

Success in creative services requires several qualifications. You must have an ear for recognizing great songs and the ability to connect songs with the appropriate artists to potentially record them. You must have close personal contacts within the music industry, self-confidence, and an outgoing personality. Strong people skills will enable you to work well with a variety of personalities, both inside and outside the company, and to deal with them in a positive and friendly way.

A DAY IN THE LIFE

Bomar's workday begins with a 9 A.M. meeting with his creative staff. They listen to the new songs that were turned in the previous day by their staff writers and cast the songs (decide which song to pitch to which artist). They discuss scheduled meet-

Read Billboard, Music Row, American Songwriter, *and other trade magazines to become familiar with the industry players.*

"Be a friendly face. Don't be too pushy. Remember the Golden Rule and treat other people like you want to be treated. Be the kind of person you would like to encounter if you were the person in the hiring or signing position."

"There are going to be a lot of ups and downs in publishing. You have to be committed for the long haul. Don't let yourself get discouraged when you're in those valleys, just keep working towards that next hill."

ings to play songs for various artists, producers, managers, A&R personnel, and others, and what type of songs those individuals want. During the course of a day, Bomar often meets with writers looking for songwriting deals and may begin negotiating terms. He also meets with the firm's staff songwriters to listen to a newly written tune, hear their pitching suggestions, or simply lend an understanding ear when they are discouraged. Throughout the day he interacts with the business, administration, and legal departments, and handles a variety of managerial and analytical tasks.

POINTERS FOR THE JOB SEARCH

Bomar suggests that a good way to get into music publishing is through the music business program at a university or college. In Nashville, the two top schools are Belmont University and Middle Tennessee State University in Murfreesboro. "Not only do you get a good education, but through the internships, you make a lot of contacts, and over the years I've hired many, many people that I met through their internship at my company." Internships give students a chance to get inside a company, where the staff gets to know them and sees how they work. "If you're the kind of person they'd like to have on an ongoing basis, many times, after the internship is over, it turns into a job when there is an opening."

Another good way is to attend writers' nights to meet songwriters and publishers, and begin to network within the industry. Through those contacts, you may hear of an opening or meet someone who can give you a recommendation.

THE LEAST FAVORITE THING ABOUT THIS JOB:

"When somebody has a problem, I tend to be the guy they go to."

THE BEST THING ABOUT THIS JOB:

"Being involved in music and being involved in songs. It's about the songs and the people—that's the joy of doing this kind of business at a company like this (Sony/ATV Music). It's hearing these great songs. We have a song currently rocketing up the charts, recorded by Martina McBride. It's called "Love's the Only House." It is written by Tom Douglas and Buzz Cason. Tom writes for us. I remember the day in one of our 9 a.m. sessions, we were listening to the new songs and that song came on and it just knocked me out. It was just a stand out. Of all the others, that one just stood out that day as being greatness."

CASE STUDY:

WOODY BOMAR, FORMER VICE PRESIDENT/GENERAL MANAGER CREATIVE SERVICES, SONY/ATV MUSIC PUBLISHING; PRESIDENT, GREEN HILLS PUBLISHING

Woody Bomar grew up in a tiny southern town 60 miles from Nashville, writing songs, playing in local bands, and dreaming of one day being like Elvis Presley. "I grew up listening to music and loving music. After school I'd stop by Hatfield's Drug Store and put money in the jukebox and listen to brand new records." While attending Middle Tennessee State University near Nashville, he got the chance to play some of his songs for music publishers. He was drafted right after college and served a year stateside, and another year in Vietnam. During that time he produced a television and touring show for the Army's Entertainment Division and continued to write songs and submit them by mail, and eventually one was recorded. After he was discharged, Bomar returned to pursue his career in songwriting, but quickly became discouraged. When an opportunity to write ad copy at a Nashville advertising agency presented itself, he took the job.

Ten years later, when Bomar was executive vice president and only wrote songs as a hobby, Loretta Lynn cut one of his tunes. The cut gave him the confidence to return to his dream of working in the music business. In 1979, he resigned from the all-consuming world of advertising "to become a full-time out-of-work songwriter."

"I thought that I would find a job in the music business pretty quickly because I was a pretty sharp young man. I didn't realize when people say 'Don't quit your day job' it's because it's going to take you a year or two to find a job. I didn't believe that. I thought I was so sharp that somebody would snatch me right up." While he looked for a position, Bomar took freelance advertising work to make ends meet, and a few more of his songs were recorded. A year and a half later, in 1981, he landed a full time job as a song plugger at Combine Music, pitching the catalogs of Kris Kristofferson and Tony Joe White, among others. During the next six years, some of his own songs were picked up as album cuts and for films, including number one hits for Conway Twitty and Joe Glazer. But Bomar came to realize that his greatest talent lay in song plugging. Naturally gifted with a likable personality and friendly disposition, he loved the personal interaction and problem solving that were involved in this work.

Bomar had been promoted to general manager at Combine before he left in 1987 to form Little Big Town Music, with partner Kerry O'Neil. The timing was perfect. Combine Music soon came up for sale, and Bomar was able to lure away some of its best writers, including Bob DePiero and John Scott Sherrill. The following year he signed Steve Seskin. During the next 11 years, Little Big Town's writers garnered 17 number one singles and more than 30 Top Ten albums. As the business grew more successful, Bomar found that his attention was increasingly taken up by administrative duties, leaving little time for the creative aspects that he loved.

In 1998, Sony/ATV Music approached Bomar about buying out his company's song catalog, and again, the timing was perfect. Ready for a new challenge, he sold the catalog and went to work at Sony, managing the creative department's four song pluggers and the city's largest roster of songwriters. Bomar left Sony in 2006 and returned to independent music publishing with the formation for Green Hills Music Group in early 2007. He is a recipient of The Nashville Songwriters Association's President's Award. *www.greenhillsmusicgroup.com*

CREATIVE MANAGER • PROFESSIONAL MANAGER • SONG PLUGGER • VICE PRESIDENT CREATIVE SERVICES

JOB OVERVIEW

The goal here is to discover and sign new writers and exploit the catalog of songs. Additionally, you want to further develop the careers of signed writers.

As EMI Vice President of Creative East Coast, Paul Morgan's main duties are to find and sign new talent, whether they are artist/writers, producer/writers, or songwriters, to work with the company's roster of staff writers, and to exploit the catalog. It is crucial that Morgan keep abreast of when artists are recording, who is producing their record and for what label, so that he can pitch songs to them or arrange for a co-write with one of his staff writers. It is important for him to maintain relationships with record company A&R staff, producers, artists, managers, and attorneys.

PREREQUISITES

To be successful, you must have an ear for great songs and the ability to match the song to the right artist. Strong personal contacts are necessary with A&R people, artists, managers, producers, and anyone who selects material to be recorded. You should be friendly, outgoing; self-confident, self-motivated, and driven to succeed. It is helpful to have a love for songs and a working knowledge of diverse styles and of the history of recordings. An understanding of publishing contracts and main deal points is important as is the ability to negotiate.

A DAY IN THE LIFE

Morgan begins his day by checking his incoming mail, which may include a CD requested from a band he is interested in signing, or artist material that an attorney has sent him. He prioritizes the music and then listens and responds to it. "I try to get through five or six tapes in the first hour and a half of the morning, and then I spend quite a bit of time working with the roster [staff writers]." Morgan listens again to new songs from his writers and goes through older catalog, while analyzing a pitch sheet of artists and record labels who are looking for particular types of songs. When he hears a song that inspires him, that he feels would be great for the artist, he fills out a pitch form and sends it to the tape library so that a tape or CD can be made and sent out as soon as possible.

CAREER TIPS

If you are a non-musician, learn about the fundamentals of music so that you have a better understanding of composition and song structures. The more you know about music, the easier it will be to talk with artists and writers about their songs.

Study Billboard *and other music trade magazines to learn who is who, what songs are being recorded, who wrote them, and who produced them.*

POINTERS FOR THE JOB SEARCH

Competition for a job in the music industry can be fierce, so you have to be determined and resilient to disappointment. "A lot of people begin as interns and don't get a salary. I would recommend even that as a way in. In essence that is what I did for a year. In the evenings I went out and scouted talent for no money. I was only given expenses, but for me it was great because I was doing something I really wanted to do and somebody else was taking care of the bills."

CASE STUDY:

PAUL MORGAN, SENIOR DIRECTOR, CREATIVE SERVICES, CHERRY LANE MUSIC PUBLISHING

In 1983, Paul Morgan was working a 9 to 5 clerk's job in the pension department of a huge firm in England, never thinking that his dream of a career in music was possible, when through a distant acquaintance, he was able to get an interview with a music agent. "The fact that I knew someone who knew someone who knew someone that worked in the industry suddenly sparked my interest. As soon as there was a slim chance, I was on it immediately." Although the agent had no job to offer, the meeting proved the adage of "being in the right place at the right time" true. One week later, the head of Atlantic Records walked into the Warner Brothers music publishing office, where the agent's wife worked, and asked if anyone knew of a young man interested in scouting talent for the American market. Word got back to Morgan, who came in for an interview. Instructed to return with his ten favorite singles the following week, he proved he had an ear for talent when a song by The Gang of Four prompted the Atlantic executive to place an excited call to the United States office to acquire it.

Continuing to work his day job to pay the bills, Morgan saw three to four bands every night for the next year, bringing in acts like New Order, Dream Academy, and The Cult, all of which Atlantic passed on. When these acts were immediately signed

VOICES OF EXPERIENCE

THE LEAST FAVORITE THING ABOUT THIS JOB:

"As I look at my cluttered desk, I'd have to say it's the minor details that I like the least. The administrative side—those things tend to bog me down. My real role here is, first and foremost, to be proactive with the roster and acquire new acts, etc. I'm very thorough; I leave nothing to chance. It means I spend a little bit less time listening to music."

THE BEST THING ABOUT THIS JOB:

"The idea of finding someone that has yet to be discovered by anybody else, and being able to take that vision of what I see that they can become and help to nurture that within the artist or the songwriter. Hopefully, in the long term, see that writer or artist fulfill their dreams. Frequently, people that want to be a rock and roll star have wanted that for an awfully long time. To see those dreams become fulfilled is a wonderful thing."

elsewhere and achieved huge success, Atlantic finally recognized Morgan's talent and gave him a full time position.

Morgan moved to EMI Records in 1987, originally hired as a talent scout, but within a month he was given four acts to A&R when his immediate supervisor suddenly left the company. Having to sink or swim, he worked on the albums of Talk Talk (which went platinum), White Snake, Saxon, and New Model Army (which produced four Top Forty singles). A move to Polydor Records had him working with Siouxsie & the Banshees, resulting in their first Top Twenty United States hit, "Kiss Them For Me." Morgan found he had a talent for developing acts that other people signed, but not such good luck convincing the label to sign acts he discovered. Although he brought in acts like Radio Head, PM Dawn, and Nirvana (all of which found success elsewhere after Polydor passed on them), after three years Morgan was fired "for not finding any new talent." Questioning whether he still wanted a career in A&R, he moved to Los Angeles for a brief stay in 1990 to try his luck.

Shortly after returning to England, Morgan got a call from EMI Publishing, who had just taken over Virgin Records' song catalog, asking if he was interested in working for them. Released from the responsibility to sign new acts, Morgan was able to concentrate on what he did best: developing talent. Ironically, as his artist signings of the past few years will attest, he has discovered that he also has a gift for finding talented songwriters. His marriage to an American woman prompted Morgan's 1995 move to EMI's New York office, where in 2000 he was named vice president of creative, East Coast. During Morgan's tenure at EMI, he signed Third Eye Blind, Bubba Sparxxx, and Chumbawumba. After several years with EMI, he left to accept a director of creative services position with Cherry Lane Music Publishing in New York. In 2007, he was promoted to senior director of creative services, where he is involved in new acquisitions, exploiting the catalog, and helping the current roster to pursue recording opportunities. *www.cherrylane.com*

LIBRARY MANAGER • TAPE ROOM MANAGER

JOB OVERVIEW

In this position, you manage the library of songs and are responsible for receiving and logging into the computer system new song recordings and lyrics. Further duties include ensuring the demo session master tapes are copied and stored, overseeing the complete music publishing library, working with the staff who make tape copies, and interfacing with the creative staff. A major publisher like Sony/ATV Music may have anywhere from 50 to 100 staff songwriters and a catalog of between 120,000 to 250,000 songs.

PREREQUISITES

To succeed, you should possess basic computer ability, be organized, detail oriented, self-motivated, and have a positive, friendly attitude.

A DAY IN THE LIFE

By choice, Lee Swartz arrives at the office early, before other staff members arrive. "I have a basket that songwriters put the new material in. The first thing I do is check-in new songs so they are ready to go into the listening meeting our pluggers have each morning. If there are any songs that have not been completely cataloged from the previous day, I will take care of that. Throughout the day there are special orders. We recently sold a catalog, so I have to track down all of those songs and get them to the new owner." Although Swartz is not responsible for the lyrics, he receives them from the writers with the demo and paperwork, and then forwards them to the appropriate departments.

POINTERS FOR THE JOB SEARCH

Move to where a hub of the music business is located. No one will hire you from a resume or telephone call. You need to live where the jobs are before you attempt to interview for even an entry-level position. Select a college with a music intern program. "There is a law in Tennessee that you cannot intern unless you're getting

THE LEAST FAVORITE THING ABOUT THIS JOB:

"Learning the fine art of management, that's been the most difficult for me."

THE BEST THING ABOUT THIS JOB:

"The people I work with."

VOICES OF EXPERIENCE

college credit. It was frustrating for me to offer up my services for free, but people couldn't let me work because I wasn't getting college credit for it."

CASE STUDY:

LEE SWARTZ, LIBRARY MANAGER, SONY/ATV MUSIC

Music has always been a passion in Lee Swartz's life, although he didn't immediately consider a career in the business. He grew up in northern Pennsylvania and after serving in the armed forces, enrolled in film school at Pennsylvania State. In time, he gravitated back toward music and transferred to a school in Pittsburgh that offered music business courses.

After graduation, Swartz moved to Nashville, arriving with no job, no prospects, and no money. "I decided I would just try to make something happen. I think when you take chances, good things happen." Because he was no longer a student, Swartz could not get an internship to get his foot in the door. "I couldn't even work for free! That was very frustrating." Eventually, he found an internship with a small firm, and soon after landed a job in the tape room at Sony/ATV. When his boss later left the company, Swartz was promoted to the position of manager of the library.

FILM, TELEVISION, AND ADVERTISING LICENSING

VICE PRESIDENT FILM & TELEVISION MUSIC LICENSING

JOB OVERVIEW

In the licensing arena, you market and exploit the catalog of songs to film and trailers, television programs, commercials, advertising, and new media communities, such as CD-ROM and video games, for synchronization. You conceive and manage a variety of music marketing campaigns, and direct and motivate department staff.

PREREQUISITES

A love of all types of music, as well as a keen interest in film and television programs are essential. Here, you must be highly organized, have typing and computer skills, and the ability to compose correspondence and various marketing materials. Verbal communication, leadership, self-motivation, and creative thinking are essential. Social skills, flexibility, and a friendly and outgoing personality are extremely helpful.

A DAY IN THE LIFE

A typical day for Art Ford begins with phone calls, an average of 50 e-mails, and a half dozen packages of music sent from the territorial offices around the world. Often he will have an early morning meeting or conference call with a director, producer, or music supervisor, and lunch with a music supervisor or client. Ongoing projects include sending out music or negotiating a deal for a film or commercial, coordinating monthly marketing mailers, and working on special projects like events for the Sundance Film Festival. Each week, Ford's staff meets to listen to new music that has come in and the singles they publish that are entering the charts. When writers and artists are in town, he meets with them about their catalog and takes them to meet film and television people who potentially could use their songs. In between, Ford has inter-company duties such as budgets and other paperwork.

"This business is about relationships and being trusted." *People need to feel confident that the information you are giving them about a song is accurate and that they can trust you will follow through on the promises you make for its use.*

Study film and television soundtracks to learn the names of supervisors, composers, writers, and others in the business. Become familiar with who wrote, published, produced, and recorded songs you love.

POINTERS FOR THE JOB SEARCH

"Find a way in. Even if you can start interning with a company, you can see how the business is done and learn who the players are. If you get an assistant position,

THE LEAST FAVORITE THING ABOUT THIS JOB:

"The administrative side of the job, which I find a way to delegate and oversee as much as possible."

THE BEST THING ABOUT THIS JOB:

"The short attention span quality of this business; I love the speed that it runs at. I like things that either pay off or don't pay off and you can move on quickly. I love that we make money for our songwriters and we defend their rights. I love being able to take care of my clients, which for the most part are my friends."

you're in a perfect position to really take care of people and build some great relationships. If you can't get a job with a publisher, try working for a music supervisor. A music supervisor deals with the publishers, record companies, and managers, and you get to see the whole problem-solving side of the job."

CASE STUDY:

ART FORD, VICE PRESIDENT OF FILM AND TELEVISION MUSIC, BMG MUSIC PUBLISHING

Art Ford began his musical odyssey as a drummer at age 11. By the time he was 15, he was playing professionally and touring with bands that opened for artists like Pat Benatar, Bob Dylan, and Tom Petty, until a car wreck ended his drumming career in 1985. Ford put in a short stint as a record producer, then as an independent talent scout in the Northwest, searching out grunge groups for Atlantic Records, and then touring as a road manager with bands like Ratt, L.A. Guns, and Poco.

After moving to Los Angeles, Ford landed a position in A&R for MCA-distributed Impact Records, working with acts like The Fixx and Southside Johnny and the Asbury Dukes. He created a job for himself when he discovered that there was no one assigned to field phone calls from film studios regarding licensing masters for sound tracks. After successfully placing songs in films like *The Bodyguard* and *Point Break*, Ford found that he loved the fast-paced, "I need it yesterday" energy of the film and television music business. Recognizing the need for a broader range of material, he worked out an agreement with the president of MCA whereby he was allowed to broker independent consulting deals with outside record labels and publishing houses. With song catalogs representing pop, rock, alternative, rap, and country material to draw upon, Ford quickly established himself as the one-stop source for film and television sound track licensing. In addition to his MCA salary, he was paid consulting fees by the catalogs he represented, as well as commissions on songs he placed.

Ford realized that if he could break into music supervising for films, he could be both the buyer and the seller. In return for supervising a small film for Synergy Productions, he obtained a letter of introduction that allowed him to get meetings with the presidents of the major publishing houses, leading to a subpublishing deal with Sony Music. Impressed by Ford's entrepreneurial spirit, in 1993 BMG Music's Danny Strick offered him a job running their film and television department.

Initially, Ford was a one-man operation. In order to service his clients and keep track of the thousands of songs in the BMG catalogs, he set up a song search computer database. Recognizing the power of the Internet, he convinced his employer to bankroll the launch of an on-line song search engine to the film and television community, becoming the first publishing house to do so. The success of the innovative user-friendly and service-oriented database established BMG's reputation within the industry as a proactive, artist-friendly music publisher. Ford's department grew to include its own marketing division dedicated to gaining exposure for BMG artists.

After seven years with BMG, Ford left his powerful position to launch his own company, June St. Entertainment in 2001. The firm catered to film and television music supervisors and advertising agencies, who "are always in crisis-management mode" when it comes to finding songs for specific projects. With a solid understanding of the needs and tight schedules of music licensees, he used cutting-edge Internet-based technology to create a song search engine where clients could search for music by artist, title, lyric, year, mood, gender of vocalist, or any other combination of prompts. The password-protected interface allowed clients to access information 24/7 from their own computers. When a potential song is identified, the user can preview the song instantly, burn it onto a CD, and cut it to picture.

In just over a year, the company placed songs in such films as *A Walk to Remember, My Big Fat Greek Wedding, Goldmember/Austin Powers 3,* and *Charlie's Angels: Full Throttle* and in commercials for Coca-Cola, Nike, Old Navy, and UPS.

In response to several offers to handle all of the music supervision and licensing responsibilities for feature films and other projects, Ford formed Ford Music Services. He has served as a music consultant on *xXx: State of the Union, Walk the Line,* and *Waist Deep.* "I put music in movies and get paid for it," Ford says, "Come on, that's a great job to have."

BUSINESS AFFAIRS

LEGAL AND BUSINESS AFFAIRS • FINANCE • HEAD OF FINANCE/ADMINISTRATION

JOB OVERVIEW

Those who work in business affairs are responsible for legal and financial management of the company's assets. They draft, negotiate, and approve contractual agreements, and are responsible for the acquisition and exploitation of assets. Business affairs protects against copyright infringement.

PREREQUISITES

You should have a law degree or substantial legal background, with knowledge of worldwide copyright law. You should be proficient in finance and have the ability to strategize.

POINTERS FOR THE JOB SEARCH

Larger firms employ legal counsel on a full-time staff basis and many also retain additional support from an outside law firm. Small publishers retain counsel or hire on an hourly or project-by-project basis for legal advice. Before finishing law school, try to find an internship in the legal department of a large publishing company, at a performing rights organization, or at a law firm with a music or entertainment department that works with publishing companies. Interning is a good way to gain experience and discover if publishing is where you want to focus your energy.

DIRECTOR CREATIVE SERVICES • PRODUCTION COORDINATOR

JOB OVERVIEW

Employees in this area of creative affairs manage the administrative side of production. They formulate the recording budget and coordinate with record label A&R administrative department for spending limits, deadlines, label copy, and recording details. They book studio, musicians and engineers, and handle any other business details as directed by the producer.

PREREQUISITES

Essential qualities include strong organizational skills, the ability to communicate well verbally and in writing, and a friendly personality.

A DAY IN THE LIFE

"When you work for somebody that has an equal amount of respect for you, that's worth more than money. That is the kind of relationship I have developed with Don [Cook, his boss]. He's somebody that I love and respect; I feel like I have a second dad in him."

Be loyal to the people you work for. Always have their back, and never say anything negative about them. If you do a good job, as they are promoted, they will take you with them. If you're disloyal, word gets around quickly, and people lose respect for you.

For Scott Johnson, a recording day begins the day before with a call to the studio to reconfirm the start time, identify the players, and note the time each will arrive. (The studio engineer is often familiar with an individual musician's preferences and can set up appropriately in advance.) He reconfirms arrangements with the caterer and assembles a package for the producer that contains lyrics sheets and demo tapes or CD copies of the songs to be cut. When recording is about to start, Johnson visits the studio and checks to make sure everyone is present and has what they need for the session. He returns at lunch time to ensure that the caterer has arrived and that everything is running smoothly. A half hour before the session is finished, he returns again to complete union contracts, time cards, tax forms, and necessary paperwork. Depending on how late it is (sessions can stretch all the way to midnight), Johnson will either return to more paperwork at the office, or take the rest of the night off.

POINTERS FOR THE JOB SEARCH

Jobs working for a producer are limited, but they are a good way to develop skills and meet producers. Get a job or internship in the A&R administration department at a record label, where you can learn the business side of production.

CASE STUDY:

SCOTT JOHNSON, FORMER DIRECTOR CREATIVE SERVICES, SONY/ATV MUSIC PUBLISHING

After law school graduation, Scott Johnson came to the realization that the legal profession was not for him. Instead, he opted to combine his love of music with a career. Johnson enlisted his father to facilitate meetings with some of his friends in the music industry in order to solicit advice. "I wasn't asking for a job, I just wanted to talk with them about what I needed to do to get one." Sony/ATV Music president/CEO Donna Hilley was one of the executives who consented to meet with Johnson. "She told me that nobody was going to hire me because I didn't know anything about the business." But recognizing his genuine desire to learn, Hilley offered Johnson a deal: if he would work for her as an intern for six months, at the end of that time she would hire him if she had an opening, or help him find a job.

On the first day of his internship, a creative department assistant announced she would be taking maternity leave and Johnson was given the temporary slot. A month into the job of answering telephones, typing letters, and other administrative support duties, Hilley recognized his hard work by awarding him a permanent position. Once on the job, he became familiar with all the company's staff writers and producers.

THE LEAST FAVORITE THING ABOUT THIS JOB:

"I like my job, there's nothing I don't like about it. I don't mind the hours, I don't mind the time."

THE BEST THING ABOUT THIS JOB:

"The most exciting part of my job is being in the studio when a song is first going down. When the musicians are out in the studio rehearsing the track. The first time a singer sits down and gets to sing it. To be there in that studio when the song comes to life. When it's played back through the monitors. When you hear that song on the radio six months later and then you see it climb the charts to number one. That's one of the coolest things, to be there when the music is basically born."

VOICES OF EXPERIENCE

One of them was Don Cook, who was experiencing great success with his production of Brooks & Dunn. When Cook was offered a senior vice president of creative position with Tree International (now known as Sony/ATV), the person he wanted to work for him was Johnson.

When Cook formed his own production label, DKC Music, Johnson became the liaison between DKC and the joint venture labels who handle promotion and marketing. While Cook handled the creative process of producing records, Johnson took care of all the business affairs and financial transactions for the company, earning the title of general manager of DKC Music. Seeking new challenges and more creative opportunities, Johnson left Sony/ATV in early 2006 to work for mega-hit songwriter and recording artist Bob DiPiero and his company Love Monkey Music. A year later, he became a full-time production coordinator, servicing eight producers. "If you can find a job where you can combine something that you love with something you get paid to do everyday," said Johnson, "that's the best thing in the world."

COPYRIGHT ADMINISTRATION AND LICENSING

JOB OVERVIEW

In this department, workers file paperwork to copyright music compositions, register songs with the appropriate performance society (ASCAP, BMI, SESAC) or Harry Fox Agency and any other collection agents or representatives. They issue appropriate licenses for use of songs (some administration personnel quote and negotiate synchronization or other use fees), collect royalties for mechanical and performance use, synchronization fees and ancillary income (commercials, advertisements, toys, and so on), and disperse payments. Administration is often responsible for collecting lyrics from staff writers, typing them, and logging them into the company system. Administrative personnel process writers' advance payments and reconcile earnings.

PREREQUISITES

A knowledge of music copyright law and a general business background are necessary.

POINTERS FOR THE JOB SEARCH

It is far less competitive to obtain a job in publishing administration than in the creative or international department. If administration is your area of interest, you stand a good chance of finding an entry level position at a large firm where you can grow. At smaller companies you may be required to also act as receptionist and creative assistant. ASCAP, BMI, SESAC, and Harry Fox Agency are also possible employers where you can gain experience.

INTERNATIONAL

SENIOR VICE PRESIDENT • VICE PRESIDENT • DIRECTOR (INTERNATIONAL)

JOB OVERVIEW

Personnel in this area manage the company's international music publishing assets. At BMG, Ron Solleveld is specifically responsible for the well-being and running of the company's music publishing concerns in Latin America, Canada, Eastern Europe (Czech Republic, Poland, and Hungary), and to some extent Spain and Asia. The executive in each respective country reports directly to him. He is involved in working to improve and enforce royalty collection laws in foreign countries, and negotiating deals to acquire or subpublish existing song catalogs.

PREREQUISITES

First, you must possess a business education, the ability to structure a budget, and knowledge of publishing laws throughout the world. Second, you should have an appreciation for all different types of music, and an understanding of the overall music industry. You should be multilingual and self-motivated and have the ability to work well with people from many different cultures.

A DAY IN THE LIFE

When he is not traveling to one of the territories he oversees, Ron Solleveld is in his New York office around 9:30 A.M. His first task is reading and responding to e-mail. Throughout the day he may be called upon to solve a crisis with one of the foreign offices, while continuing to work on strategic planning negotiations for better foreign rights for the company's catalog, and negotiating to acquire or subpublish other catalogs. One to two weeks each month, for nine months of the year, Solleveld travels around the world to work with the territories he manages.

"You need good mentors—people that take you under their respective wings."

"It doesn't hurt if you are well traveled and understand what music goes where in which country, and why certain things don't go in particular countries."

The ability to speak a second and third language is an advantage—Spanish, German, French, Japanese.

CAREER TIPS

POINTERS FOR THE JOB SEARCH

"One of the most important things is to learn different languages. Oddly enough, you find a lot of Dutch people in international positions because of the Dutch education system. You have to learn four languages before you can graduate. If you aspire to do something international, it wouldn't hurt to at least have your Spanish, German, and French handy." Strive to get any position at a major publishing company and then express your desire for working international.

CASE STUDY:

RON SOLLEVELD, VICE PRESIDENT OF INTERNATIONAL, BMG MUSIC PUBLISHING WORLDWIDE

Born in Java and raised in Holland, Ron Solleveld is the son of the founding president of Polygram Music. Even though he grew up around the music business and had his father as a connection, he began his professional career at the bottom. He served a six-month internship in 1967 as an assistant's assistant of international repertoire at a small music publishing company in Paris. "At night I would go around to discotheques, hand delivering newly released product. Doing a little promotion."

After returning to Holland for mandatory military service, Solleveld studied international business, earning a scholarship in 1971 that afforded him the opportunity to study at Kent State University. "It was my first encounter with American culture. It was the year after the shootings at Kent and it was still a pretty sad place, but it was an amazing experience." While there, he completed his undergraduate work and earned a master's degree in business administration.

VOICES OF EXPERIENCE

THE LEAST FAVORITE THING ABOUT THIS JOB:

"Saying 'no' to people. Constructive criticism is one thing, but sometimes there are people that come in and they are incredibly happy with what they have created, but it doesn't look like it is ever going to go anywhere. I hate to tell them and burst their bubble."

THE BEST THING ABOUT THIS JOB:

"To see something that we built up in country 'A' cross over to country 'B,' and become a success there as well. We put things together in South America that became hits in Asia and vice versa. I really like to see when something crosses over. In other words, developing worldwide hits. That is a lot of fun."

In 1973 Solleveld went to work for Chappell Music in New York as assistant to the international manager. Promoted when his boss returned to France, he eventually became the general manager of Intersong USA. During this time, he also acted as international manager for Chappell Music. In 1977, he accepted a London post to head the Intersong International Desk, making deals outside the country of origin and North America for all worldwide Intersong agencies.

Solleveld returned to the United States in 1980 and went to work for CBS Songs as the liaison between the international and domestic divisions. A year later he moved to RCA Records to rebuild their publishing company after an ill-advised sale of their United States catalog. As publishing was not considered important at RCA at the time, most of his duties involved looking after the licensed labels, among them Jive, Motown, and Virgin, for the Latin American and Asian markets. In 1984, he was named president of Toronto-based Sunbury-Dunbar Music Publishing (now BMG), RCA's Canadian music publishing arm. There he became involved in the Canadian Country Music Association and served as secretary/treasurer of the organization.

RCA Music Publishing became BMG Music Publishing in 1986, and two years later, Solleveld was asked to return to New York to help organize the company's various international activities into one cohesive musical publishing effort. Serving as vice president of International BMG Publishing, worldwide, Solleveld had specific responsibilities over Canada, Spain, Latin American, and Eastern Europe.

Solleveld left his post with BMG in 2002, to join performing rights organization BMI as vice president, international. Eight months later he was promoted to senior vice president, international. Solleveld oversees all of BMI's international activities with an emphasis on relationships with foreign performing rights organizations. The key to his success is an ability to establish relationships with songwriters, composers, and music publishers around the world. *www.bmi.com*

SENIOR VICE PRESIDENT • VICE PRESIDENT • DIRECTOR (INTERNATIONAL ADMINISTRATION)

JOB OVERVIEW

The focus here is to facilitate communication between the company's American office and their foreign offices and affiliates throughout the world. They should ensure that each has the necessary paperwork to protect copyrights and collect appropriate earnings of both the firm's catalog and songs that they subpublish outside the United States. Administrators also provide notification of new writer and artist signings, catalog acquisitions, and newly released records, film, television, and advertising that contain songs published by the firm. They should interface with owners of catalogs the firm subpublishes.

PREREQUISITES

To succeed, you should have a broad knowledge of the music publishing business, an understanding of foreign publishing rights and societies, strong verbal and written communication skills, and the ability to multi-task.

POINTERS FOR THE JOB SEARCH

A working knowledge of music publishing is a requirement for an international position. Apply for any administration or clerical position within the publishing company and once in, express a desire to work in international. You might also work for one of the performing rights societies to gain some skills and knowledge, and then look for an opening with a publishing firm.

RECORD COMPANY

The record company discovers, signs, develops, and records musical talent. It oversees package design, manufacturing, and distribution of the artist's recorded product and creates marketing, publicity, video, and promotional campaigns to maximize sales.

Major record companies have a full roster of artists signed to the company and a large staff to promote them. Major labels are often owned by a large corporation that also includes a distribution company to deliver the recorded product to retailers. Smaller, independent record companies either affiliate with a major label distribution company, or use an independent distributor to deliver their records to retail outlets. They have a much smaller roster of artists, and a staff of employees who fill multiple job functions.

This chapter is divided into 12 sections: Executive Office (major or large label); Executive Office (smaller or independent label); A&R (Artist and Repertoire); A&R Administration and Production; Creative Services; Promotion; Sales; Marketing and Artist Development; Publicity and Media Relations; Emerging Technologies and Interactive Media; Business and Legal Affairs, and Licensing; and Human Resources and Support Staff. Though basically similar in structure, individual record companies' department names and job descriptions may differ slightly to fit their specific needs.

EXECUTIVE OFFICE
(MAJOR OR LARGE LABEL)

CHIEF OPERATING OFFICER • PRESIDENT

JOB OVERVIEW

The executive office manages and directs the vision and daily operations of assigned company holdings.

PREREQUISITES

Executives need a well-rounded knowledge of the music industry. They must possess the foresight, reputation, integrity, experience, and drive to formulate a strategy and direct its execution.

POINTERS FOR THE JOB SEARCH

"Professional persistence, with a heavy emphasis on professional. People need to believe that you have some discipline and can conduct yourself in a way that is socially acceptable. Gain an understanding of how the business works. That will help you concentrate your efforts and protect you from people that might take advantage of you. On the persistent side, don't think you're going to make it in the first 90 days. Have a nest egg so you can continue to be persistent."

CAREER TIPS

"I believe people either live up to or down to expectation. I try to hire people that I think are great and help them become greater. Believe in them and give them the support that allows them to grow."

Everyone makes mistakes—successful people realize they are going to make mistakes and they use them as growth opportunities. Learn from your mistakes.

"In this business you have to have integrity. People need to know you're going to do your absolute best to be fair, finding a way that both of us can succeed and both of us can get what we deserve."

"I always conduct my business life in such a way that I wouldn't be embarrassed if I had to explain to my mother something I had done."

CASE STUDY:

TIM DuBOIS, FORMER PRESIDENT AND CO-FOUNDER, UNIVERSAL SOUTH RECORDS

"I grew up playing music," says Tim DuBois, who was raised by schoolteacher parents in the northwest corner of Oklahoma. In high school he began to write songs, a talent that later became his entry into the music business. At Oklahoma State College he studied accounting and planned to continue on to law school. With a wife and two small children to support upon graduation, he shelved the idea of becoming an attorney and instead earned his master's degree in accounting, taking a job as an auditor at a CPA firm in Dallas. From there, he was hired as senior financial analyst for the Federal Reserve Bank. DuBois' time in Dallas proved to be another important step toward his future musical career. "That is when I first became interested in music that had country roots. I didn't grow up listening to The Opry. I was strictly into rock and roll music. It was in my early twenties, there in Texas, that I discovered the music that eventually led me to Nashville."

Inspired by the sounds of country music, DuBois began to write songs again. His thirst for knowledge led him to the local library in search of information about the business side of music. "I read every book I could get my hands on." Through diligent study he came to understand the basics of how the industry worked. *Songwriter* magazine proved especially helpful in alerting him to the pitfalls that await aspiring writers. Returning to Oklahoma State in 1974 to pursue a doctoral degree, DuBois became acquainted with several people who later would prove influential to his music career, including future production partner Scott Hendricks. He also discovered that his musical talents were as a songwriter, rather than as a vocalist. A year later, having

THE LEAST FAVORITE THING ABOUT THIS JOB:

"Any time you grow a company, you have to change directions and you have to sometimes rebuild. You make decisions that impact people's lives, letting them go because they don't fit anymore. That is the hardest thing I've faced. Quite often it's not about whether or not the person did a good job. It's a tough business decision forced upon you and you have to do what's good for the company and for the majority of the people working there."

THE BEST THING ABOUT THIS JOB:

"I love songs. I love songwriters. I love working with people who have that creative spark. Finding a great song and being excited about it, thinking about who can record it. Looking for songs for a specific artist and finding a great song."

VOICES OF EXPERIENCE

secured several appointments with music publishers, he made his first visit to Nashville. While not received with open arms, DuBois made a few contacts, managed to generate some interest in one of his songs, and got some good advice. One publisher advised, "If you really want to do this, you're going to have to move out here, but you need to come with your eyes wide open to the fact that you probably won't make it." He told DuBois to come prepared with a game plan, another way to make a living, and to be persistent.

Setting himself a two-year limit to succeed as a songwriter, DuBois got a job at the University of Tennessee in Nashville in 1977. At night he taught classes in accounting and by day he wrote songs. After two years of frustration, despite getting several album cuts, he was ready to return to Oklahoma. A chance meeting with another songwriter convinced him to give it one more try. Within the year, he had been signed to his first publishing contract, and one year later had written three number one songs: "Midnight Hauler" (Razzie Bailey), "Love in the First Degree" (Alabama), and "She Got the Gold Mine, I Got the Shaft" (Jerry Reed). "Those three songs changed my life as a songwriter. I set a goal to always have something in the charts, going up or coming down, and for the next three years, I did."

Having achieved a level of success, DuBois and a group of friends began writing songs that rode the line between pop and country. Believing in the songs despite a lack of interest from the country music community, he put together a band to perform them. After many trials, Restless Heart was born. With $50,000 of his own money invested and an eight-song demo album he had produced, DuBois and partner Scott Hendricks began shopping the band at record labels. Only RCA's president, Joe Galante, saw the group's potential. As producer of the band's records, DuBois recovered his investment on the first album, saw the next three albums go gold, and wrote his fourth number one song, "The Bluest Eyes in Texas." When the group's management deal went sour, DuBois became their manager as well. Searching for a partner, he connected with the prestigious Los Angeles pop and rock management firm Fitzgerald Hartley Company, facilitating the opening of their Nashville office in 1985. The firm expanded the Nashville operation by signing Foster & Lloyd and Vince Gill.

Frustrated that the demands of managing left little time for songwriting, DuBois hooked up with Gill, who at the time was frustrated by his own inability to break into the country market. They wrote three songs in one week, including "Oklahoma Swing," a hit duet by Gill and Reba, and "When I Call Your Name," which became Gill's breakthrough single and DuBois' fifth number one song. In 1988, DuBois realized that the pressures of managing, writing, and producing for Restless Heart had become too much. He took stock of his life and decided to simplify. Divesting his interest in the band, he was considering opening a publishing company when Arista Records contacted him about heading up a country division. Not really wanting the job, but eager to meet label head Clive Davis, DuBois took the meeting and wound up getting the job. ("When I read all those books about the music business back in the mid-70s, one of them was *Clive: Inside the Music Business*.")

After assembling his team, DuBois signed Alan Jackson and Exile the first year, Brooks & Dunn, Diamond Rio, and Pam Tillis the second year, and by the third year, had made Arista the number two label in Nashville. During the boom years of the early 1990s, Arista opened a second country label, a Christian music division, and a Latin division. All of these were either sold or reabsorbed into the Arista Group as the country market began to slump later in the decade. After launching the Wilkinsons in 1998 and Brad Paisley in 1999, the label was back on track.

Taking stock of his career, DuBois once again was looking at opening a publishing company, when a restructuring at Gaylord Entertainment, owners of the Grand Ole Opry, offered a new possibility. Released from his contract at Arista, DuBois was appointed president of the creative content group in 2000. Six months later, DuBois left Gaylord to pursue other interests.

In early 2002, DuBois teamed with mega-hit-producer Tony Brown—Brown has produced more than 100 No. 1 singles for artists that include Wynonna, Reba McEntire, Vince Gill, Trisha Yearwood, and George Strait—to launch Universal South Records. The first full-service, major start-up label in over a decade, the label was a joint venture between DuBois, Brown, and New York-based Universal Records.

The two executives share a commitment to expanding the marketplace for new music. Under their leadership, the roster featured both country and rock acts, including Joe Nichols, Marty Stuart, Shooter Jennings, and Lee Roy Parnell. DuBois left the label in early 2007 to "attend to family matters." *www.universal-south.com*

PRESIDENT/GENERAL MANAGER • VICE PRESIDENT/GENERAL MANAGER

JOB DESCRIPTION

At The Atlantic Group, Ron Shapiro managed and directed all aspects of the company's worldwide operations, beginning at the point an artist is signed to the label through the marketing and sales of the music in the United States and abroad, and overseeing the administration and human resources concerns.

PREREQUISITES

Good communication skills are essential. You must be able to articulate a point of view powerfully and succinctly on the phone, before a group of people, and in writing, whether it be a press release, a letter or e-mail. Other important qualities include an outgoing and friendly personality, the ability to motivate others, a knack for spotting gifted and unique artists, a broad understanding of the music business, and strong contacts within it.

A DAY IN THE LIFE

Each day in Ron Shapiro's life is a new and exciting adventure. Like all executives, he receives external and internal mail, e-mail, faxes, and telephone calls that he responds to throughout the day. He attends a variety of meetings both on a company and a corporate level. One hour might be a sales and marketing strategy to plan the launch of Jewel's next album, the next could be a legal department meeting to negotiate a new contract for an employee. He is also involved in music industry organizations, events, and charities.

POINTERS FOR THE JOB SEARCH

"First, you have to have conviction about what you want to do. Your conviction can have no holes in it. You have to be 100 percent sure that you want this and that you want it more than any other career that you can have. From there you have to go with no ego and be willing and open to opportunities. Lots of people come in my office and say they only want to do A&R; they don't want to work in promotion. I almost never hire them. You have to be willing to do anything that doesn't compromise your moral code. My attitude is you have to get in however you can and learn everything you can about yourself and the business. If you're smart and work hard, you'll impress people and opportunities will come."

CAREER TIPS

Develop a positive personality and attitude. "In the entertainment business your job is to sell other human beings and their work. You can't do that without some enthusiasm and energy in your aura; some happiness and strength in your dialogue with everybody."

"Never say 'never' and never take 'no' for an answer. When I moved to the West Coast my family said, 'You'll never make it in entertainment. It's impossible. You have no connections.' But I did. Then, when I wanted to get out of publicity and do other things at a record company, everyone said, 'It never happens. Publicity people never get to run record companies.' Every time people tell you something has never been done or can't happen, don't believe them. Just believe that you can and be willing to work really, really, really, really hard and take the risks that come. A lot of people believe you can't have everything, but you can make all your dreams come true professionally, personally, spiritually. You just have to accept that you can't have it all, all of the time."

CASE STUDY:

RON SHAPIRO, EXECUTIVE VICE PRESIDENT/GENERAL MANAGER, THE ATLANTIC GROUP

At 21, Ron Shapiro left Vassar College and moved to Los Angeles in 1986 with about $2000 in graduation money, not knowing how he would translate his love of music and television into a career. Several weeks later, he saw an ad in the UCLA *Daily Bruin*, for a public relations or English major to work at an entertainment public relations firm specializing in music. Not really knowing what public relations was, but having a degree in English and loving music, he applied. The job was for an assistant to Sarah McMullen, publicist for Elton John, who hired Shapiro on the basis of his writing skills. It seemed somewhat appropriate that this should be his first job in the music business, given the fact that the first record he ever bought was *Goodbye Yellow Brick Road*.

From McMullen, who had just left a large firm to open her own business, Shapiro learned in two years what would have taken ten years elsewhere. He went from being tour publicist to account executive, working with clients like Bryan Adams, Elton John, and Roy Orbison. When McMullen branched out into corporate public relations, Shapiro was assigned to handle newly appointed BMI President, Frances Preston. The two clicked, resulting in an offer to run BMI's West Coast publicity department, where a year later he was promoted to writer/publisher relations execu-

VOICES OF EXPERIENCE

LEAST FAVORITE THING ABOUT THIS JOB:

"There is still no better way (albeit the Internet is booming) to get music heard around the world than through the major record label system. All these companies are owned by big corporations now and are dominated by quarterly earning reports for Wall Street. People want profitability and they want it on a quarterly basis. That is hard to do when your product isn't corn flakes, when it has a heartbeat."

THE BEST THING ABOUT THIS JOB:

"I believe that music changes the world. Music is the sound track to everyone's lives. Try and do anything, from watching a movie to getting married, without music. It entertains and it also moves you, it enlightens you and it can teach you. The greatest part of my job is being able to work everyday with brilliantly gifted people who create that music. Those people are touched by God in some way, and given a gift. I like to help them use that gift in a way that can really make a difference in the world. That's a very exciting and powerful feeling."

tive. "I had all this experience dealing with superstars touring on the road and learned how to do publicity. Now I was learning all about performing rights and how important BMI, ASCAP, and SESAC are. I learned about the world of the songwriter, how they make money, and what their place in the music industry food chain is. It was a great experience."

After a couple of years at BMI, Shapiro wanted to learn about the record business. About that time, MCA Records was reorganizing their West Coast office, and he landed the job of national publicity director. "I went there having experience that a lot of record company executives don't have. I understood publishing, performing rights, independent publicity, management, and the touring business. I had this whirlwind four years with McMullen & Company Public Relations and at BMI. That taught me a lot." Quickly promoted to vice president, Shapiro spent four years learning the record business, handling day-to-day artist and corporate public relations, and marketing.

During a campaign to promote the reunion of Belinda Carlisle and the Go-Gos, Shapiro met their manager, Danny Goldberg, who had just been made head of Atlantic Records. Goldberg offered him a job, which after a few months, turned into the general manager position over the West Coast office. During the following year, Shapiro was instrumental in signing several artists, including Jewel. In 1995, parent company Time Warner shook up Warner Music Group, of which Atlantic Records is a part. When the dust settled, Shapiro found himself in New York, promoted to senior vice president and general manager of The Atlantic Group.

It took two years of 16-hour work days to learn the ropes, but Shapiro was up to the challenge. Under Shapiro's leadership, Atlantic Records boasted a major league roster that included Jewel, Brandy, Kid Rock, Matchbox 20, Sugar Ray, Tori Amos, and the cast albums of numerous Broadway productions, among them *Jekyll & Hyde*, *Hedwig & The Angry Inch*, *Scarlet Pimpernel*, and *Smokey Joe's Cafe*. Shapiro was promoted to executive vice president and general manager in 1997. Three years later, he and Craig Kallman were named co-presidents.

In early 2004, parent company Warner Music Group restructured its recording and publishing interests and Shapiro exited the label. The always positive Shapiro remarked, "When I walked out of 1290 [Sixth Avenue] for the last time, I thought, 'I've had the greatest experience in the world. I'd gone from publicity to president.'"

Shortly after leaving Atlantic, Shapiro received a call from Universal Music Group Nashville co-chairman Luke Lewis about managing up-and-coming Mercury Nashville artist Julie Roberts. Respected for nurturing artists' careers and his ability to get radio airplay for nonstereotypical acts, Lewis thought Shapiro possessed the right combination of strengths to become a successful artist manager. "At Atlantic, I often felt like I was an internal manager to certain acts, like Jewel, Brandy, P.O.D., or Matchbox Twenty."

Ron Shapiro Management and Consulting LLC was formed a few months after Shapiro's departure from Atlantic. In addition to artist management, Shapiro was hired as a consultant for AOL Music and Clear Channel Entertainment. He was also named president of Artist Den, a New York-based company started by venture capitalist Mark Lieberman that includes Artists Den Records and Artists Den Performances. "You should always approach [a project] with an attitude of changing the marketplace or changing the culture," Shapiro says. "At Atlantic, the minute the gatekeepers told us 'no' was the minute we started to have a good time."

CHIEF OPERATING OFFICER • PRESIDENT • CHIEF EXECUTIVE OFFICER

JOB DESCRIPTION

Ultimately responsible for managing the day-to-day operations of LaFace Records, Mark Shimmel concentrates his efforts on long term promotion and marketing strategy of label-signed artists' careers. He is heavily involved in each artist's touring plans and spearheads label, radio, and retail support. Internet projects are another scope of focus for him.

PREREQUISITES

Executives must have a solid understanding of the music industry and strong personal contacts within it. They must be able to discover new talent and to strategize the necessary marketing and promotion. Executives must motivate and manage personnel and skillfully negotiate deals. "Resiliency. The industry can burn people out. Your ability to go in every day and move past the arguments and battles; each day you have to recharge and revive yourself."

A DAY IN THE LIFE

There is no typical day in the life of Mark Shimmel. He may meet with LaFace Records' co-presidents Antonio "L.A." Reid and Kenneth "Babyface" Edmonds, followed by a promotion and marketing meeting to strategize a campaign for the new Toni Braxton release. Then there might be a contract negotiation or agent meeting about one of the label artist's touring plans. Between meetings he returns telephone calls, responds to e-mail, faxes, and other correspondence, and deals with pending deals or problems. He may telephone radio programmers about airplay on a new single or talk with a manager about sales figures and promotional ideas. Often he travels to New York, Los Angeles, and other cities to see artists perform. While there, he spends time with some of the key radio people in the market and schedules other business meetings.

"A critical component of being successful in the music industry is you need to figure out how to recharge your energies. One of the best ways is to really enjoy the people that you work with. You want to make it an environment where people are not afraid to sit in a room and come up with a crazy marketing idea, where they are free to give off their thoughts, because you may have to go through 25 ideas before you get the winner."

"The entertainment business is probably the most documented of any industry. You walk into a magazine shop and there are 15 magazines every month that can help expand your knowledge of it. Read every one of them. Immerse yourself in the business. Every month I sit and read all the trades: Billboard, Spin, Rolling Stone, Variety, Gavin, *and I read the* Living Arts section of The New York Times *and the Calendar section of the* Los Angeles Times, Entertainment Weekly, Time. *It's a lot of work, but I never feel when I walk into a meeting that I don't have a working knowledge of lots of the music/entertainment industry. It is really important to take advantage of the wealth of information that is out there."*

POINTERS FOR THE JOB SEARCH

"Sometimes this industry takes you where it wants you to go rather than the other way around. The key thing is, wherever you go and whatever the opportunities are, you need to make the most of them. You absolutely have to be fully dedicated to whatever task you're working on at that particular time. If you're good and if you get a little bit lucky, people will notice and will open up opportunities. I've never looked at any of the things I've done as steps toward something else. Every job I've held in this business I dedicated myself to thoroughly and passionately and just through circumstances of life and business, other opportunities opened up."

CASE STUDY:

MARK SHIMMEL, SENIOR VICE PRESIDENT OF MARKETING AND ARTIST RELATIONS, ARISTA RECORDS

Initially, Mark Shimmel wanted to be an actor. After hanging out at Yale Drama School and working a few dinner theater gigs in his early twenties, he realized that he was much more passionate about music than acting. He moved to Los Angeles in 1981 and found work in a small booking agency that sold talent to military bases, but quickly discovered that it was not what he wanted to do. After running his own successful agency, enabling him to bypass the mailroom and the assistant positions, he was hired as a full-fledged booking agent by Regency Artists, before moving to International Creative Management (ICM).

In search of a new challenge, Shimmel left the talent booking business to open a company specializing in corporate sponsorship. He set up deals for Jimmy Buffett with Corona Beer, Bill Cosby with Kodak, and George Michael with Coca-Cola. A job lining up sponsorship for Arista Records' anniversary show at Radio City Music Hall segued into negotiating broadcast rights with CBS Television, and Shimmel established a friendship with Arista label head Clive Davis. After scoring such major deals, Shimmel felt there was no way to top his own success, and began looking for a new challenge. While settling a disagreement between George Michael and Coke, he realized that he was more comfortable representing the artist's point of view. He went to work with Michael's management team for several years, until the artist's dispute with Sony was settled at trial.

After opening his own artist management company, Shimmel got involved with the urban music market and later merged his firm with artist manager Rob Kahane, whose clients included George Michael, Morrissey, and Jody Watley. Together, they launched Acme Records in 1993, with Shimmel being named senior vice president and general manager.

Shimmel left to form another management company, with John Denver, Broadway composer Frank Wildhorn (*Jekyll & Hyde*), and others as clients. The signing of Arista recording artist Tony Rich brought him into contact with Antonio "L.A." Reid and Kenneth "Babyface" Edmonds, founders of Arista subsidiary, LaFace Records. In 1996, Reid approached Shimmel about a change of career. Already having a relationship with Arista and its founder, president and CEO, Clive Davis, and impressed with the creative energy at LaFace, Shimmel moved to Atlanta and signed on as the label's chief operations officer.

LEAST FAVORITE THING ABOUT THIS JOB:

"I have to say 'no' a lot. Having to say 'no' because there are certain things that become economically unfeasible."

THE BEST THING ABOUT THIS JOB:

"The ability to provide leadership. The power to execute ideas and get things done; to be able to focus money and resources into a very specific area whenever I want to, when it is feasible. The ability to sit down with an artist and lay out a marketing or game plan, predict how their record will develop, and see the plan executed and done almost perfectly. There is a real sense of accomplishment in that."

VOICES OF EXPERIENCE

In 2000, Reid was named president and CEO of Arista Records in New York, succeeding Davis, and Shimmel went with him, becoming senior vice president of artist relations. Eighteen months later, he was promoted to senior vice president of marketing and artist relations. Reporting directly to Reid, Shimmel oversees product development and marketing duties for all Arista artists and acts as a day-to-day liaison between the label and its talent roster. *www.arista.com*

EXECUTIVE OFFICE
(SMALLER OR INDEPENDENT LABEL)

GENERAL MANAGER • OPERATIONS MANAGER • PRESIDENT
(INDEPENDENT LABEL)

JOB DESCRIPTION

These executives oversee the day-to-day operation of the record label. At independent label HighTone Records, Darrell Anderson not only manages, but performs many of the tasks under his direction. He oversees radio promotion, marketing and sales, stock maintenance and shipping, and management and training of staff. He is also the first step in the A&R process.

PREREQUISITES

Two important qualities are the ability to multi-task and an engaging telephone personality. "When I hire people, I want to talk to them on the phone more than I want to meet them in person because I want them to convince me that they ought to have a job on the telephone."

CAREER TIPS

Develop a confident, but friendly, telephone personality.

Once hired as an intern or in any entry-level position, talk with those around you and learn the responsibilities of each person. Stay busy and look for opportunities to assist others with their workload. Make yourself indispensable.

A DAY IN THE LIFE

Darrell Anderson arrives at his office around 6:30 A.M. His first chore of the day is to check the label's web site and read through his e-mail. Sometime in the morning, Anderson meets with the label owner to discuss ongoing projects. Throughout the day he talks with label artists and venue personnel about purchasing tickets to the artists' performances. He contacts radio stations to set up advertising campaigns, and checks on the staff to be sure they are meeting deadlines for promotions, mailings, and other projects. Through it all, Anderson resolves any problems that may occur.

POINTERS FOR THE JOB SEARCH

"Intern. Intern. Intern. Intern. Everybody who is working for me right now started out as an intern. You get an idea of whether you're going to like the job or not, and the company finds out if they like you or not. If you're in a city where there is a record label, find out if you can stuff envelopes, answer telephones, do anything that needs to be done, so you can surround yourself with people who are in the business."

CASE STUDY:

DARRELL ANDERSON, OPERATIONS MANAGER, HIGHTONE RECORDS

Darrell Anderson got his start at age 15 in a suburban California "mom and pop" music store, selling records, cassettes, and eight-tracks. "It was halfway between San Francisco and Sacramento. It was a little store that my father had helped the owner build. My mother was their first employee, my sister their second, and I was the third." At 18 years old, he was promoted to store manager, and when the shop later became part of a chain, he transferred to manage a store in Ohio. He quit after five years, returning to the West Coast with plans to get out of retail. The next year, realizing that he missed the business, he went to work for the small Rainbow Records chain, teaching employees how to sell records at five locations in San Francisco and Oakland.

VOICES OF EXPERIENCE

THE LEAST FAVORITE THING ABOUT THIS JOB:

"People can't believe this, but going to shows is my least favorite thing. I get up at four in the morning. When you go to a show that starts at midnight and you have to work the next day, it makes it a little tough. I got into the record business because I like records, not concerts. I love seeing the artist and I love seeing them play, but I don't like the hours you have to keep to go to shows."

THE BEST THING ABOUT THIS JOB:

"Working for a company where I'm not embarrassed of what I do. I get to work records that are good records. I can hold my head up and say, 'We may be little guys but we make good records.' I work with nice people, who are intelligent and hard working. I like surrounding myself with people who have convictions."

In 1987, after seven years with Rainbow, a local record salesman urged Anderson to interview with a music distributor for a position doing promotional work with local radio stations. After a year on the job, he heard that HighTone Records was looking for someone to do national promotion. He applied, but was told that the position had been filled. When that person quit a month later, Anderson was offered the job and over the past 12 years has risen to the position of operations manager. He oversees marketing and radio promotion for the label's roster of artists. *www.hightone.com*

CHIEF EXECUTIVE OFFICER • PRESIDENT/GENERAL MANAGER

JOB OVERVIEW

These executives chart the direction of the company and oversee daily operations. As president of a new independent label, Monty Hitchcock is hands-on with everything from answering the telephone to signing new artists. "My main responsibility is to make sure that marketing plans, budgets, and relationships with the artists are developed, and that budgets and plans are adhered to."

PREREQUISITES

To succeed, you need a solid understanding of the music business and substantial knowledge in the areas of distribution and marketing, creativity, problem solving, multi-task abilities, self-motivation, management qualities, communications skills, and strategic planning.

A DAY IN THE LIFE

No day is like any other in the life of Monty Hitchcock, but some of his daily tasks include responding to e-mail and faxes, and returning phone calls to artists, managers, attorneys, and other executives. He has regular meetings with his marketing, promotions and sales staff, artists who are signed to the label and their managers, and others who might be pitching new artists or presenting a marketing opportunity. He may review a contract, approve artwork, listen to newly recorded music or songs being pitched to an artist, negotiate a television special, or help unload a shipment of CDs that has just arrived.

CAREER TIPS

Be true to your word and do everything you say you will do. It is a very "who you know" industry. If you are not true to your word, everyone in the industry will soon know it, and they won't want to work with you.

POINTERS FOR THE JOB SEARCH

Whether you want to be in management or someday run a record label, work in every facet of the business and gain an understanding of what an agent does, how publishing and performing rights fit into the picture, what marketing, promotion, and salespeople do, and so forth. Gain a concept of what role each person plays.

CASE STUDY:

MONTY HITCHCOCK, PRESIDENT, EMINENT RECORDS

"I played drums from the time I was 13," says Monty Hitchcock of his musical beginnings. He grew up in Carthage, Tennessee, and knew he wanted a career in music from the first time he was paid for playing. "I knew I would never get into any other business." After attending college to appease his parents, he went right back out on the road. One night in 1983, during an extended gig in Las Vegas, he was in a lounge watching the drummer of a small jazz combo, when it occurred to him that he would never play as well as this musician, who had been performing in this dive for eight years.

Returning to Nashville, he found work in video production and by 1986, Hitchcock was on the road almost continuously as a production/lighting technician, juggling the touring schedules of Roseanne Cash, Sweethearts of the Rodeo, the O'Kanes, and Vince Gill. While touring with Emmylou Harris at about the same time, he continually looked for ways to increase production values, cut costs, and make traveling easier. His suggestions led to a job as Harris' road manager in 1991, and later to the formation of Monty Hitchcock Management to guide the careers of Harris, Jon Randall, Sweethearts of the Rodeo, and others.

After several years of being pressed to start an independent record label, by the late 1990s Hitchcock felt the time was right. He divested himself of his management

THE LEAST FAVORITE THING ABOUT THIS JOB:

"The downside is that you can't give everybody what they want. It's hard to make an artist understand that there is a whole lot more to the business than just making great records. You've got to have a team, a manager, an agent and a desire to go out there and work."

THE BEST THING ABOUT THIS JOB:

"I hear a tremendous amount of great music. That's what got me in the business, period; the fact that I loved to listen to music."

VOICES OF EXPERIENCE

responsibilities and opened Eminent Records in 1998. The label's first release was Emmylou Harris' *Spyboy*, a live concert recording. Struggling to carve out a solid niche for the label, Hitchcock left Eminent in 2000. Returning to artist management, he opened M. Hitchcock Management and reunited with Sony/Epic recording artist Jon Randall. *www.mhmgmt.com*

ARTIST AND REPERTOIRE (A&R)

SENIOR VICE PRESIDENT • VICE PRESIDENT (A&R)

JOB OVERVIEW

Doug Howard and Nancy Jeffries discover, sign, and develop musical talent for their respective record labels. They screen potential songs for their artists, oversee the recording process, and find the right producer and studio. Once the record is finished, they work with each label department to ensure the music and artist are presented and marketed appropriately.

PREREQUISITES

To succeed, you need the ability to spot talent and develop and nurture it to be successful. You should be able to bridge the gap between the creative and business sides of music and have a firm understanding of the recording process. Strong personal contacts with publishers, producers, and songwriters are essential. You should be able to recognize great songs and to match them with the appropriate recording artists.

A DAY IN THE LIFE

Throughout the day, Nancy Jeffries listens to the ever-growing mountain of demo tapes she receives, meets with publishers and writers pitching songs for artists on the roster, and with attorneys, managers, and others pitching new artists. She speaks with the artists she is responsible for to check where they are in the recording process, to set up meetings for them with prospective producers, and to talk about material they are looking for. She may stop by the studio to hear a new recording or mix, or attend a company business meeting, or one about an artist she represents. At night Jeffries attends performances by label artists or those auditioning for a deal.

Some constants in the life of Doug Howard are attending marketing, sales, and promotion meetings. "This allows me to hear what radio is saying about our projects; what reviewers have written." If he has an artist in the studio, he drops by to ensure everything is running smoothly. Throughout the recording process he continues to listen to songs in case something great comes in. He sorts through a massive amount of e-mail and tries to catch up on telephone calls. On any given day Howard meets with songwriters, song pluggers, producers, potential artists, and individuals pitching new artists. As a senior executive, he handles a variety of administrative tasks and participates in industry events and seminars. Howard's primary goal is to listen to songs and find hits for the artists signed to the label, and that is where he directs his energy whenever possible.

POINTERS FOR THE JOB SEARCH

"In the A&R field, it's very rare that somebody gets a chance just because someone likes them. You have to get yourself in people's sights and prove to them that you have some ability to spot talent, and then once you've spotted it, you have the ability to nurture it and bring it along. It's not an easy job to apply for. If you want to be in A&R and you can't find a job, then find work booking a club, managing an artist, or working at a college radio station. Something where you have to select music and you can show people that you selected it in a way that was advantageous. Then people will be more receptive than if you just come in and say, 'I can pick a hit.'"—NJ

"I think it's vital that you move to a music center. Take a vacation and check out some place like Nashville or Los Angeles. It's unfortunate to have to tell somebody in Little Rock, but you have to live in a music center. That may be a sacrifice, so be prepared for that."—DH

"In A&R, I think it's very helpful if you have some grounding in music. Not just to know what a hit is; that's not enough. You need to know what makes it a hit or a great piece of music. You need to be able to recognize what kind of personality can handle what's going to happen to them; can they handle the success? You have to have a grounding in the business side of music as well."—NJ

"Be feisty. No one is going to come over to you and say, 'Oh, you're great! Let's make you an A&R person.'"—NJ

"Having the sense of melody and why one song stands out more than others. I really think that can be learned, but it comes from really listening. If you surround yourself with great music, those good things surface when you're out listening to demos. Focus on that."—DH

"Listen. Listen. Listen. Be a fan of music, first and foremost. It doesn't matter if you're a country fan or pop fan or whatever. I find the more diverse you are, the better."—DH

"Working in A&R administration is a good way to get your foot in the door. I think it gives you a fantastic base to work from. You really get to know the nuts and bolts."—NJ

CASE STUDY:

NANCY JEFFRIES, SENIOR VICE PRESIDENT A&R, ELEKTRA ENTERTAINMENT

"I was a singer," says Nancy Jeffries. "I sang with a band in the late sixties and early seventies." This native New Yorker's band, Insect Trust, cut two albums before she decided that the aspect of music she enjoyed most was producing records. While searching for work in 1974, she discovered that the world of the recording studio virtually excluded women. With money running low, she applied at a temporary secretarial agency, listing all of her past skills in concert promotion and recording, and landed a job working for the head of R&B A&R at RCA Records. "It didn't take him

THE LEAST FAVORITE THING ABOUT THIS JOB:

"The piles of unsolicited demos. Demo listening: I think that is everybody's least favorite part of the job. In the A&R world there is always a constant battle to keep up with the demos coming in. It's the most boring part."—NJ

"The fact that because there is only one of me, I don't see my dear friends as often as I'd like. My schedule is such that I can't return every phone call. I miss a lot of my old relationships with friends I worked with as a publisher."—DH

THE BEST THING ABOUT THIS JOB:

"I love finding somebody and watching their career happen. To work with somebody that when you first saw them had only two people in the audience and by the time you're done, they're playing a stadium—that's amazing."—NJ

"I've had a lot of great opportunities to work with nice people. The bosses I've had, for the most part, have been very creative people. That has allowed me to do things that are a little bit left of center."—NJ

"I get to make a living making music, working with musicians, artists, and writers. I can't think of anything better than that. I'm also surrounded by friends at this office; people I've known for years."—DH

long to realize I had no office skills, but I could talk on the phone to his clients about what they were doing in a way that took a weight off him, so they let me stay." Her boss moved to another label nine months later and she was promoted to A&R administration for several years.

When her efforts in signing an important act failed to get her promoted out of administration and into the creative side of A&R, Jeffries threatened to quit. Rather than lose her, RCA gave her the desired promotion. Later, she moved to A&M Records, to work A&R for label head Jordan Harris. While there, she signed Suzanne Vega and matched Iggy Pop to record with David Bowie. When Harris and Jeff Ayeroff opened the American office of Virgin Records, Jeffries went with them, and signed Lenny Kravitz, Ziggy Marley, and Keith Richards, among others. In 1990, Jeffries moved to Elektra Entertainment as senior vice president of A&R to work with such established acts as Linda Ronstadt, Natalie Cole, and Jackson Browne, and to sign new talent.

CASE STUDY:

DOUG HOWARD, SENIOR VICE PRESIDENT A&R, LYRIC STREET RECORDS

Raised in Mississippi cotton country hearing musical refrains drifting out of Memphis, Doug Howard fell in love with music at an early age, knowing from childhood that he wanted to go to Nashville. As a teenager, he had a job at a local radio station that introduced him to *Billboard* magazine, where he first learned about the business side of music. After going to Nashville in the 1970s to attend David Lipscomb University, he transferred into Belmont College's music program, where he met many people he would later work with, and interned in the mail room of a small Christian publishing company. After graduation, he worked three jobs simultaneously and put out the word that he wanted to get into music publishing. When college friends recommended him for a song plugger position at Welk Music, an independent publisher, Howard jumped at the chance to interview.

"It was kind of funny because Bill [Hall] sat on one side of the room and Roger [Sovine] sat on the other side, so that I couldn't see them both at the same time. They asked all the questions you ask a guy you're sizing up to work for your company, but then they just stopped and said, 'We'll be in touch.' It was just the coldest." Normally, Howard would have just said "thank you" and left, but not this time. "This mattered so much to me that I stood up and said, 'Y'all have to understand that I'm your guy.'" Seeing Howard's passion, they hired him. Over the years, Hall became a mentor and even sent Howard to Vanderbilt University so he could earn an MBA to increase his business credentials.

By 1988, Howard sensed that the industry and the times were on the brink of change, so he made a bold career move. He temporarily left the business and enrolled at George Washington University to pursue a law degree. While attending classes, he gained experience by working at a legal firm in Washington, D.C., knowing that he wanted to return to the music business. In the meantime, Welk Music was sold to Polygram, and just as Howard was finishing his studies, he got a call from the head of Polygram North America, offering him a position in Nashville, which they held for six weeks until he graduated.

In 1997, when Disney decided to open Lyric Street Records, Howard's college friend, Randy Goodman, was named president and enticed him to come aboard as senior vice president of A&R. One of the label's biggest successes is Rascal Flatts; other artists include SHeDAISY, Josh Gracin, and former *American Idol* finalist Bucky Covington.

Howard was elected president of the board of governors of the Nashville chapter of Recording Academy in 2004 and served a two-year term. In 2005, Lyric Street's parent company, Disney, announced it was opening a Nashville office of Disney Music Publishing. Howard was named senior vice president and general manager, affording him the opportunity to return to his roots in publishing and developing songwriters, while retaining his A&R duties at the label.

SENIOR VICE PRESIDENT INTERNATIONAL A&R • DIRECTOR INTERNATIONAL A&R

JOB DESCRIPTION

The purpose of the A&R department is to find and develop new talent. The specific role of the international A&R department is to scour the world for artists who have the potential to break in America and secure rights to release their music in the United States. Some artists may come from the label's foreign affiliates, while others may be signed to another label group and not have a deal in place for America. International A&R is also involved in adapting the artist's material to fit the market. For instance, the first 'N Sync record had four songs recorded that do not appear on the European release, to make it more appropriate for the American market.

"I've been in the music business for 26 years and I still love it like I did in the beginning. You've got to have a love and passion for it to be successful."

"Trust your gut to make decisions for you. Pay attention and seriously consider the messages your gut is telling you."

PREREQUISITES

To succeed, you must have the ability to recognize and develop international artists who have the potential to achieve success in the American market.

A DAY IN THE LIFE

For Dave Novik, the day begins with telephone calls to overseas markets to discuss new signings and discover leads on talent of interest to him. "I'm constantly getting e-mail from new artists offering music, sometimes sending an MP3 file of songs so that I can download and listen." He may attend a meeting about the marketing campaign for an artist to ensure the project is set up correctly. Throughout the day he listens to as much music as possible. He attends concerts and showcases for bands both locally and out of town. Daily he meets with managers, publishers, lawyers, and others wanting to talk about their artists. Mornings, before he arrives at the office, and weekends, are devoted to listening to the overwhelming amount of music he receives on a daily basis.

POINTERS FOR THE JOB SEARCH

"International A&R is not a job that you can train for, so you have to find your way into the organization somehow. Become an assistant. Become a college intern. There are programs offered in many colleges and universities around the country that have music business courses. Start out by getting some kind of training and understanding of the business. Then, it's starting at the bottom and building yourself up in an organization."

CASE STUDY:

DAVID NOVIK, FORMER SENIOR VICE PRESIDENT INTERNATIONAL A&R, RCA RECORDS; SENIOR VICE PRESIDENT A&R, UNIVERSAL CLASSICS GROUP

When it became apparent that he would never learn to play the guitar, London teenager David Novik transferred his love of music to working as a deejay at the local youth club. Within a few years, he was entertaining at parties with a mobile sound

---

THE LEAST FAVORITE THING ABOUT THIS JOB:

"I hate cigarette smoke [in clubs]. I have asthma and I don't like my clothes to smell. I hate that I don't have enough time in the day, or night, to listen to music. That's probably the biggest problem that I have as an A&R person: trying to find the time to listen to music."

THE BEST THING ABOUT THIS JOB:

"I love hearing a song, or an artist, or a vocal performance that sends shivers up my spine. It doesn't happen too often but when it does, it is amazing. The feeling of finding something special, seeing it as a finished record presented to the market, and then ultimately working—that is an exciting moment. Seeing the response from radio or, more importantly, the public who go out and buy it. Seeing a great first week in Sound Scan. Those things make me feel great."

VOICES OF EXPERIENCE

system, all the while learning everything he could about the bands, producers, and record labels that generated the music he played. A 1974 interview at newly opened Virgin Records failed to produce a job offer, but the interviewer helped Novik get another interview at Magnet Records that resulted in an offer. Hired initially as a messenger/office boy, he was promoted through the ranks to A&R talent scout.

After eight years at Magnet, Novik joined CBS Records in 1982, and worked with artists such as Paul Young and Psychedelic Furs. A couple of years later he was offered a position with CBS International in New York. "I jumped at the chance because I had never been to America. I loved American music and wanted to be part of that scene." In New York, he worked with such acts as Men at Work and Nina Hagen, and when given the opportunity to expand into international territories, he learned that some of them needed A&R help. Acting on this information, he secured an interview with the head of the Australian office, and ended up being hired as the head of A&R for CBS Australia in 1985. After three years of building up the Australian market, and working with the band Midnight Oil, he was offered a job as vice president of A&R for Epic Records in Los Angeles.

Following a year working with artists like Indigo Girls and Social Distortion, Novik was offered a job in New York, co-heading the A&R department at Columbia Records. Despite the problems of shared management, he worked with Michael Bolton, Mariah Carey, and Judy Collins until 1991. Hired as the senior vice president of A&R at RCA Records in 1992, he became senior vice president of A&R international in 1995, and was involved in the signing of Natalie Imbruglia and 'N Sync, among others.

After ten years with RCA, Novik left in 2002 to pursue other interests. He opened a consulting and production company and served as executive producer on the Grammy Award-winning CD, *Wire*, recorded by the band Third Day.

Novik returned to the corporate music world in 2005, when he was appointed senior vice president A&R for Universal Classics Group. Based in New York, Novik is responsible for discovering new artists and projects in the classical crossover and adult music genres and the development of new soundtrack opportunities for the Universal Classics Group of labels. He is also involved in the creative aspects of existing artist projects and recordings released on the various international classical labels. *www.new.umusic.com*

DIRECTOR • SENIOR DIRECTOR (A&R)

JOB OVERVIEW

Atlantic's Rich Christina and Arista's Pete Ganbarg specialize in different genres of music, but their primary roles are similar. They discover new talent, facilitate the artist signing with the label, and develop music for release. Within that scope, they help find material for the artist to record, help select the right producer and engineers, and oversee the entire recording process, including whether to record on digital or analog tape. They also guide the artist through the process of imaging and marketing. Christina is involved in finding already recorded material, and artists from foreign markets, to release in the United States.

The story of how Santana's hit song "Smooth" came to be is a perfect example of what an A&R person does. "I got a call one day from a friend of mine who was working with a new songwriter that had written a song with Santana in mind, and asked if I had a few minutes to hear it," explains Ganbarg. The writer came to the label and played the song for Ganbarg, and although he didn't think the lyric was right for Santana, he liked the music. He suggested that the writer leave a copy of the music and let him find someone else to write new lyrics. "I called a music publisher friend and I played him the music without the lyric over the phone." The publisher liked what he heard and suggested one of his writers, Rob Thomas from Matchbox 20, to take a crack at writing the words. The music was sent to Thomas and the resulting song, "Smooth," earned a 1999 Song of the Year Grammy for Santana and Thomas, who also sang on the recording.

PREREQUISITES

You should have an overall love and appreciation of music, an understanding of how the industry works, and contacts within it. The ability to find and nurture recording talent is essential.

A DAY IN THE LIFE

Rich Christina's day begins the night before, going through trade magazines and other material to research records that are doing well, or showing potential throughout the world. When he arrives at the office the next morning he makes calls to and e-mails record companies, artists, attorneys, and other international contacts about records that interest him. Because he deals with R&B, rap, pop, and pop rock, he rarely attends shows to discover talent, like rock and country A&R people do. Instead, he deals more with producers, songwriters, and studio-based artists. By noon he starts taking meetings with songwriters, producers, or attorneys who have artists they feel would be great for Atlantic Records. Throughout the day he listens to music (including on the drive to and from the office), attends interoffice meetings, and returns phone calls. He works with artists on various recording projects, including film sound tracks.

"I usually get in around 11 in the morning," says Arista's Pete Ganbarg. "I'll check in with my projects that are recording in the studio, speak on the phone to all the producers, artists, and writers involved with a specific project." Next he verifies radio airplay, sales, and press on any projects currently in release to get a sense of what is working and what needs some help. Throughout the day he listens to songs or meets

"An A&R person is only as good as the new talent he discovers. So, the future is definitely bright for young people who have a desire and skill to be able to identify amazing new talent."—PG

Put a smile on your face and do whatever you're asked with a positive attitude so that people will want to work with you. It is a very competitive business. If you're not positive and easy to work with, particularly when trying to get your foot in the door, you'll be replaced by someone else who is.

Hang out in clubs and attend showcases, and listen and look for new talent that knocks you out.

with the rest of the A&R department, or the head of the label. At night he often sees a band showcase or a concert by one of the label artists, or stops by a recording studio.

POINTERS FOR THE JOB SEARCH

"When you're an intern, you've got people's attention for six months. In that time you've got to look for ways to stand out and fit in." Look for areas of the company where someone is needed to complete a task that is not being covered. "Don't try to do another person's job better, that won't fare too well with the person that already has that job, and the record company will just see that as redundancy. Come in and carve your own path."—RC

"Immerse yourself in music. Listen to every record that comes out. Know who produced it, who wrote the songs, what label it's on. If you're doing that, you're going to be on top of what's going on and in a position to be turned on to new and exciting things that will hopefully lead you to a connection that helps you find a job."—PG

CASE STUDY:

RICH CHRISTINA, SENIOR DIRECTOR A&R, THE ATLANTIC GROUP

By the time he entered college, Rich Christina had amassed an extensive record collection, which afforded him the opportunity to make money working as a deejay. At Rowan University he studied advertising and hated it. "I was going to leave school for a year so that I could mentally regroup and decide what I was going to do with my life." A discussion with a relative who pointed out, "You love music. There must be something you can do in music," influenced Christina to switch his major to mass communications and set his sights on working for a record company. Through a fraternity brother who worked in the video department at Atlantic Records, and who happened to be in the right place at the right time, Christina got a shot at working for the label. His friend walked into the human resources office just as a call came from the dance department in search of an intern with deejay experience. Christina was recommended.

Determined to turn the internship into a full time position, Christina volunteered for extra work and began looking for a way to create an opportunity. "I had researched the music business enough to know that it's very difficult to get into, and I figured this was my one and only chance to turn this into a job. I did whatever they asked me to do with a smile on my face and in the meantime I looked around the department to see where there was a hole, something that wasn't being covered." At the time, radio stations were giving club deejays their own shows, and airing remotes

THE LEAST FAVORITE THING ABOUT THIS JOB:

"The thing I like the least about the music business, or my job specifically, is that there is a high failure rate. I don't know the exact number, but around 90 percent of all records produced don't perform; they don't make their money back. It's hard when you work with someone for a year or two and they put their heart and soul into a record; they've waited their whole life for this opportunity and nothing happens. I hate failing for other people; not being able to help them fulfill their dreams."—RC

"Sometimes there is a lot of red tape and bureaucracy that you have to deal with in any corporate business. The music business is becoming much more business oriented."—PG

THE BEST THING ABOUT THIS JOB:

"I love music. I always have, since I was a small child. I love the fact that I can make a career out of something I love. You only have one life to live so you might as well enjoy every moment."—RC

"I love being able to create something and watch it grow and be successful. There is nothing more thrilling than finding a record or an artist that you think is fantastic, coming up with a great single, the photos come out great, the video is fantastic, and launch it and it sells a million records."—RC

"I like hearing a song and working with the writer or the artist to get that song to be a hit, hearing it on the radio, and going into the record store and seeing people buy the record."—PG

from clubs. Christina recognized an opportunity to get records played through servicing the club deejays and calling on them to promote records. He approached his boss with the idea and was given the go-ahead to begin making calls. Within a year, nearly every label was doing the same thing. Later, this became a way for the label to discover talent and sign record deals for music that was being played on the club scene.

When the first record he found became a Top Forty success, Christina stepped up from intern to a position in promotion and A&R. A year later, when Everything But The Girl's "Missing" sold three million copies worldwide, he was able to leave promotion and move into A&R full time. In addition to his work with individual acts, Christina has also been involved in sound tracks for several films, including *Space Jam* and *Dr. Doolittle*. www.atlanticrecords.com

CASE STUDY:

PETE GANBARG, SENIOR DIRECTOR A&R, ARISTA RECORDS

In his early teens, Pete Ganbarg discovered *Billboard* magazine at the local library and his fate was sealed. He immersed himself in reading the record charts to find out which records were currently popular and began to amass a record collection. He began to work as a deejay at parties around Rockland County, just outside Manhattan. Because he loved being a deejay, a good campus radio station was one of his prime requirements when it came time to select a college.

On his first day at Wesleyan University, Ganbarg went to the radio station and basically spent the next four years there as its music director, overseeing the music, programming, and whatever else needed to be done. Over time, he also began booking acts for campus concerts, and managed several local bands.

Armed with some significant music business experience and an education degree in high school English as a backup, Ganbarg got a job doing radio promotion for an independent New York record label. He landed the job on the recommendation of a college friend. A year later, the same friend arranged an interview when his father was starting up SBK Records. Ganbarg began as an entry level A&R manager, and during the next eight years, he was promoted to vice president of A&R, and saw the label merge with EMI Records. When EMI closed their American offices, he moved to Arista Records as senior director of A&R, where he oversaw the multiple Grammy Award winning album *Supernatural Santana*.

In 2001, Ganbarg joined Epic Records as senior vice president A&R, where he signed and developed new artists and worked with the label's existing roster. While there, he signed rock band Revis and worked on releases of Michael Jackson, Celine Dion, and Keb Mo's 2005 Grammy Award winning CD *Keep It Simple*.

Ganberg left Epic in 2003 to open Pure Tone Music, a full-service music company. His A&R consulting clients included Arista Records, Virgin Records, Warner Brothers Reoords, RCA Records, and Burgandy Records. Banbarg has A&R'd CDs for Taylor

Hicks, Daughtry, Santana, Aaron Neville, Donna Summer, Kenny G., and Chaka Khan. *www.puretonemusic.com*

MANAGER • SENIOR MANAGER (A&R)

JOB DESCRIPTION

Managers scout new talent for the label to sign and find songs for them to record. Because Renee White also serves as Tony Brown's (label president and a producer) assistant, her main focus is as a facilitator of information to and from him. She prioritizes and schedules appointments and phone calls requested by him or other individuals. White makes him aware of internal and external office correspondence, and briefs him about information that requires his response. She accepts and delivers music he needs to hear and coordinates his travel arrangements. Essentially, White's goal is to help Brown's business life run smoothly.

PREREQUISITES

One of the most important traits of an assistant/A&R manager is flexibility because the workday revolves around coordinating the needs of another person. It is important to know who is who in the industry in order to prioritize calls and appointments. A positive and friendly attitude, clerical skills, the ability to multi-task, and confidentiality are essential requirements.

Study music trade magazines and learn who is who in the industry, particularly the names of song-writers and publishers. Read album label copy and become familiar with who wrote, produced, and played the songs on the album.

CAREER TIPS

A DAY IN THE LIFE

White begins most mornings helping her boss go through the list of phone calls that need to be made and returned, and channels people through the office who need to meet with him. When he is in the recording studio, she stops by with anything pertinent that he might need, such as papers to sign, phone calls to make, charts to review. Throughout the day she deals with e-mail, faxes, and other correspondence. She fields telephone calls from publishers, songwriters, producers, artists, managers, attorneys, label executives, and others, and takes appropriate action.

POINTERS FOR THE JOB SEARCH

"Be flexible and open to opportunities, even working in the mail room. If you work hard, you can move up." Another good starting point is as a receptionist, where

LEAST FAVORITE THING ABOUT THIS JOB:

"The only thing that is not a dream about this job is that I have to be here every day. There is no traveling involved and I do have the wanderlust."

THE BEST THING ABOUT THIS JOB:

"I like being in the thick of a lot of interesting things happening. For instance, last night I attended Michael McDonald's record release party. Last week I went to a Bruce Springsteen concert. It's fun being around so much talent. It's a lot better than insurance work, I'm telling you."

you can become familiar with people calling in to the label, and can gain experience dealing with a variety of personalities.

CASE STUDY:

RENEE WHITE, FORMER SENIOR MANAGER OF A&R, MCA RECORDS NASHVILLE; A&R, VANGUARD / SUGAR HILL RECORDS

Detroit native Renee White had been studying painting at Wayne State University when she decided that she had suffered through enough cold winters. While visiting a friend in Nashville, she found a job with the first of several insurance companies. Hating the work, she moved on to a pawnshop where she learned the diamond trade. After eight years of selling wholesale diamonds and custom jewelry, the birth of her daughter sent White searching for a job with medical insurance and benefits. The secretarial skills she had honed working for insurance companies helped her to land a job at Welk Music Publishing (later bought by Polygram Music) answering telephones and copyright administrating. She loved the creative energy of the music business and quickly got to know many of the major songwriters in town.

In 1990, after eight years of struggling to make ends meet, White decided it was time for a change. She quit with the idea of returning to painting, but missed the structure of an office job after only one month. She put together a resume, dropped one off at MCA Music, and the next day got a phone call from a friend offering her a job. She was hired as executive assistant to Tony Brown, president of MCA Records Nashville. Working for Brown, White had an opportunity to work closely not only with the label's roster of artists but also with songwriters, publishers, and producers. She earned more responsibility, searching for and screening songs, and was rewarded with a promotion to senior manager of A&R.

With Brown leaving MCA to co-found Universal South, it was time for White to spread her wings, taking on A&R responsibilities for Vanguard/Sugar Hill Records. *www.sugarhillrecords.com*

A&R ADMINISTRATION AND PRODUCTION

VICE PRESIDENT • SENIOR DIRECTOR
(PRODUCTION AND A&R ADMINISTRATION)

JOB OVERVIEW

These administrators manage and oversee A&R administration and production departments. At Arista Nashville, Susan Heard oversees a staff of four people who are responsible for the payment of all recording costs, including artist and producer advances, and recoupable expenses, such as video. Approval of recording budgets, and responsibility for the master tape vault, also fall under her direction. She and her staff gather and check the production credit information that appears on each release, such as producer, engineer, and musician, publishing and songwriter information, and so forth, and deliver it to the creative department. Heard's department ensures that the production master finds its way from the mastering studio to the manufacturing plant. They arrange for film of the paper inserts to be sent to the printers, and oversee the manufacturing of cassettes, CDs, and singles.

PREREQUISITES

To succeed, you should have experience in A&R administration for a label, studio, or producer, and an understanding of the entire recording and manufacturing process. The ability to manage and motivate people is essential.

A DAY IN THE LIFE

Susan Heard starts her day by checking voice mail as she drives to the office and e-mail upon arrival. Throughout the day Heard meets with her staff, reviews and approves budgets and expenditures, and attends meetings with other department heads. "I try to plan ahead and set the course for the projects and once the course is set, the rest of the department

Stay abreast of changes in recording technology. "If the production and A&R administration department don't keep up with technology innovations, we are doing a tremendous disservice to the company because what the artists and producers are turning in as masters will become inaccessible for the record label."

CAREER TIPS

VOICES OF EXPERIENCE

THE BEST THING ABOUT THIS JOB:

"My real love is the recording process. That just fascinates me."

can maintain the course. I put out the fires along the way."

POINTERS FOR THE JOB SEARCH

"Experience is the best teacher. Hang out in a studio or join whatever organization you can to learn more about the recording process."

CASE STUDY:

SUSAN HEARD, SENIOR DIRECTOR PRODUCTION/ A&R ADMINISTRATION, ARISTA RECORDS NASHVILLE

"I have always been involved in music," says Susan Heard. "I played clarinet in band for ten years, studied classical piano for twelve years." So it was no surprise that she chose music as a major when she enrolled at Baylor University. In her junior year, Heard changed her emphasis to radio and television communications, serving internships in both radio and television news, before completing her undergraduate work in 1982. After graduation, she went to Los Angeles where she made contacts at recording studios through friends, but was unable to find a job. Within 24 hours of returning to Texas, she got a phone call from one of those contacts, offering an interview.

Without a definite job, but wanting to live in Los Angeles, Heard made the move. Upon her arrival, she interviewed and landed the job of production assist-ant and session booker to Grammy Award winning producer Bill Schnaye, and remained at his recording studio for two years. "I had a great time working at the studio and seeing the inner workings of how records are made. It was fascinating, hanging out with incredible musicians." Session work with the band Toto led to an introduction to the group's management team of Larry Fitzgerald and Mark Hartley, which in turn led to a five-year job with Fitzgerald Hartley Company as an administrative assistant.

Heard's new job gave her experience in many different areas, from publicity to publishing to tour promotion, with groups as diverse as the Jacksons, Glenn Frey, Toto, and Paul McCartney. The firm opened a Nashville office in 1985, partnered with songwriter/producer Tim DuBois. With a second child on the way, she quit her job in 1989 to sort out her next career move. Heard's husband, also in the music industry, lost his job soon after. When a string of promising offers failed to pan out, the couple decided that they would starve slower in Nashville than in Los Angeles. Heard relocated in 1990, once again without having a job in place.

After a round of interviews, she was hired as A&R administrator for Christian label Sparrow Records. Three years later, DuBois, now head of Arista Records' Nashville office, hired her to transfer the label's A&R administration from the New York office and head up the department. When Arista bought Reunion Records in 1994, Heard was charged with setting up and hiring staff for an in-house production department. After that, she became senior director of production and A&R administration. In 2000, Heard followed DuBois to Gaylord Entertainment Company to become vice president of production.

MANAGER A&R ADMINISTRATION • DIRECTOR OF A&R ADMINISTRATION

JOB OVERVIEW

The job of A&R administration begins when the producer and the artist are in the recording studio. You must track recording costs and process invoices, and receive and log in all masters, parts, multi-tracks, mixes—all tapes and CDs—from the recording session. Other duties include arranging for production parts to be cut and sent to the manufacturing plant; logging in and archiving all master tapes, videos, CDs, and so on, and overseeing the archive of recording and video masters.

PREREQUISITES

To succeed, you must have computer data entry skills and be detail oriented with strong organizational skills. You need the ability to communicate clearly with both business and creative individuals.

A DAY IN THE LIFE

A major portion of the day for RCA's Lawrence Loring is devoted to processing bills from studios, producers, engineers, and others. "There are always requests for video or audio masters from the vault and I control that like a librarian. All of our tapes are bar coded, so when I get a request that someone needs a TV track to a certain song—Martina McBride doing Letterman or something—I'll go through our vault tracking system and find those tapes [which are sometimes stored offsite or even out of state]." Loring also accepts delivery of recording projects as they are completed, logging in all the mixes, masters, multi-tracks, and

"Have a good, well-rounded music background—knowing all types of music."

Listen to songs by staff writers and become familiar with their catalog. Even though you're not responsible for pitching songs, knowing the catalog will open up opportunities for you and earn you the respect of the writers and others you work with.

CAREER TIPS

so on. He also ships video or audio masters, and orders master parts for manufacturing from various mastering facilities.

POINTERS FOR THE JOB SEARCH

"Go to school locally and become familiar with people, companies, and artists. Nashville is a big family and everybody knows everybody."

CASE STUDY:

LAWRENCE LORING, MANAGER A&R ADMINISTRATION, RCA LABEL GROUP/NASHVILLE

"Music has always been a hobby of mine. I grew up in Strongsville, Ohio—the home of rock and roll. I made a point of becoming familiar with all types of music, whether it be classical or country or pop or rock, and I enjoyed all types of music." Two years into the premed program at Miami University, Loring decided medicine was not his passion. He returned home and enrolled in a community college, where one course sparked his interest: an introduction to the recording industry. "I took that class and fell in love with the thought that there was a way for me to take what I like doing in my personal time and make a career out of it." Loring researched colleges that offered a four-year degree in music and chose Middle Tennessee State University because of the school's relationship with Nashville's music community.

When it came time to intern at a music company, Loring focused on record labels, interviewing at Capitol and RCA, where he landed a slot. Begun in 1989, Loring's internship was split between the A&R administration department and the production department. He completed a second internship at producer Brent Mayor's publishing company.

It took Loring nearly a year after graduation to land a full time job in the industry. He had remained in touch with contacts made at RCA and when a position

THE BEST THING ABOUT THIS JOB:

"Although the job description may be specific, there have not been any two days exactly the same. I think part of that is because our product is really people and every person, every artist, is different. So every situation is different; every studio we work with is different, and every producer is different. That always keeps it interesting."

became available in 1992, he got a call. In his new job, his time was divided between the production department, where he had interned, and the finance department/building operation. One of his primary duties was working as an assistant in the tape vault. He was promoted through the ranks over the course of eight years to assistant to production, production coordinator, manager of production, and currently, manager A&R administration. "I like the whole recording and production side of the business. The next step for me would be to move up to department head."

PRODUCTION MANAGER • PRODUCTION AND OFFICE MANAGER (INDEPENDENT LABEL)

JOB OVERVIEW

The production manager takes over the manufacturing master at the mastering studio, ships it to the plant, and then follows through all the way up until the finished product is shipped to the distribution warehouses. The production manager also coordinates with creative services to get their film shipped to the printing plants, the graphics printed to meet up with the CDs and cassettes, and have them assembled and sent to the warehouses.

The production and office manager orders and stocks office supplies, processes invoices, and helps where needed, which may involve answering telephones. The office manager also obtains mechanical licenses, oversees royalty payments, and is involved in artist imaging for photo and video shoots. These staff work with the art director and designer on CD and video packaging, and other promotional pieces, and oversees the design, printing, and manufacturing process. Assembling and mailing press kits, promotional CDs, and other materials is also part of this job.

A DAY IN THE LIFE

Throughout Dawn Bryant's day she answers and routes telephone calls, greets artists, managers, and others coming to the label for meetings. She may talk with the art director about a CD cover design,

CAREER TIPS

"Make sure you truly love the business and you believe in the artist(s) that you work with. You can't be motivated by money because the money goes up and down." You may land a job that pays well, and then the company suffers a major cutback, and you're faced with taking a pay cut to secure another job.

"Don't ever burn a bridge. At some point, you will work again with somebody that you've worked with in the past and you don't want any bad feeling or bad words between you."

order more stock from the manufacturing facility, assemble promotional packages, or sit in on a staff meeting.

POINTERS FOR THE JOB SEARCH

Strong secretarial skills may enable you to find an entry-level support position. Be willing to start as a receptionist, secretary, part-time assistant, or mail room clerk to get in the door of a record label. Then work hard with a good, positive attitude. When an opening becomes available, you will be a proven asset to the company.

CASE STUDY:

DAWN BRYANT, PRODUCTION MANAGER AND OFFICE MANAGER, EMINENT RECORDS

A three-week temporary receptionist job at a Fort Lauderdale, Florida radio station was Dawn Bryant's introduction to the music business. Two years later, she had moved up to morning show producer, researching topics, writing bits, and occasionally reporting. "We were the number one station in south Florida, so we had constant dealings with artists like Gloria Estefan, Huey Lewis, and Michael McDonald."

A divorce and the desire to move to another environment led Bryant to Nashville. "Even though I had built a small career in southern Florida, it really meant nothing in Nashville. If you don't know someone, it's nearly impossible to get in. I worked as a hostess and bartender at the restaurant at night and started doing temporary work during the day. Whenever the agency got a call from the music industry, they sent me." A call to temp at a business management firm, O'Neil Hagaman, led to a one-year job in reception, office, and administration work. "[While] there I met Monty

THE LEAST FAVORITE THING ABOUT THIS JOB:

"*There is no stability in the music business. You're hot one day and the next day you're not, depending on how successful the artist is you're working for. If something happens—they lose their deal or don't sell as many records—the next thing you know, you lose your job.*"

THE BEST THING ABOUT THIS JOB:

"*I love the perks. I remember one night sitting on a bus in Austin, Texas with Shelby Lynne, Bruce Hornsby, Asleep at the Wheel, and Willie Nelson, just chatting. I got to go to Tricia Yearwood's wedding and sat next to Johnny Cash. You get to meet people you really admire and respect. I've gotten paid to travel and do some really cool things.*"

Hitchcock, who was managing Emmylou Harris at the time, and he hired me as his assistant."

The time with Hitchcock was an important learning and growth period for Bryant. When Magnatone Entertainment opened a record label, management firm, and publishing arm, she was ready to spread her wings. "I started in the management side. We got a lot of flack about the conflict of interest—our artists that were on the label were also managed by us, and eventually they shut the management division down." After Magnatone, Bryant joined TLE Management, artist Tracy Lawrence's attempt to manage other artists, but the firm was closed down six months later. Bryant landed back at Magnatone, working as creative services coordinator for the record label, but within ten months the label folded. Several other independent labels closed at that time and she found herself competing in a flooded market of laid off employees, and had to take work outside the music industry.

Eventually, Bryant received a phone call from a contact she had made while looking for work. There was an opening at Moress, Casmus Management, and she secured the job as Stan Moress' assistant. A year and a half later, she got a call from former boss Monty Hitchcock, offering her a job with his new label, Eminent Records, proving the truth of Bryant's advice that "you never want to burn a bridge," because you will probably end up working with the person again. *www.eminentrecords.com*

CREATIVE SERVICES

SENIOR VICE PRESIDENT • VICE PRESIDENT • DIRECTOR (CREATIVE SERVICE AND VIDEO)

JOB OVERVIEW

The creative services office is responsible for the imaging, art direction, and design of CD and cassette covers, media advertising, and other collateral material. At RCA Label Group, Mary Hamilton directs and oversees staff and freelance artists who are responsible for the physical image in print, video, and other forms of the label's artists. They are literally charged with making the artists' hair, makeup, clothes, and lighting look good for the camera, and ensuring that the appropriate image is projected in print and video.

PREREQUISITES

"You have to be open to change. You have to be capable and willing to put yourself on the wavelength of the person who is at the helm. Communication: being able to get numerous people on the same agenda. Art direction and international diplomacy [are] kind of the same thing."

"*Ultimately, if you want to do something, you can. The opportunities are there. You just have to put forth the effort and you will find a way for it to work.*"

Take some classes in video production; learn about photography; study design and art direction—become well-rounded and well-versed in these areas. In addition to reading music trade magazine, read about fashion trends. Watch videos and stay abreast of what others are doing.

"*You have to be willing to take what comes and if you feel a bit over your head, great—enjoy the swim. You can do the doggy paddle or you can do the breast stroke.*"

A DAY IN THE LIFE

On a non-shoot day, Mary Hamilton stops off to check on the retouching of a photo shoot before she arrives at the office between 9:00 and 9:30 A.M. Most days begin with returning phone calls to managers, hair and makeup stylists, photographers and others, trying to lock in times for a photo or video shoot. Then there are meetings to ensure everyone has the same concept and vision in mind. She meets with photographer and video director reps who come to show their clients' portfolios, attends various departmental and interoffice meetings, and reviews and approves budgets.

THE LEAST FAVORITE THING ABOUT THIS JOB:

"*I hate the politics!*"

THE BEST THING ABOUT THIS JOB:

"*The challenge of having some participation in the creative process of taking a new artist and finding what about that human being is appealing—what people will become infatuated with—and trying to project that on film, in print, or video.*"

POINTERS FOR THE JOB SEARCH

Build an appropriate portfolio. Don't fill it with random projects from art school. Find a local band and offer to design their CD, or redesign CDs already on the market to get experience. "I look at so many portfolios of graduating students who don't have any idea of what reality is. It is going to take them a few years in the field to learn. You've got to be willing to pay your dues."

CASE STUDY:

MARY HAMILTON, VICE PRESIDENT OF CREATIVE SERVICES/ VIDEO, RCA LABEL GROUP/NASHVILLE

Mary Hamilton arrived in Nashville with little more than the clothes on her back, some college art training, and a four-year-old son to feed. "We didn't have a place to stay, not a job, not anything." Her one contact in town worked at a publishing house, where she was hired as a freelance illustrator of children's books. Brought in-house in 1977, she took advantage of the opportunity to learn every aspect of the printing business, and was later promoted to art director. "I was illustrating and doing mechanicals back in the days before the advent of computer graphics. It was old school, where you spec'd the type, got it set, cut it up, pasted it, and laid it in. It was very labor intensive."

After seven years in book publishing, Hamilton needed a new challenge. Through a friend, she got an interview at RCA Records and was hired as director of creative services. At the time, the label had no in-house art department, so the total responsibility fell on her shoulders. As she had done previously, Hamilton learned everything she could about her new job, which meant talking to the product development and marketing departments, photographers, stylists, graphic artists, printers, and everyone else involved, to learn about *their* jobs. As the liaison between the artistic and the commercial sides of the business, she felt it was essential to be able to speak both languages.

About four years later, she approached her boss with the idea that artist videos, which had previously been a separate entity, should be integrated into the same image concept as all other media. Her boss, convinced of the wisdom, as well as the cost savings behind the idea, promoted Hamilton to vice president of creative services/video for the RCA label group. *www.rcarecordslabel.com*

PROMOTION

VICE PRESIDENT OF PROMOTION • NATIONAL PROMOTION MANAGER

JOB DESCRIPTION

The promotion department develops and executes radio promotion campaigns. Lori Holder-Anderson is responsible for obtaining radio airplay in all pop formats, which includes Top Forty, Hot AC, and Modern AC. She manages and directs the field staff to ensure that the promotional campaign is implemented.

PREREQUISITES

To succeed, you should have strong verbal communication skills, be focused and self-motivated, and possess a high level of personal integrity.

A DAY IN THE LIFE

Monday is generally the longest day for Lori Holder-Anderson, beginning at 6 A.M. when she checks the *Monitor* charts and the daily and weekly Broadcast Data

CAREER TIPS

"Volunteer for things. There are so many people that become concerned that it's not their job or they aren't being paid to do it. I think that you will be a more valuable employee, the more you know and the wider your experiences."

"I caution people to think long and hard about taking this type of job. Make sure you know what you're getting into. How demanding, how consuming it is. Your boyfriend will leave you. Your cat will run away. Your plants will die. You won't have a personal life. Not everyone can deal with the fact that it is an incredibly consuming thing, especially for the first two years. The amount of rejection and frustration is staggering."

"Read as much as you can about the record business: about sales, about promotion, about marketing. Whether it's a trade magazine or on-line source, just read and try to absorb as much information as you can, no matter how much you think you already know. Once you start doing promotion, the first two years are an extraordinary learning curve. The more you can prepare yourself for that, the better."

Service (BDS) reports. She forwards it to her field staff and gives chart information to label staff. In the morning, she talks with the radio consultants and independent promoters to exchange chart information, assess the status of target stations, and plan strategy. Throughout the day, she advises the field staff and independent promoters as radio stations add, drop, increase, or decrease record rotations. She talks with the sales and marketing departments to discuss production issues related to upcoming singles promotions, receives sales and account reports, and exchanges other significant information. In between, she telephones radio stations, reads a variety of trade magazines, sifts through and disseminates incoming information that could affect airplay, and approves expenses, travel, and vacation requests from the field staff. At the end of the day, she resolves any advertising needs.

POINTERS FOR THE JOB SEARCH

"I've hired lots of people over the years that came through intern programs who were willing to work for free because they wanted to learn."

CASE STUDY:

LORI HOLDER-ANDERSON, VICE PRESIDENT OF PROMOTION, WIND-UP RECORDS

Planning to be a doctor, Lori Holder-Anderson needed a job in her senior year of high school and found one at a Portland, Oregon Top Forty AM radio station. Willing to work weekends and the after midnight shift, she fell in love with the work, getting involved in compiling charts and calling record stores. Her interest and willingness to work brought increased opportunity to learn many aspects of the business.

Following a year at Stanford University, Holder-Anderson found she missed radio work, so she moved back to Portland to continue her studies and work part time at the radio station. Over the next four years her career moved at remarkable speed. She relocated to Seattle to accept an assistant's position at the WEA branch office. She returned to radio as music director of a Seattle rock radio station for a year, then moved to Los Angeles to become associate Album-Oriented Rock (AOR) editor at *R&R* magazine. Holder-Anderson decided she wanted to work for a record label and took a local promotion job at ABC Records for several months before landing a position at Epic Records in 1978.

After nine years at Epic, Holder-Anderson decided it was time to return to the Northwest. She took a job with A&M Records in 1987 doing local promotion in Seattle, and after a year convinced her boss to create the position of national field director for her. She continued to work from Seattle, and during the next ten years, she was made vice president of promotions operations, and then vice president of pop promotion.

In 1998, Holder-Anderson left A&M to form a promotion consulting company, acting as *de facto* head of pop promotions for Wind-up Records, Squint Entertain-

THE LEAST FAVORITE THING ABOUT THIS JOB:

"Dealing with people who continually reset the bar you have to reach in order for them to take you seriously; who continually change the rules of engagement, if you will, when it comes to their participation in your record."

THE BEST THING ABOUT THIS JOB:

"Helping guide and direct a group of people to accomplish things that they never imagined they would accomplish. I love to take a really tough record and just go for it. The most fun is a real challenge, where the odds are against you and people think it can't be pulled off and you prove that they're wrong."

ment, and Restless Records. She also helped amazon.com with the opening of its on-line music store. In 1999, she signed on full time at Wind-up Records as vice president of promotions. *www.winduprecords.com*

SENIOR VICE PRESIDENT • VICE PRESIDENT (NATIONAL PROMOTION)

"Have passion for the music and artists, and loyalty to teammates."

"Hire great people and let them do their work. Don't be intrusive and get in their way. Be there as a resource, but not a block. Help them overcome obstacles and hurdles."

"Don't worry about money and all the other extraneous stuff. Do what you love and money will tend to follow."

JOB OVERVIEW

The promotion department obtains radio airplay for label artists. Larry Pareigis manages and directs the promotion and marketing efforts to ultimately obtain maximum airplay for Monument label artists.

PREREQUISITES

To succeed, you must possess self-motivation, a friendly and outgoing personality, honesty, flexibility, and the ability to manage and motivate others.

A DAY IN THE LIFE

Each of Larry Pareigis' days brings a new set of challenges. Immediately after arriving at the office, he makes phone calls to his independent promotion people and promotion staff to gather information about how radio is responding to the records they are currently working. He meets with Jack Lameier, the senior vice president of promotion for Sony Music, to re-evaluate current strategy. Throughout the rest of the day, Pareigis is on the phone with radio stations and his field staff to exchange information to obtain more airplay. During the week he attends meetings with other label executives to keep abreast of publicity, sales, television appearances, touring dates, and artist information that might help generate more excitement with radio stations. At least one-third of the year, Pareigis is on the road visiting radio stations across the country, often taking new artists in to meet the station personnel. He also attends the yearly Gavin Convention and Country Radio Seminar.

POINTERS FOR THE JOB SEARCH

Get involved at your college radio station to gain some experience. Secure an internship or entry level position with a radio station, or in promotion at a record company. "You have to have a burning passion for promotion. If you do, then go for it."

CASE STUDY:

LARRY PAREIGIS, FORMER SENIOR VICE PRESIDENT RADIO PROMOTION, SONY MUSIC NASHVILLE; PRESIDENT NINE NORTH RECORDS

Larry Pareigis discovered music through the crystal radio sets he built as a child, and fell in love with the songs that came to him at night from far away places. He got a job as a deejay at an AM radio station in Savannah, Georgia in his first year of high school. When his family moved to Tennessee two years later, he found work at a small station outside Nashville, and was promoted to full time music director after graduation. During college, he worked as a deejay at an AM rock station in Nashville, attended classes in the morning, and slept in the afternoon. He pulled the late night shift on weekdays, and worked 7 P.M. to midnight on Saturdays.

After graduating from Middle Tennessee State University, Pareigis got a job as a part-time deejay at legendary WSM-FM in Nashville, where eventually he was promoted to music director over both the AM and FM stations. At that time, CMT and TNN cable television net-

THE LEAST FAVORITE THING ABOUT THIS JOB:

"People who are either close-minded or do more talking than listening."

THE BEST THING ABOUT THIS JOB:

"Working with people who care and genuinely want to forge partnerships. I'm blessed with a great group of teammates, artists, and managers to work with. Sometimes I get to sit back and admire their handiwork, and that's really cool."

VOICES OF EXPERIENCE

works were just starting up their operations. Owned by the same parent company as WSM, the networks hired Pareigis on the side as a consultant for their early music video programming.

In 1990, Pareigis took a job with an Albuquerque, New Mexico station. From there, he hopped to Sacramento, California where he oversaw two country stations and a hot talk station under one roof, then moved on to a station in San Francisco. When hit producer Garth Fundis was tapped to head the Nashville office of Almo Sounds, he offered Pareigis the chance to leave radio and head up the label's promotion staff. Unfortunately, the Nashville office proved a short-lived enterprise. Just as it was closing down, Pareigis was invited to join the promotion team of Sony Music's revitalized Monument label as vice president of national promotions. One of his biggest successes at Monument has been breaking the Dixie Chicks.

Sony consolidated its Nashville-based labels in 2002. In the restructuring efforts, Pareigis was promoted to senior vice president of Epic/Monument. Sony Music later separated promotional duties for its labels, moving Pareigis into the senior vice president or radio promotion for Columbia position. In 2003, Sony merged with BMG to form the second largest music company in the world. Amid layoffs and reorganization of Sony BMG, Pareigis remained in place, serving as senior vice president of radio promotion for Sony Music Nashville.

In early 2007, Pareigis exited Sony BMG to launch virtual record label Nine North Records. As president of the new virtual label, Pareigis is involved in every aspect, from scouting and signing artists, A&R, marketing, and promotion. He hired a team of radio marketing professionals, but others will be hired on an as-needed basis. "We'll be aligned with several highly experienced professionals who can bring sales, marketing, public relations, digital, and artist development skills to the mix on an à la carte basis. This business format will allow us to work with acts from the ground up and with less of a safety net. We may even expand to other genres." *www.myspace.com/ninenorthrecords*

SALES

SENIOR VICE PRESIDENT OF SALES • VICE PRESIDENT OF SALES

JOB DESCRIPTION

People in sales positions are responsible for sales of music and video released by the label. Neal Spielberg's job is to manage and direct the sales, advertising, and merchandising campaigns for Warner Bros., Inc. Nashville, which includes the Asylum, Reprise, and Warner Brothers labels. He is also the liaison for the labels, distribution, and the retail account base.

PREREQUISITES

To succeed, you should have excellent communication and problem solving skills, the ability to motivate others, and to follow through on a project. Flexibility, honesty, and an engaging personality are important.

A DAY IN THE LIFE

A typical day for Spielberg is spent attending meetings to exchange ideas and strategize promotion for the label's artists. He is on the phone with his field sales staff and the distribution company to provide all the information needed to sell the label's records. This information is gathered through telephone calls and meetings with an artist's management and agent, and the publicity, promotion and video departments. Success is measured by increased radio airplay, planned television appearances, current tour schedules, a recently completed sponsorship deal, or anything else that might increase sales of the artist's record. On any given day Spielberg deals with budgets, projections, sales forecasts, co-op advertising, merchandising, and consumer advertising.

"If you're thinking about getting into sales, be excited. If you're not excited about what you're doing, get out. Be passionate about what you do, otherwise find something else to do."

"Your job is only part of what you do with your life. It's important that you stay in tune with your community, your city, your church or synagogue, and your family. Work is one piece of your life; don't let it consume your life. It's important to have a balance."

LEAST FAVORITE THING ABOUT THIS JOB:

"Being away from my family as much as I am, even though I love to travel. That's the human element, the love/hate thing. I love to travel, but I have a problem being away from my family."

THE BEST THING ABOUT THIS JOB:

"The music—that's really what it's all about—I love the music. There is nothing like watching a new artist blossom. To see new artists develop, find themselves onstage and the fans start to sing their songs back to them. There is nothing like having a brand new artist go from an unknown to selling a lot of records and becoming a celebrity or star. Getting new music, whether it's from an established artist or a new one, that is the part I love the most."

POINTERS FOR THE JOB SEARCH

"Fight for what you want and don't give up. When I got out of college I wanted to be in music, but the business was in turmoil. So I took other jobs, but I kept my focus on the record business and read and kept in tune."

CASE STUDY:

NEAL SPIELBERG, FORMER VICE PRESIDENT OF COUNTRY MUSIC SALES AND MARKETING, WEA

The night that 13-year-old Neal Spielberg saw the Temptations perform changed his life. "I was just mesmerized, both by their performance and songs—everything. I was already into music, but when I went to that show and saw them perform, at that moment I knew I needed to be in the music business." He learned the retail side of the trade selling eight-track tapes in his father's music stores, and from his uncle, a Warner Elektra Atlantic (WEA) sales manager. While majoring in radio and television at the University of Arizona at Tucson, he established the campus' student chapter of the National Academy of Television Arts and Sciences (NATAS) and served several internships, including writing ad copy at a local radio station. The station's sales manager became a mentor, and taught him about sales and special promotions through work on a Ringling Brothers, Barnum and Bailey Circus account.

After graduation in 1978, Spielberg landed a job at WEA's Los Angeles office and relocated to southern California. Before he could even begin work, he was laid off due to an industry downturn. With no jobs available in the record industry, he took a department store sales position and taught ice hockey lessons at a local rink while he planned his next move. Tapping the relationship he had earlier established while working on the circus account, he landed a job in 1979 as regional marketing director for Ringling Brothers, Holiday on Ice, and Ice Follies, based out of Florida. After two years, he took a job as area sales representative for a company that supplied videos and Atari video game accessories to rental outlets. "It was all mom and pop owned stores back then. I traveled in my car up and down the state of Florida, picking up leads from the company and other video store owners." Through a company buyout, he ended up working for Warner Home Video, who in 1983 transferred him to their Nashville office as a WEA sales representative to handle both video and music sales.

Finally involved in the music business, Spielberg was the perfect candidate when Warner Records' Nashville office created a full time sales and marketing position. Hired in 1984 as national sales coordinator, he initially oversaw video and music sales for just the Warner Brothers label, but over time, the Atlantic, Asylum, Giant, and Curb labels were also added. In 1999, Spielberg was made vice president of sales for Warner Brothers' Nashville division, including the Reprise and Asylum labels. His title later became vice president of country music sales and marketing, WEA (the parent company of Warner Brothers).

The Internet has afforded opportunities to market independent artists and labels in a way that was not possible prior to the early 2000s. Seeing the possibilities to carve out his own niche, Spielberg departed WEA in 2003, after 21 years with the label. He opened Spielberg Consulting, a marketing and sales company. The firm's clients include Equity Music Group, Compendia Records, and Lolton Creek Records.

MARKETING AND ARTIST DEVELOPMENT

SENIOR VICE PRESIDENT MARKETING

JOB DESCRIPTION

Staff in these areas oversee all aspects of marketing artists and their music. They are responsible for coordinating the efforts of the creative services, marketing, and publicity departments (which include packaging, video, advertising, and sales campaigns) to ensure the consistency of imaging between artists and their music, and to maximize the contributions of each to ultimately increase sales.

PREREQUISITES

To succeed, you should have flexibility, and the ability to manage and motivate people. You need to have a creative eye for imaging and an ear for music. You must be able to strategize an all-encompassing marketing campaign, and have a clear understanding of how each department at the record label works. "You have to have a sense of what an artist is about; being able to find the unique traits of each artist. We're not manufacturing Ford trucks here, where every truck will be the same, just a different color and interior. There are so many dynamics that separate artists from other artists."

A DAY IN THE LIFE

"I have the best laid plans for my day," says Fletcher Foster, "but they never work out." On his drive to the office he begins making calls to artist managers and continues to do so throughout the day, sometimes meeting with some in person. He arrives at the office around 10

"I've always had great people working for me. I give them the freedom to just do their jobs. I'm not the type of boss who watches over them. If I hired the right person, I know I can put my trust with them to perform."

"You have to be flexible. You don't get to choose the artists you work with. At a record company, you are given artists to work with and you have to be able to treat them each as individuals and find their strengths."

A.M. and resolves any crises from the night before that demand an immediate response to the media. At some point he responds to e-mail and faxes, returns phone calls, listens to new music, watches new videos, plans marketing strategy, and reads trade magazines. Throughout the week Foster attends publicity, production, artist development, marketing, and other meetings with the label staff.

POINTERS FOR THE JOB SEARCH

Foster's path toward senior vice president of marketing began in the publicity department. Because the position manages several different departments, the best course is to pursue an internship or any entry level position, then learn all you can and do a good job so that when an opening arises, you will be hired or promoted.

CASE STUDY:

FLETCHER FOSTER, FORMER SENIOR VICE PRESIDENT MARKETING, ARISTA RECORDS NASHVILLE; SENIOR VICE PRESIDENT AND GENERAL MANAGER OF UNIVERSAL SOUTH RECORDS

Before he was ten years old, Kansas native Fletcher Foster cut a record that got local country radio airplay and caught the attention of the Association for Retarded Citizens (ARC). He became a junior spokesperson for ARC, and cut several more records to raise funds in his region. After his parents vetoed schools in New York and Los Angeles, he entered the music program at Belmont College in Nashville. He supported himself by recording advertising jingles and served an internship at Sony Music. "That was really where I learned the business end of the music business," Foster said. "The foundation of what I know now, I learned there."

Foster graduated at a time when the country music industry was in a slump. He worked three part-time jobs at the Country Music Association (CMA), Mercury Records, and Sony Music, before landing a full time position as a junior publicist at CMA, writing for *Close Up* magazine. He then moved to Sony as manager of publicity and worked his way up to director of artist development.

VOICES OF EXPERIENCE

THE LEAST FAVORITE THING ABOUT THIS JOB:

"What annoys me the most are the preconceptions that certain things supposedly have to be done a certain way."

THE BEST THING ABOUT THIS JOB:

"It is really gratifying to be able to have somebody get signed to the label, knowing it's been their lifelong dream to be an artist, and to be a part of that and really see them become successful. It's hard when it doesn't happen, but when it does, it's just an amazing feeling."

Foster moved to Los Angeles in 1993 to work for Arista Records, overseeing the label's West Coast promotion activities at a time when Whitney Houston and Toni Braxton were achieving their first big successes. His primary responsibilities involved lining up media appearances for the label's artists, including Houston, Braxton, Annie Lennox, TLC, and Kenny G. He landed alternative rock band Live their first television appearance on *Saturday Night Live* which helped launch them toward triple-platinum success. After three years, he hired on at MCA Records, staying for two years while the label underwent major personnel changes. Released from his MCA contract early, Foster returned to Nashville in 1998 and was soon hired as president of artist development at Arista Records. He was promoted to senior vice president of marketing about 18 months later during a change in label management.

During his tenure at Arista, Foster was responsible for getting several artists their first national network exposure, including Alan Jackson on the Grammy's and Billboard Awards shows, Pam Tillis on *The Tonight Show*, and Brooks & Dunn on *Arsenio Hall Show*. "At the time, Arsenio was key to Arista because we had so many R&B/Urban artists on the roster. But the show didn't book much country, so it was really a coup to be able to showcase Brooks & Dunn to a brand-new audience early in their career," Foster recalled.

He also executive produced the soundtrack for the Miramax film *Happy Trails*. The album featured performances by Keb Mo', Joan Osborne, Pam Tillis, Emmylou Harris, and BR549, and earned two Grammy nominations.

Foster moved to Capitol Records/Nashville and served as senior vice president of marketing where he was instrumental in the success of Keith Urban, Dierks Bentley, Trace Adkins, and others. He arrived at a key point in Urban's career. Through television appearances and an intense industry awareness campaign, he raised the singer's profile. Due in part to Foster's marketing plan, Urban won the CMA Horizon Award and the ACM New Top Male Vocalist Award.

In late 2006, he was appointed senior vice president and general manager of Universal South Records. *www.universal-south.com*

SENIOR VICE PRESIDENT • MARKETING DIRECTOR (STRATEGIC MARKETING) • VICE PRESIDENT (SPECIAL MARKETS)

JOB DESCRIPTION

These marketers exploit catalog master recordings and handle Internet marketing. At BMG Latin, Guillermo Page coordinates efforts between BMG and the record clubs, such as BMG Direct and Columbia House, and oversees the exploitation of the company's catalog master recordings and all Internet related activities.

"You really have to be bilingual and bicultural. In the United States, we work four or five different markets and they are very fragmented. We have a Mexican culture on the West Coast, a tropical culture in New York [Colombians, Dominicans, and Puerto Ricans], Colombians and Cubans in Miami, and in Chicago a mixture of all those cultures. Each market behaves differently and you need to understand those differences."

PREREQUISITES

To succeed, you should be proficient in Spanish and English, and have an understanding of Latin markets, both outside and within the United States. You need to be creative and have strategic planning and computer skills, coupled with an understanding of Internet sales and marketing.

A DAY IN THE LIFE

Page begins his day reading and responding to his 30 to 40 e-mails from the European, Latin American, and United States offices, and various accounts. He works with the Internet staff to ensure they have the artist information they need, or specifics about a promotion or tour. He attends meetings with different departments to plan and implement marketing campaigns.

POINTERS FOR THE JOB SEARCH

Learn a second language and study the international charts so you become familiar with artists and companies. Read all you can about foreign music markets so that when you apply for an internship or entry-level position, you have some basic knowledge, and a language skill, to offer an employer. "Every BMG company has an international exploitation manager who handles our repertoire for every country that has a BMG presence."

CASE STUDY:

GUILLERMO PAGE, VICE PRESIDENT OF COMMERCIAL DIVISION, SONY BMG LATIN

Guillermo Page began his career in the music business at age 16 at Velvet, the independent record company his father owned in Venezuela. He began as an assistant in the recording studio division and rose to general manager of the label. In 1989, at age 22, he moved to the United States and entered the University of Miami, where he eventually earned a bachelor's degree in international finance, marketing, business management and organization, and an MBA in international business and marketing. Between studies, he handled sales and production coordination at Rodven, an independent Latin label. He moved to Vedisco Records in 1993 to become general manager, and in 1999, left to join BMG U.S. Latin as strategic marketing director.

In early 2005, Guillermo became vice president of Sony BMG Latin's commercial division. Among his duties are designing and implementing direct response campaigns and exploiting the Latin catalogs of Sony and BMG.

THE BEST THING ABOUT THIS JOB:

"There is not a single moment that I feel bored on the job; it is always changing. We are working with different artists every day, so it's not like selling a standard product. The way you market each artist is different."

VICE PRESIDENT • DIRECTOR • MANAGER (INTERNATIONAL MARKETING)

JOB OVERVIEW

This office coordinates and manages international marketing efforts for American signed artists. Yumi Kimura serves as the artist and product information liaison between Warner Brothers Nashville and the label's offices around the world. She assists each office in deciding which product is appropriate for release in their country, and helps maximize publicity and marketing efforts.

PREREQUISITES

To succeed, you should have computer and written communication skills, proficiency in a second and third language, and an understanding of foreign markets. A basic knowledge of the music industry is necessary.

A DAY IN THE LIFE

The first task of the day for Yumi Kimura is to check e-mail. While she may speak via telephone with individuals about specific projects and needs, the Internet is the most efficient method of communicating information, charts, and marketing plans to people in different time zones. Throughout the week, Kimura attends staff meetings where she gains information about the label artists to pass on to the international markets, and meets with individual artists and their managers to form a game plan for international marketing and sales.

"Want it bad. You have to have organizational and communication skills—that is very important—but actually getting in, I think the person who wants it the most, gets it."

You need to have at least a second language, and a third or fourth language is even better. Courses in international business are particularly helpful.

POINTERS FOR THE JOB SEARCH

Find a college with a music business department and a good internship placement program. Study the business side of music and enter a label through the internship program.

CASE STUDY:

YUMI KIMURA, INTERNATIONAL MARKETING MANAGER, WARNER/REPRISE NASHVILLE

As a teenager in Japan, Yumi Kimura fell in love with American music. She knew at an early age that she wanted a career in the music business, and wanted to be closer to its origin than her native country would allow. She learned English as a foreign exchange student, spending four summers in Texas, and following graduation from high school in Tokyo, moved to California to continue English classes. After researching schools that offered degrees in music business, she was accepted into Middle Tennessee State University's program.

Kimura served two internships during her final year at MTSU. The first was at a record company in Japan, where she learned the workings of the foreign market. The second, at Warner Brothers Records in Nashville, became a permanent position upon graduation. While multiple language skills are not a requirement, fluency in several languages was instrumental in Kimura's rise to international marketing manager.

VOICES OF EXPERIENCE

THE LEAST FAVORITE THING ABOUT THIS JOB:

"If I work on a project very hard and believe in it, but it doesn't work in the marketplace, sales wise, it's very, very frustrating. [In other businesses] if you work hard and do your best, you get good results. It doesn't work that way in the music industry."

THE BEST THING ABOUT THIS JOB:

"I love the people. I love the variety of job tasks I have. I get to travel and go to foreign cities. I get to work with people of all different cultures."

PUBLICITY AND MEDIA RELATIONS

SENIOR VICE PRESIDENT • VICE PRESIDENT
(MEDIA RELATIONS OR PUBLICITY)

JOB OVERVIEW

Publicity personnel manage and direct media relations for the company and artists. Bob Merlis, spokesperson for Warner Brothers Records, directs and oversees all media endeavors for individual artists and the company as a whole. Under this broad umbrella is the creation of press releases, biographies, promotional literature, and all media related services.

PREREQUISITES

Although not all publicists can write, the ability to compose a press release or biography is a major plus. You need good verbal communication skills and a friendly, outgoing personality.

CAREER TIPS

When you're starting out, "I think it's good to work for a big company because you get to see the big picture with all the possibilities."

Take creative writing and other classes that will help you to hone your writing skills.

A DAY IN THE LIFE

Much of Merlis' day is spent working on the telephone. He focuses on talking with artists, managers, and various media people, obtaining information and listening for opportunities to plug into an appropriate media campaign. He may issue a press release, be required to make a statement to the media on behalf of the company, or devise a game plan for an artist's upcoming release. He attends meetings with other department heads and corporate executives, and relays information to the company's offices around the world.

POINTERS FOR THE JOB SEARCH

"If your inclination is to write, then get yourself published in newspapers and magazines or on line. Get your feet wet and know who the players are. Start in an assistant type position and get some kind of an overview. You may discover you don't like it."

CASE STUDY:

BOB MERLIS, SENIOR VICE PRESIDENT WORLD WIDE CORPORATE COMMUNICATIONS, WARNER BROS. RECORDS, INC.

A record collector from an early age, Brooklyn native Bob Merlis was fascinated by the label copy and album notes found on the recordings. "I read all the material found on a single or album: the inner sleeve and liner notes, publishing credits and all of that. The Motown label had a map of Detroit and Atlantic Records had little figures on the singles sleeve. It all fascinated me; anything to do with music I found interesting."

As a student at Columbia University, he auditioned for a deejay slot at the campus radio station, but was rejected. He ended up programming the jukebox in the student union and promoting concerts on campus, working with some of the top pop acts of the mid-1960s. After only three days of journalism school at U.C. Berkeley in California, he was convinced that his true interest lay in music. He headed to New York to search for a job. "I just beat the pavement. I looked in the phone book for all the record companies and then through the trade magazines." He contacted every company that would let him in the door and was finally offered a job as an office boy at *Record World* magazine. Upon reporting to work two weeks later, he discovered that the job had been filled. The editor, impressed that Merlis wanted a job in the music business badly enough to move across the country to be an office boy, made him an assistant editor instead. Not knowing what the position entailed, he learned on the job. "I got to interview different people and write articles about musical topics. That's how I got in the music business."

After three years, Merlis was hired as a junior publicist at Warner Brothers Records in 1971. Again learning on the job, he was instrumental in introducing classic English rock acts like T-Rex, Black Sabbath, and Deep Purple to America. He left in 1973 for brief stints at a small Warner distributed label and RCA Records, before returning to Warner Brothers in 1974.

Merlis moved to Los Angeles in 1975 to head up the publicity department at the label's home office. In addition to his department head duties, he personally handles publicity for John

THE LEAST FAVORITE THING ABOUT THIS JOB

"Meetings—I try to go to as few meetings as possible. I'd rather be talking to people in the media, artists, and management."

THE BEST THING ABOUT THIS JOB

"The proximity to people who make music is what got me into the music business."

Fogarty, Neil Young, and Chris Isaak, among others, and has risen to senior vice president of worldwide corporate communications.

The AOL and Time Warner merger brought major cutbacks and restructuring to the music divisions. In 2001, after 28 years with Warner Bros. Records, Merlis exited. "I never bounded around," he said. "I never took any other offers because they weren't as good as what I had."

With nearly 30 years of experience in the music business, Merlis opened his own consulting firm, M.f.h. (Merlis for hire). He also co-founded Memphis International Records, an independent blues and roots-oriented label. *www.bobmerlis.com*

BUSINESS AND LEGAL AFFAIRS

SENIOR VICE PRESIDENT • VICE PRESIDENT (BUSINESS AND LEGAL AFFAIRS)

JOB OVERVIEW

This office handles business and legal affairs and oversees the daily operation of specifically assigned departments or the entire company. In her capacity as senior vice president of operations, Susan Genco is responsible for the day-to-day legal and business affairs for all the labels under the Capitol Records Group, which includes Capitol, Capitol Nashville, EMI Christian Music Group, EMI Canada, and Blue Note Angel. She is also the senior vice president of operations for Capitol, and oversees sound track, film, and television licensing, business development, including office services and Internet technology, and Capitol Records Studios.

PREREQUISITES

Besides having a law degree and experience in the music business, Susan Genco cites fairness and personal relationships as keys to her success. "I feel that both on a creative and business level, if you can come up with a way to structure something where everybody benefits, you'll have better long-term success and better long-term relationships with people. Also, imposing the same standards on yourself that you would impose on other people. If you expect someone to work really hard and produce, you have to do the same yourself."

A DAY IN THE LIFE

"My day starts between 8 and 9 A.M.," says Genco. She sorts through the massive number of internal e-mail communications and scheduled telephone calls to negotiate various deals. She participates in creative meetings to determine whether the company will release a particular sound track, or license music to a film or television program. "I sit in on the weekly marketing meetings where we develop the company strategy. We look at all of our current projects and decide how we've gotten where we've gotten, and where we are going to go." Throughout the day she may be called upon to negotiate deals or offer input, both at a creative and business level.

POINTERS FOR THE JOB SEARCH

"The advice given to me was, you should take a job at a law firm; if you can get into their entertainment group or their music group, great. But if you can't, you should make sure you go to a firm that has one and then try and move over. Generally, the same is true for boutique law firms, the ones that handle just music or just entertainment. Record companies have small staffs and they don't want to spend a lot of time training. They would rather you go and get a couple of years of good corporate training, so that when you come to them you're able to hit the ground running."

CASE STUDY:

SUSAN GENCO, FORMER SENIOR VICE PRESIDENT OPERATIONS, CAPITOL RECORDS; VICE PRESIDENT OF BUSINESS AFFAIRS, WARNER BROTHERS RECORDS

Susan Genco grew up in Buffalo, New York, greatly influenced by the music she heard on the local college radio station. Later, as an economics major at Wellesley

"Don't be discouraged. I was living in New York and quit my job and moved to Boston to go to law school. I was incurring all this debt—law school isn't cheap—and when I got there, people were very pessimistic about my ability to get a job in the music business. I was crushed, but over the years I've spoken to a lot of people and everyone who has really wanted to get into music has eventually gotten a job. You should just persevere and really stick to it. If you're enthusiastic, you will find something that you really like."

"Find out as much as you can about a position or different opportunities. Talk to as many people as you can, read as much as you can, discover if your skills and personality are well suited for a particular position."

"You should be up to speed in terms of new media and how that is changing the industry. Stay abreast of what's going on in the industry before you're even a part of it. The more you know about your future job or the industry that you want to work in, the more likely you are to find something that you'll be happy with."

College in Boston, she indulged her love of music by working as a deejay at the campus radio station, and hiring bands for campus concerts. After graduation, she took a bank job, but quickly found that she missed being involved with music. "I knew that I wanted to be in music. I had always been involved in music, behind the scenes. I unfortunately never had enough talent to do anything else." On the advice of co-workers, she decided to go to law school as a way of gaining entry to the music business.

Following graduation from Harvard Law School, Genco supplemented her skills with classes in entertainment law at Boston College School of Law. While there, she begged an internship at Rounder Records to get record label experience, ending up in the promotions department. "It had nothing to do with business affairs, it was just to get inside a record company and see how it worked." Her summer breaks in New York were split between an internship at a law firm and one in publicity, and later in business affairs, at Arista Records. After graduating in 1993, Arista hired her as director of business affairs, later promoting her to vice president.

In 1999, Genco decided a move to Los Angeles was in order. She took a job at EMI Records as senior vice president of business affairs for the Capitol Records Group. When she began working there, she discovered that the deputy president of Capitol Records was an acquaintance from her days at Arista. The previous working relationship led to her other duties as senior vice president of operations.

Genco departed Capitol Records in late 2001 to become senior vice president of business and legal affairs at Warner Brothers Records.

VOICES OF EXPERIENCE

THE LEAST FAVORITE THING ABOUT THIS JOB:

"The hardest thing about this job is that it is sometimes very hard to switch gears. When I need to be focused on something that takes a lot of concentrated time, whether it's sitting and trying to find a song that would fit a movie, or it's negotiating and drafting a complicated agreement, those things take a concentrated chunk of time. Due to the diverse nature of my job, it's hard to find those chunks of time. It's more like getting 15 minutes or a half hour here and there. That's the hardest thing; the best thing and the hardest thing is switching gears so quickly during the day."

THE BEST THING ABOUT THIS JOB:

"The diversity and the variety. I do such a wide variety of things and that keeps things very, very interesting. The job uses all of my resources and it challenges me. I can see more than one side when I'm thinking about a deal; I can evaluate it on a strategic business level and also on a creative level."

LICENSING AND BUSINESS AFFAIRS

JOB DESCRIPTION

The licensing and business affairs office handles licensing of label-owned master recordings for exploitation, primarily through repackaging and synchronization. At Sony Music Special Products, Vinny Tabone clears master recordings of albums the label group manufactures, including compilations, premiums, CDs, boxed sets, and reissues. He is responsible for both the products released by Sony, or those licensed to another company. He researches Sony artist contracts for marketing restrictions, negotiates fees for off-label cuts, and obtains other related permissions. Tabone is also responsible for licensing Sony master recordings for CD-ROM, Internet, and new technology use. He handles licensing of Sony Music Special Product masters for worldwide synchronization rights to television, film, and home video. He negotiates fees with motion picture studios, independent music supervisors, advertising agencies, and various other licensees.

PREREQUISITES

To succeed, you should have computer proficiency, interpersonal and communication skills, and the ability to multi-task. You should be self-motivated with good organization skills, inquisitiveness, flexibility, and an understanding of master licensing.

CAREER TIPS

"Keep up on current events, because the conversations around the water cooler are very important to forming solid working and personal relationships. Reading the newspaper every day can help you start conversations with people so you have some kind of relationship with them. It gives a whole different perspective on how you're viewed by people."

"Showing up to work on time is very important. It tells people that you're interested in your job and that you want to be there. If you constantly show up late or call in sick, it's a bad reflection on your work ethic. If you're not happy with your job, you should leave and find something you really enjoy."

"Don't be afraid to ask questions. No one knows everything. Everyone has their little niche of knowledge, from the top person of a company to the bottom rung on the ladder; they each have their specialty."

A DAY IN THE LIFE

Much of the day, Tabone is in his Sony office sitting at the computer, researching details for various projects, responding to e-mail requests for quotes or other information, preparing quotes, and completing other tasks. Throughout the day he works on multiple projects with attorneys, visors, film studio executives, advertising agencies, and other employees, to bring them to completion.

POINTERS FOR THE JOB SEARCH

"Go to the library and research your area of interest to become familiar with every aspect of the area you want to work in. Remember that old saying: 'information is power'? Information *is* power, especially in this business."

CASE STUDY:

VINNY TABONE, DIRECTOR OF LICENSING AND BUSINESS AFFAIRS, SONY/BMG MUSIC SPECIAL PRODUCTS

While gazing longingly at drum kits in the Sears catalog, six-year-old Vinny Tabone was bitten by the music bug. "I knew from an early age that music was going to play a big part in my life." He spent 22 years as a working rock musician, recording and touring with a number of New York City area bands. During eight leaner years, he supplemented his income working in retail music outlets and then decided to look into the business side of the industry. With a two-year college degree already under his belt, he enrolled at the State University of New York at Oneonta. Counseled by his father to make industry connections while still in school, Tabone attended a guest lecture and met music veteran Ann Ruckert, who ran an industry referral service.

THE LEAST FAVORITE THING ABOUT THIS JOB:

"The work load can become pretty overwhelming at times."

THE BEST THING ABOUT THIS JOB:

"The daily interaction with other lovers of music. Every day we're constantly talking about music, in the hall, at lunch, or working on specific projects. All aspects of the business, from songwriting to artist agreements to manufacturing and distribution, we cover it all. I feel very lucky to be surrounded by such terrific people. I love getting up in the morning and coming to work."

VOICES OF EXPERIENCE

Upon graduating with a BA in music business, Tabone met with Ruckert, who led him to a job as a contract administrator with Diamond Time. At Diamond Time, Tabone cleared rights and permissions from artists and record labels for the Rock and Roll Hall of Fame, a monumental Time-Life Music project entitled *The History of Rock and Roll*, and several educational projects for Sony Music.

In 1996, following two years of building a relationship with Sony Music, Tabone was offered the position of associate director of licensing and business affairs for Sony Music Special Products. He was later promoted to director of licensing for Sony/BMG Special Products.

VICE PRESIDENT • DIRECTOR • MANAGER (BUSINESS AFFAIRS AND LEGAL AFFAIRS)

JOB OVERVIEW

This office oversees business and legal affairs. In the most basic form, Jennifer Jones is responsible for knowing the specific parameters of contracts, such as the label's obligation to the artist, and vice versa, both materially and financially. She negotiates new deals and ensures that current contractual commitments are fulfilled. She also handles licensing and synchronization fees.

PREREQUISITES

To succeed, you should have good communication, negotiation, organizational, and mathematical skills. You need an understanding of contracts and deal points, and must have the ability to work with a variety of personalities. Beneath it all should be a love of music.

A DAY IN THE LIFE

Jones' daily activities can be summed up in two words: contracts and communications. Each day she receives calls from artists who have questions about their recording budgets, status on a video, royalty statements, or other contract-related business. She may respond to a request to use a song in a film or

CAREER TIPS

"Read the music trade magazines. Go down to your local bookstore or magazine rack and get a Billboard *and an* R&R. *Know about the climate in the music business."*

"My intuition was always to pursue the companies that did the types and styles of music that I was interested in. That made a big difference for me."

Learn the roster of artists for the company you are applying to. Know a little about the history of the label and the names of the key executives. Do your homework before you apply for a job.

television program, review label copy for an upcoming CD release for legal sound-ness, make comments and check legal obligations on a contract or other document, and work with other departments on day-to-day business.

POINTERS FOR THE JOB SEARCH

"If you're in school now, I would follow my preference of music style and seek out those types of companies and the people who are directing them, for unpaid or paid internships, part-time positions, any kind of involvement."

CASE STUDY:

JENNIFER JONES, BUSINESS AFFAIRS MANAGER, CAPRICORN RECORDS

As the daughter of a strict Baptist minister in a tiny Kentucky town, Jennifer Jones' early musical influence was limited to the vinyl singles she and her mother secretly listened to when her father was away. Although she was too young to under-stand that her destiny lay in the music business, she knew what she wanted to do from a very early age. "I sort of knew I would be working with them [entertainers] in some service-oriented capacity."

Her interest continued to grow, and lead her to study radio broadcasting and communications at Western Kentucky University. She transferred to Belmont College in Nashville after hearing that it had a good music business program, and immedi-ately landed an internship in the tape copy room of Screen Gems, an affiliate of EMI Music Publishing. "I made the tape copies, cleaned the machines, and delivered the cassettes to different companies and producers. It was a good experience because I got to meet a lot of people." After a second internship as the singles buyer at a Camelot Music branch store, she took a third post in the pop promotion department of MCA Records, tracking airplay at radio stations and working with artists like Jody Watley and Tiffany. While there, she heard of an opening with an independent promotion company based in Nashville. Although the firm's manager initially was looking for a male candidate, Jones' persistence in calling him finally won her a job working up promotional giveaways in support of album releases.

THE LEAST FAVORITE THING ABOUT THIS JOB:

"Sometimes you run into people who aren't even open to the idea of nego-tiation."

THE BEST THING ABOUT THIS JOB:

"Working in the film and television realm; seeing what new things are in production and turning them on to our music. We have a strong roster and I really enjoy working the music and getting it placed."

VOICES OF EXPERIENCE

Jones graduated in 1988 and pursued a career in pop music, with interviews in both New York and Los Angeles. While deciding between offers in each city, she was offered a job with Gold Dust Records in Atlanta, through a connection she had made while interning at MCA. Working for the small label, Jones got experience in every aspect of the music business: contracts, promotion, publishing, management, A&R, and so on. Gold Dust folded in 1991 and Jones returned to Nashville to put together a successful freelance promotion business for emerging rock and alternative rock acts. When Liberty Records later opened a rock division, she was hired to work in the A&R department, but soon left when it became clear the label had little interest in supporting the new enterprise.

After a round of phone calls to friends, Jones landed at RCA affiliate BNA Entertainment for seven months as art director over video production and packaging. Upon hearing that alternative rock label Capricorn Records was establishing a business and legal affairs department in their Nashville office, she pursued a position with them and was hired in 1994. The label moved their offices to Atlanta in 1997, and Jones moved with them as director of business affairs.

HUMAN RESOURCES AND SUPPORT STAFF

SENIOR VICE PRESIDENT • VICE PRESIDENT • DIRECTOR (HUMAN RESOURCES)

JOB OVERVIEW

Human resources personnel manage and oversee employee relations, including employee negotiations, orientation and training, benefits and compensation, and performance management. David Gilbert is responsible for the traditional functions of a human resources director, such as salary planning, hiring and training staff. (At BMG insurance and financial benefits are handled by another department.) He is involved directly, or through an attorney, in negotiating new and renewed contracts, and in negotiations to end contracts early. Under his direction at BMG Entertainment are specific regions for the label, the Latin division, music publishing worldwide, classics, and a small group of New York based international staff.

PREREQUISITES

You must have a knowledge of, or experience in, human resources; an understanding of compensation, training, benefits, and organization development, and the ability to work in a constantly evolving environment. You should have the ability to be diplomatic and work with a variety of personalities. Good negotiation and communication skills, combined with a passion for music, are essential.

A DAY IN THE LIFE

"Because I deal with people all over the world, I could choose for my day to never end," says Gilbert. When he isn't on the road for the company, he usually arrives at the office at 7:30 A.M. to make calls to Europe and Asia. Each day he spends at least a couple of hours on e-mail. Throughout the day he may deal with a contract on a salary issue, or provide information for a report in New York or Germany. He makes time for strategic planning, reviews hiring needs and salary budgets, and conducts an interview or two. He also meets with colleagues to get up to speed on any information he might have missed while traveling, which takes up 50 percent of his time.

"Know human resources from a technical standpoint. Be comfortable with ambiguity and chaos. Learn to be comfortable having to make decisions without having all your ducks in a row, not having all the best information in hand. Know that you are going to make mistakes and get over it, but try not to make the same mistake too many times."

Learn about the structure of a record company and the music industry so that you have a general understanding of the business.

POINTERS FOR THE JOB SEARCH

Study human resources in school to gain a working knowledge of business and legal issues, then take whatever entry level position you can find in a human resources department to gain practical experience. Look for paid opportunities, or for internships in human resources, at a music company.

THE LEAST FAVORITE THING ABOUT THIS JOB:

"There is a certain amount of office politics, but that is not unique; I don't think the music industry has a monopoly on that."

THE BEST THING ABOUT THIS JOB:

"Variety—the variety of the music, the variety of the people, the variety of situations that I encounter. I like the pace, which is fast."

CASE STUDY:

DAVID GILBERT, VICE PRESIDENT HUMAN RESOURCES, BMG ENTERTAINMENT

David Gilbert grew up with a love for music, and spent ten years learning piano, but had no idea he would one day work in the music business. After a childhood of bouncing around the country wherever his father's aerospace engineering career took him, Gilbert graduated college in the mid-1980s and took a job as personnel director of YMCA in Taiwan. "When I got on the plane I couldn't even use chopsticks, let alone speak the language." Two years later in 1990, after a crash course in Mandarin, he found a position with Levi Strauss working in human relations (HR) over the Asian/Pacific region, based out of San Francisco.

After an assignment in the Philippines, Gilbert found himself in Singapore in 1997. While at a Levi's event, he was approached by a headhunting agency that told him about a music company with a regional HR position to fill. Gilbert was hired by BMG Music in the summer of 1998 and relocated to Hong Kong, finally able to combine his early enjoyment of music with a job. Originally the company planned for him to work three years in Hong Kong before returning to the United States, but their needs changed and he was posted to the New York office after only a year.

OFFICE MANAGER (SMALLER LABEL) • RECEPTIONIST

JOB OVERVIEW

At MCA Nashville, Willie Mayhoe is the face and voice of the company. She greets everyone coming into the MCA office, answers incoming calls, routes them appropriately, takes messages, handles concert ticket buys for the company, schedules appointments, and provides other office support.

PREREQUISITES

To succeed, you need good people skills, a friendly telephone manner, the ability to perform several tasks at the same time, and excellent organizational skills.

A DAY IN THE LIFE

"I have to be on the console at 9 A.M.," states Willie Mayhoe. She fields all incoming calls, which can be an enormous task particularly on days when something significant has occurred in an artist's life and she has to screen calls from fans and the media. If the phone traffic is light, she may coordinate tickets for an upcoming concert, book the conference room, or make other appointments for label executives. She greets people arriving for meetings and directs them appropriately.

"If you see an artist is performing somewhere or doing a showcase, go to that showcase and meet people. Introduce yourself. You might meet someone who has a friend that's looking to hire someone. Network and meet as many people as you possibly can."

"Treat everybody with respect, whether it's the man coming in to deliver the paper, or the president of another company. I've known people that started out as interns or song pluggers that are now corporate executives."

"Do not treat the receptionist like she's stupid. She can help you. She can get you in to see people. If you're nice to the person at the front desk, they are more likely to go the extra mile to help you."

POINTERS FOR THE JOB SEARCH

Find a school with a good music business course of study and network. "It's worth your time to enroll in just a class so that you can get the opportunity to do an internship and meet people. There are many people who started out as interns. I was one of them. Networking is key. Get out and meet as many people as you can."

CASE STUDY:

WILLIE MAYHOE, RECEPTIONIST, MCA RECORDS NASHVILLE

Among the citizens of Virginia's Blue Ridge Mountains, families didn't come much poorer than that of Willie Mayhoe. She grew up in a household where no one else could read or write, and fell in love with the music of Tammy Wynette and George Jones at age eight. She dreamed of going to Nashville, even though she had no idea where that was. Later, she attended Ferrum College for a year, then took a job in a grocery store, and trained to become a manager.

Out driving on the evening of her 21st birthday, Mayhoe and a friend spotted Earl Thomas Conley's tour bus and followed it to a hotel in Salem, Virginia. The two planted themselves in the hotel bar and waited for a musician-type to appear. Mayhoe made her first industry contact that evening: Conley's bass player. When she told him about her love of country music, he offered to help her in any way he could. Inspired to make her dream a reality, she researched schools and was accepted to Belmont College. She packed up her few belongings, and with her final $750 paycheck in hand, boarded a Trailways bus headed for Nashville in 1987.

THE LEAST FAVORITE THING ABOUT THIS JOB:

"Being called 'honey, babe, sweetheart, and dear.' Part of the job is having to deal with people who think that because I'm the reception-ist, I'm not intelligent."

THE BEST THING ABOUT THIS JOB:

"When a new artist is signed to the label, I get to see them blossom from being an unknown to becoming a major superstar."

In her second semester, Mayhoe landed an internship at MCA Records, in public-ity and marketing. Her diligence and enthusiasm motivated her supervisor to pay her for extra assignments. After filling in for the receptionist at lunch breaks, she was offered the position full time when it became available. Impressed by the number of zeros in the salary, she quit college in 1988 to work full time. Over the years, Mayhoe has become known on Music Row as the voice of MCA. As the person who frequently decides who gets access to senior management and who does not, she is often referred to as the second most powerful person at the label. After seeing firsthand how every aspect of the music business operates, in 2000 she returned to college in the evenings to pursue a degree in entertainment law. *www.umgnashville.com*

RECORD DISTRIBUTION GROUPS AND RETAIL

The distribution company receives finished musical product—such as CDs, cassettes, singles, and videos from the record company—and is responsible for selling and delivering it to retail and on-line outlets. The parent company for most major labels also owns a distribution company to handle the needs of all the company's owned and affiliated labels. Independent record companies either align themselves with a major distribution company, or contract with an independent distributor to deliver their product to retailers.

Retailers receive the music product from the distribution company, work with the record labels to create sales and marketing campaigns, and sell product to the public.

DISTRIBUTION

SENIOR VICE PRESIDENT • VICE PRESIDENT (SALES)

JOB DESCRIPTION

Distribution executives manage sales campaigns and the distribution of music products. Alan Shapiro oversees the day-to-day sales operations of all WEA-distributed product (which includes all labels and divisions of Warner Brothers Inc., Elektra Entertainment, and The Atlantic Group), ensuring that product is in retail outlets on the planned release date, and managing a staff of more than 90 sales representatives.

To be a successful salesperson, you must treat everyone like a potential friend. "People are willing to do things for you if you treat them like human beings."

"My management style is to make people around me relax and avoid tension. I think if you joke with your fellow workers, you get a lot more out of them. It takes the edge off things."

SPECIAL SKILLS

To be successful, you should be people-oriented, have a sense of humor, and be able to motivate people. Experience in retail music sales or record company sales is important.

A DAY IN THE LIFE

Monday morning Alan Shapiro's first point of business is to check sales figures for the previous weekend. He focuses on orders for new product, including quantities, and reviews which titles stores have and have not ordered. He calls his field staff to discuss sales strategy and reviews sales of special promotions and discount programs. Then he meets with his boss to review sales progress title by title. In the afternoon, Shapiro formulates activities for the rest of the week and talks with each record label about new releases, radio airplay, television appearances, and any other promotional information that might help the field sales staff. Throughout the day he handles phone calls and various managerial duties.

LEAST FAVORITE THING ABOUT THIS JOB:

"The toughest thing for me to handle is the intense pressure. There is so much money being put into records, and rightfully so, but when a record isn't happening, it's really tough to face the labels and tell them."

THE BEST THING ABOUT THIS JOB:

"Our new releases come out on Tuesday and it's a whole new ballgame every week. Every day there are new stories to tell. Vitamin C added 85 radio stations last week and we picked up another 80 stations this week. Faith Hill is crossing over to pop and she has two Pepsi commercials. To break a brand new artist is very rewarding."

POINTERS FOR THE JOB SEARCH

"This is not an easy business to break into. I came up through retail, which is one way. My boss picked records in the warehouse. The president of our company put up posters. The CEO started out putting up posters; he was a merchandiser. You have to get in somebody's face and say, 'Give me a shot.' If you have any moxie on the Internet, that might be a way in. Everybody wants to be a vice president the day they come out of school. I think you have to work your way up and be patient, and jobs will open up for you."

CASE STUDY:

ALAN SHAPIRO, SENIOR VICE PRESIDENT SALES, WEA CORPORATION

Brooklyn native Alan Shapiro first fell in love with music while listening to the great radio disc jockeys in the heyday of 1950s rock and roll. He went through junior college on a baseball scholarship, and then decided that he needed to finish his education in a warmer climate. When he left New York for the first time in 1966, and arrived in Houston, Texas to study market research, he was surprised: he loved it. When his tuition loan money ran out in his junior year, he found work in a Disc Records store, then just breaking into the Texas market. Although he was called into the Army Reserves after only three weeks on the job, his employer was sufficiently impressed with his work to promise him a position after his tour of active duty. Shapiro returned to his former work place as general manager, and as the chain expanded, he was promoted to district manager.

Shapiro became WEA music sales representative in 1973 and continued working the Houston market. In 1977, he moved to Western Merchandisers, the area's largest retail music outlet, but was lured back to WEA in 1980 as sales representative of newly organized Warner Home Video. He returned to WEA's music division a year later as sales manager of the Houston office, then moved to the Dallas office in 1987.

After years of resistance, Shapiro agreed to move to the Los Angeles office in 1990, where he was later promoted to vice president of music sales. In 1995, when he was offered the general manager position at Giant Records in Nashville, his employer agreed it was a once-in-a-lifetime opportunity, and released him with their blessing. In 1997, WEA contacted Shapiro and offered him his former position in Los Angeles. He moved back in 1998 and was promoted to senior vice president of music sales in 1999. *www.wea.com*

"Seek out a mentor. Find someone who will guide you through your learning curve."

"Loyalty is a critical thing to learn." Never say anything negative about your boss or the team you work with. Support one another through good and not-so-good decisions. Look for ways to help others succeed, and it will come back to you in dividends.

"Manage your expectations. People come in and they get discouraged, or the job isn't what they think it should be in the beginning. Patience is important, and diligence and tenacity."

RETAIL

RETAILER • ON-LINE RETAILER • ON-LINE STORE VICE PRESIDENT • MANAGER OF MUSIC

JOB DESCRIPTION

Retailers direct and manage sales efforts of music product to the public. At Best Buy, Ted Singer develops the strategies for on-line music sales. He coordinates between Internet technology resources and publishing, merchandise planning, and finances to maximize on-line sales efforts.

SPECIAL SKILLS

To succeed, you must have the ability to work in a chaotic atmosphere. You should be self-motivated with plenty of people skills and creativity. You should be able to strategize ways to use new technology to increase sales efforts.

A DAY IN THE LIFE

About half of Ted Singer's time is devoted to discussions with lawyers who are negotiating, drafting, or reviewing contracts. He gathers information for the web site and decides how it will be presented. Throughout the day he handles phone calls and attends meetings internally and with potential business partners.

LEAST FAVORITE THING ABOUT THIS JOB:

"Sometimes the politics drive me crazy, but I love the business. I think that occasionally even the things I love drive me crazy."

THE BEST THING ABOUT THIS JOB:

"My favorite part of the job is free records. I've been very fortunate to work in the record business and be able to raise a family and live relatively comfortably. I don't think that many people get the opportunity to work in a business that they love and make enough money to support their family comfortably."

POINTERS FOR THE JOB SEARCH

Be open to opportunities where you can gain experience, such as small record stores or on-line retailers. "Don't pick your job based on a genre of music, but pick it based on the opportunity to learn about music. I've worked in country and folk radio, did a reggae and an African radio show, worked in urban and rock record stores and at Tower Records, and I just never made the distinction about music."

CASE STUDY:

TED SINGER, SENIOR MANAGER, DIGITAL MEDIA SERVICE, BEST BUY

As a teenager growing up outside Philadelphia, the only thing that truly engaged Ted Singer's attention was the music he heard on the radio. Once out of high school, he drifted around the country for several years before settling into a job stocking record bins at a Warner Elektra Atlantic (WEA) warehouse. He immediately fell in love with the record business, memorizing the liner notes of every album and pouring his salary into a spectacular record collection. "You were allowed to buy ten records every two weeks for $1.82." After a skid of records was dropped on his foot, he left warehouse work and enrolled at a Philadelphia radio school in 1976, working nights answering the telephone for a deejay he had listened to as a kid.

Following a miserable year of spinning disks at a country radio station in Hobbs, New Mexico, Singer moved to Phoenix, Arizona. He found a job on public radio doing a weekend folk music show, and worked at a downtown record store during the week. Several years later, he and two partners opened Charts Records, and added two more locations over the next six years. When the stores were sold in 1985, he went to work for the buyer, and moved to Rhode Island to manage the Midland Records chain.

Six months into his new position, a Minnesota entrepreneur offered Singer a job opening in an innovative video and music chain called Tidal Wave. He began with only a borrowed desk, a set of blueprints, and a list of telephone numbers, and within eight and a half years, he had opened 14 stores. Thoroughly burnt out by this time, he quit and took six months off to plan his next career move.

Singer put together a self-marketing campaign whose quirky sense of humor appealed to the management at Best Buy. Always able to operate well in chaos, he took over the special projects that no one else wanted or understood. In 1997, he was drafted to expand the company's web site into an on-line music store, which continues to evolve as one of the industry's most innovative operations. "We created a download storefront on the Web," said Singer, "utilizing a platform that makes it easy for consumers to access their favorite music digitally." Singer was rewarded for his success with a promotion to senior manager of Digital Media Service. *www.bestbuy.com*

CHAPTER

5

RECORDING

When you read the liner notes of an album or CD, you realize how many people are needed to make a single recording. The four sections of this chapter—Production, Studio and Equipment, Production Assistants and Companies, and Musicians—discuss the jobs involved in the recording process.

PRODUCTION

Producers, engineers, mixers, and mastering engineers all require technical and creative skills, a thorough knowledge of the recording process, and an ear for music.

PRODUCER • RECORD PRODUCER

JOB OVERVIEW

The producer is ultimately responsible for the quality of the finished recorded sound, and is involved in both the business and the creative side of making the recording. Business tasks include working closely with the record label and manager on budgets, schedules, and deadlines. Creative elements include selection of songs (some producers co-write with the artist), studio, engineers, musicians, musical arrangements, mixer, and all other aspects of the recording process.

Although his primary function is creative, Little Dog Records president Pete Anderson is also responsible for the business aspects of running the label, in addition to the normal duties of a producer. He decides which artists are signed to the label, when their records will be released, and produces most projects.

SPECIAL SKILLS

"Because I've been a singer," says producer Chris Farren, "I understand the emotions and the feelings of having a set of headphones on and being on the other side of the glass from where the music is coming out. I understand what it feels like when the headphones don't fit right, you're not feeling good, you're singing as hard as you can but it doesn't sound right, or you don't understand what the producer wants from you. Because I've felt like that, it allows me to communicate with singers better than nonsinging producers."

A producer must understand both the creative and business aspects of making records. He must be able to communicate with the engineer and musicians in technical and musical terms, and with label executives on the business matters.

CAREER TIPS

Being in the position to hire musicians, Anderson looks at people and asks, "Are they responsible? Are they polite? Do they have a car? Do they have a phone? Do they have good equipment? Are they low maintenance?"

POINTERS FOR THE JOB SEARCH

"I don't think you decide to be a producer. I think you either are or you aren't. I think my biggest piece of advice is to be as objective as you can about yourself and your talent. Try not to go down the wrong path for too long of a time. I wanted to be an artist; I wanted to be a singer/guitar player/harmonica player. I wasn't a good enough singer, but I could be a good producer. If you're not succeeding, there must be a reason. Be objective."—PA

"Do anything and everything in the music business that you can do. Absorb as much music and as many different influences as you can. Make yourself as multifaceted and valuable as you can. Go in and produce someone's demo. Do it for free. Just get in the studio and work and experiment."—CF

CASE STUDY:

PETE ANDERSON, PRESIDENT, LITTLE DOG RECORDS; PRODUCER AND MUSICIAN

From the time he first saw Elvis Presley perform on television, Detroit native Pete Anderson fell in love with the sound of the guitar. "I just loved how the guitar looked. I've always been in love with the sound of it." At age 16, inspired by the music of Bob Dylan, he bought his first instrument and taught himself to play. Although he went to art school, that interest soon faded away and was replaced by music. "Music became a creative outlet for me."

He moved to Los Angeles in 1972 and, not knowing anyone, began making the rounds of jam sessions and band auditions, playing blues and writing songs until landing a gig with a touring bar band. Next came a stint working in a music store that led to gigs sitting in with country musicians. Anderson continued to play, worked his way up to better gigs, and made a name for himself. In 1983, Dwight Yoakum hired him as a sideman for club dates.

Yoakum's sound was so different from what was currently heard on radio, that the band was fired from every gig they played. With Yoakum on the verge of giving up, Anderson convinced him to self-finance a six-song album that was distributed locally, and won immediate critical praise. Yoakum was opening for the Blasters on a cross-country tour when Warner Brothers Records caught his act, and signed him to a deal. The resulting album, *Guitars and Cadillacs*, which Anderson produced and played on, garnered several hit singles and went gold.

As time went by, Anderson's studio work with songwriters and recording artists turned more and more into producing, until in 1993, he opened Little Dog Records. The label gave Anderson the creative freedom to sign and develop artists that he believed in. Beginning with one artist and a toll-free telephone number, Anderson

VOICES OF EXPERIENCE

THE LEAST FAVORITE THING ABOUT THIS JOB:

"I resent the fact that people get into positions of power and have absolutely no taste or talent or reason to even have that job, other than some other guy with no talent hired him."—PA

"The fine tuning—the little tweaking part of getting the vocal and the mix right. You just have to get so inside the music, you feel like you're pulling out a microscope. Also, the crazy kind of political things you have to deal with. Like when the label doesn't want a song, but the artist does."—CF

THE BEST THING ABOUT THIS JOB:

"I love songwriters. I love hearing a great song. I like the music I work with, the musicians, and the opportunity to be creative and work with creative people."—PA

"I like tracking: being in the room with great musicians and having that energy spiral into something magical. I love being in a live music setting where there are four, five, or six musicians all playing at once. It's like the sum is greater than the individual parts."—CF

took out some ads and did his own marketing. As he continued to expand and sign new talent, he made distribution deals, first with Rounder Records, then with Polygram. He realized the enormous potential of Internet sales, and Anderson decided that a single distributor was not the way of the future, opting instead for multiple independent distributors by region. Little Dog releases represent a wide range of American roots music ranging from honky-tonk, blues, country, and folk to rock and Latin. Anderson also released his solo projects "Working Class," "Dogs in Heaven," and "Daredevil" through the label.

In addition to playing and producing his own blistering solo recordings, the Grammy Award winning Anderson has produced such artists as Michelle Shocked, k.d. lang, Sara Evans, Lonesome Strangers, Joy Lynn White, and Meat Puppets. *www.peteanderson.com* and *www.littledogrecords.com*

CASE STUDY:

CHRIS FARREN, PRODUCER/WRITER AND PRESIDENT COMBUSTION MUSIC

Chris Farren discovered that music exerted a powerful force over him at a very early age. From the piano lessons he began at four years old, to the guitar, trombone, and saxophone, which he later mastered, to the club bands he played in during high school and college, his entire life was consumed by music. "Music just had a strangely powerful allure for me." He enrolled at East Carolina University, but when the course work began leading him toward classical music, he switched his major to English, and focused on creative writing as a way of advancing his interest in writing songs. He graduated in 1981, moved to Los Angeles, and supported himself playing club gigs and as a session singer on demos, jingles, and backups. "I thought I was going to be a star. I thought I would pay my dues and be discovered. It was a lot harder than I thought."

Farren signed an artist/writer publishing deal with MCA in 1983 and created a niche writing for film and television during the mid-1980s. Advised that he did not fit the techno/heavy metal/glam rock image then popular, and that Nashville was the only place then embracing the singer/songwriter, he made the move, despite not considering himself a country artist. Between cutting his own albums, playing guitar and singing backup on other people's records, co-writing with some of the city's best songwriters, and the session work he continued to do in Los Angeles, Farren was able to make a decent living. He honed his skills while engineering demos of his own songs, and he added to his income by engineering and producing demos for other artists.

Between the demos Farren did in Nashville, and the film sound track work he continued to do in Los Angeles, he found himself increasingly drawn to producing. Able to write and sing the songs, play all the instruments, and produce and engineer the recordings, he found that film companies liked working with him because with one person doing it all, they could reduce their licensing fees. He quickly became as well known for the hit songs he produced, as for the hit songs he wrote.

In the early 1990s, Farren divided his time between Los Angeles and Nashville and was soon producing records for country artists Boy Howdy (three albums; two Top Ten hits), Kevin Sharp (platinum album; three number one hit singles), and Deana Carter (quintuple-platinum album; three number one hit singles; CMA Single of the Year). Along the way he also picked up *American Songwriter*'s 1997 Country Producer of the Year Award and was named *Billboard*'s number three Top Producer in Country Music.

Farren was instrumental in opening the Windswept Pacific Publishing office in Nashville, serving as creative consultant. In 2001, Farren and Ken Levitan, president of Vector Management, teamed to open Combustion Music, a publishing and production company, a joint venture with Windswept Pacific. The company has scored several No. 1 singles, including 2006 Grammy and ASCAP Song of the Year "Jesus Take the Wheel," recorded by *American Idol* winner Carrie Underwood. *www.combustionmusic.com*

RECORDING ENGINEER AND MIXER

JOB OVERVIEW

The recording engineer retrieves and stores musical data, essentially everything that comes through the microphones. These engineers select and place microphones, record the music onto analog or digital tape, and work the console. The job of the engineer/mixer is to sort out the information that has been recorded and over-dubbed, and mix it down to two or four tracks, or whatever format is needed, so that people can understand the musical statement of the producer and artist.

SPECIAL SKILLS

In addition to technical abilities and people skills, Jimmy Douglass adds, "Knowing music is important for success. When I record a live band or a live orchestra, they give me a chart. I have to be able to read that chart as I'm doing the recording."

A DAY IN THE LIFE

"On our first day of tracking," explains Tom Harding, "We'll come in and get the musicians all set up. On sessions where I'm acting as producer and engineer, I'll get everybody's sounds and then get the artist set up. Before we start tracking, we'll probably sit around an acoustic guitar, play the song, double-check keys, and allow everyone to bounce ideas off each other. Then, we'll go out into the studio and start running down the song. Once all the tracking is completed, the musicians pack up

"If you do this [engineering or producing] for the love of what you're doing, then the success, the fame, and the money will not be denied you, eventually. You have to come into this job with the love of what you're doing first."—JD

Stay abreast of changes in recording technology—read and attend gear and equipment shows.

and leave and we begin to work on vocals. After the lead vocals are done, we'll add the background vocals, and then maybe some sweetening, like adding tambourine. I'll put a lead vocal together from all the takes and let the artist hear it, and we'll decide if they need to punch a line or fix anything. After everything is recorded, it's ready to be mixed."

POINTERS FOR THE JOB SEARCH

"Do your homework in terms of knowing who makes the records you like, who makes the sounds that you like. Find out as much as you can about how they make those sounds. What other records they've done. Try to learn as much as you can about the equipment they use. Find out who does what on a session. Become familiar with the latest technology by either buying your own equipment or going to a recording school. There is no reason you should ever walk in a door, trying to get a job, and not know how the system works. Learn all that you can about the genre of music you want to work in and be ready. The keyword is, never say 'No, I can't do it.'"—JD

"You don't necessarily have to be in New York, Nashville, or Los Angeles to be a good recording engineer. With the invention of A-DATS, ProTools, and all the digital recording, you can have a great studio anywhere in the world."—TH

THE LEAST FAVORITE THING ABOUT THIS JOB:

"It's a 24-hour business and it seems that everyone should be available all of the time."—JD

THE BEST THING ABOUT THIS JOB:

"The reward of working with great talent and actually being part of putting some great music together that excites people. When you see people listen to the records that you've made and they really love the music, it's so rewarding. You can't explain the feeling. The money is great too, but in terms of a job, I get paid to sit and listen to music all day."—JD

JIMMY DOUGLASS, RECORDING ENGINEER, MIXER, AND PRODUCER

From a very early age, Jimmy Douglass had a passion for music. As much as he loved listening to it, he loved to play it even more. He took piano lessons, but taught himself to play guitar, bass, drums, and keyboards, and performed in a number of bands around Long Island, New York. While he was attending college classes, a friend of a friend got him a part-time job making tape copies in an Atlantic Records recording studio. While there, he took advantage of occasional down time to learn how to work the studio's sound and recording equipment. That knowledge, combined with his experience as a lead musician in bands, convinced him that he had the ability to become a music producer.

Encouraged by the studio staff, Douglass tried his hand at producing the demos for three bands that he hoped to help get recording contracts. He had to be convinced to double as engineer, because he had only watched others perform that function, but had never actually done it himself. When he took the final tapes to Atlantic in an attempt to get the bands signed, he was told that the label did not care for either the songs or the bands, but they were really impressed by the production. Deciding that it didn't matter what position he played as long as he got into the game, Douglass switched his focus to sound engineering and mixing, and each job led to the next.

Over the years, Douglass' skills as an engineer and mixer put him in great demand with artists like the Rolling Stones, Foreigner, AC/DC, Genesis, and Aretha Franklin, and finally led him into producing. As music evolved in the late 1980s, and came to rely more on digital technology, he found that the sound he had developed was no longer selling records. Essentially taking a year off to learn the new technology and absorb the new sound, Douglass returned to the streets, offering his services cheaply to gain experience working with emerging urban musicians. Transforming his approach, he was soon back in the studio, producing platinum projects with Missy Elliott, Lenny Kravitz, Ginuwine, Aaliyah, and Timbaland. Nicknamed Senator Jimmy D, he explains, "When you're mixing, you're often off in the room by yourself, but when you're recording you have to be a diplomat—it's so political! So I call myself 'Senator Jimmy D.'" *www.myspace.com/jimmymagicmix*

ENGINEER • SECOND ENGINEER

JOB OVERVIEW

These engineers are charged with set-up, connection, and notation of all the equipment to be used during a recording session. They serve as backup for the engineer, taking on his board duties when necessary.

"Many times, writers, management, publishers, and promotion people come into the studio. It's really helpful if you know about other people's jobs in the industry."

"A lot of people come to town and don't progress as quickly as they expect and become frustrated and quit. You've got to be willing to work hard and stick with it."

PREREQUISITES

A thorough knowledge of how to set up and use recording equipment is a must. The ability to listen, take instructions, and communicate well with an underlying positive personality are skills that will help you succeed.

A DAY IN THE LIFE

On the day of recording, Ricky Cobble arrives at the studio one to two hours before the session begins so that he can set up the equipment, including microphones, stands, any specially ordered gear. He puts tape in place and makes appropriate notations on the board. When the musicians arrive, he assists in getting them set up and miked, with all lines working properly. Throughout the session he is available to assist with anything from getting coffee to running the board while the first engineer steps away. At the end of the session, the second helps break down the equipment.

POINTERS FOR THE JOB SEARCH

"Enroll in an accredited school where you can learn about all aspects of the industry. I highly recommend learning how all the different areas of the industry work. Get into an engineering class and learn about signal flow and how the different pieces of equipment work, and what pieces of equipment you should use to get the sound you

THE LEAST FAVORITE THING ABOUT THIS JOB:

"My least favorite part of my job are the hours and being away from my family. The engineer is the first to arrive at the studio and the last to leave. The arsenal of musicians shows up after everything is set up, and once the recording is over, they leave. You're there another hour or so, tidying things up."

THE BEST THING ABOUT THIS JOB:

"The thing I love the most is working with all the musicians."

want. Then do an internship at a studio. Some people get started by working at small studios in small towns and gaining hands-on experience."

CASE STUDY:

RICKY COBBLE, FIRST ENGINEER, LOUD STUDIOS

Ricky Cobble grew up amid the country music of eastern Tennessee, and was always interested in music. At an age when all his friends were putting together bands, he knew he wanted to work in recording. Introduced by a friend to the music program at Belmont University, he moved to Nashville to attend classes and ended up serving an internship at Quad Studios. He started out doing the things that nobody else wanted to do: answering the telephone, making coffee, watching the door, and working the night shift. Soon he was setting up microphones and assisting the second sound engineer. More importantly, he was getting the opportunity to observe the recording process and see how the producers and engineers worked. When his internship was finished, Cobble was hired as house assistant, charged with the technical aspects of interfacing the studio's equipment with the additional equipment brought in by engineers for specific recording sessions.

During his four years at Quad, Cobble developed relationships with the recording teams there. When several of these people started up Loud Studios in 1994, he was brought in as house assistant, and quickly worked his way up to the second position. As second engineer, Cobble has worked with artists like Faith Hill, Tim McGraw, and Randy Travis, as well as with top-notch producers like James Stroud. He broke into the first engineer position by tracking and mixing for several developing artists, and landed his first major session in 1999 by being in the right place at the right time. When a flight delay stranded the first engineer in Hawaii, Cobble stepped into the position at the last minute to record tracks for a Clint Black album. Cobble has since engineered on albums for Faith Hill, Toby Keith, and Montgomery Gentry.

MASTERING ENGINEER

JOB OVERVIEW

Mastering is the final creative step in the recording process before the manufacture of a CD, DVD, cassette, record, or any other format that is released to the public. It is the process of transferring recorded sounds that are stored on a master tape, to a lacquer disc (or master disc) for the purpose of manufacturing recordings. "Imagine being in the studio, mixing, being finished with the recording and listening back to your mixes," says Denny Purcell. "The producer and artist have a picture in their minds of how they want the recording to sound to the public, which they lined up song by song. The mastering engineer makes that possible. The sound, time between songs, the volume of each song; we make the record palatable for the public."

"If money is your goal, your career will be short lived. Music is an art form. The most important things in music are the song, the performance, and the production."

SPECIAL SKILLS

"I think people skills helped me the most to become successful. That and diplomacy and patience."

POINTERS FOR THE JOB SEARCH

"When I started out, there weren't any schools that taught mastering. You had to find someone and become an apprentice. I don't know how much schooling you need, but I don't know if there is an engineer who would let you in the door if you didn't have some schooling."

CASE STUDY:

DENNY PURCELL, MASTER ENGINEER, PRESIDENT OF GEORGETOWN MASTERS

Growing up in a musical family in Indiana, Denny Purcell fell in love with songs through the lyrics of Bob Dylan and Joni Mitchell. "I had three Bob Dylan records: one to listen to and figure out what he said, one to play after that, and one to keep." Early on, he knew that he wanted to be involved in the creative process of music. A musician in the late 1960s, Purcell moved to Nashville in the early 1970s after gaining some initial engineering experience in New York. He drove an ice cream truck until he landed a job as second engineer at Quadrafonic Sound Studios. There he worked with artists like Jimmy Buffett, Dan Fogelberg, Linda Ronstadt, Joe Walsh, Neil Young, and many others. When Young's producer, Elliot Mazer, wanted to record the artist's Time Fades Away Tour, Purcell and Gene Eichelberger built Masters Wheels and Purcell manned the mobile studio for the next two years.

Purcell returned to Nashville in 1974. "I worked at a gas station trying to figure out how to get a job [engineering]. I remember washing the windshields of people I knew. They would ask me what I was doing and I told them I was getting back in the business. One fellow looked at me and said, 'It's nice to see people with goals.'" Persistence paid off and although

THE LEAST FAVORITE THING ABOUT THIS JOB:

"Running the business. I like to come to work and play. I haven't grown up yet."

THE BEST THING ABOUT THIS JOB:

"Getting to share a day or two with some of the most well-known people in the music business on a one-to-one level."

he didn't find work as a producer, Purcell landed a job as a mastering engineer at Woodland Mastering, which forever changed the course of his career. He began mastering gospel music, later mastered Kansas' legendary *Masque* album, and eventually ended up running the facility. "If you're a studio engineer, you might work two or three months on an album," says Purcell. "I work on a different album every day. I'm the type of person who wants to see the end of his work. It ended up that the job I found, which fed my family, is the one that is much more attractive to me than studio engineering."

In 1985 he founded his own company, Georgetown Masters, where he has mastered more than 500 gold and platinum albums for such diverse artists as Garth Brooks, Vince Gill, Yo-Yo Ma, Tom Petty, Phish, Keith Richards, Paul Simon, Trisha Yearwood, and Neil Young. In 1998, he won *Billboard* magazine's Mastering Facility of the Year award. One of only ten people worldwide who is capable of operating at this level of success, Purcell founded Mastering Engineers Guild of the Americas (MEGA) in 1998 with the mission to assist the music industry with technological issues, and to deliver to consumers accurate renderings of artist's works.

STUDIO AND EQUIPMENT

STUDIO OWNER

JOB OVERVIEW

The studio manager oversees the daily operations of the recording studio, including booking and maintaining the facility, engineering, marketing, and all administrative tasks.

CAREER TIPS

"I'm a big believer in college. I've noticed that some people that come through tech school and are just 18 or 19 aren't mature enough to handle the problems that arise. They get insulted if you say, 'Go make coffee,' whereas, for some reason, the people that have gone to college realize that is a small part of the job. I also think they are more well-rounded and can carry on a conversation that's not just about recording."

"Try to learn an instrument. You don't have to be extremely proficient at playing it, but it will help you better understand music. Learn to read chord charts and things like that."

PREREQUISITES

To succeed, you should have patience, people skills, and an understanding of business and marketing. "When you're in school studying to be an engineer and you're made to take marketing and accounting classes, you think it will never help you," says Tom Harding, "but all of that has helped me. You understand that you've got to keep your checkbook balanced. It all sounds logical and a bit silly, but you'd be surprised at how many studio owners don't understand finance and marketing."

A DAY IN THE LIFE

"The first thing I do is check to see what is booked in the studio," says Tom Harding. "If I have an outside engineer coming in, I make sure I have an assistant here before anybody arrives to get everything set up. If the session is tracking, we make sure that we've got two-inch tape on hand, DATS, and cassettes. If there are any maintenance problems in the studio, we make sure those have been taken care of. Electronics constantly need repairs; it is vital to the session that everything is working. I make sure that we've got coffee and that the machine is working. If I need to arrange for catering, I take care of that. I meet with the client and make sure everyone is happy and they have what they need. Then I might have some invoicing, bills payable, and other business to take care of."

POINTERS FOR THE JOB SEARCH

"To manage your own studio, you better know your clientele and who you are gearing your studio for first. There was a studio built just a mile from Tombstone and they spent around three million dollars making it very state of the art. It lasted 14 months. Number one, the room was too complex. Even if they were booked every day, they would not make enough money to pay their bills. Number two, they didn't

THE LEAST FAVORITE THING ABOUT THIS JOB:

"I don't think you could ask anybody about any job that they wouldn't say that the politics is what they dislike."

THE BEST THING ABOUT THIS JOB:

"I just love that point when you're putting music down for the first time, when I'm recording a band and we're in the studio for around six hours, it's gotten dark and everybody is tired, but everybody is in that zone where everything is clicking and it almost seems surreal."

have a client base to build on; they had a few people who weren't from the area using the studio. You need to have a client base so that you know certain people will come use your studio. Don't overbuild or overspend, so you're affordable and competitive in your prices."

CASE STUDY:

TOM HARDING, ENGINEER, PRODUCER, STUDIO MANAGER/OWNER, TOMBSTONE RECORDING

"My job is to give the client everything they demand to make their session go as smoothly and as technically perfect as possible," says Tom Harding. The son of an air force officer, Harding grew up mostly in Utah. After nearly flunking out of college, he followed his family to Saudi Arabia, where his father was stationed for a year, then returned to America determined to become a recording engineer. At a recording workshop in Ohio, he learned about music recording courses at schools in Miami, Middle Tennessee State University (MTSU), and Memphis State. He contacted all three and made his selection based on the fact that Memphis was the only school that sent enrollment information. MTSU sent a catalog, and he never even heard from Miami. "I was accepted to Memphis. I was cleaning out my desk drawers and packing, and threw the MTSU catalog in the garbage. It fell open in the recording department section and there was a picture of a console and the studio. I picked it up, looked at it, and said, 'Wow, this is the school that I want to go to.'"

While at MTSU, Harding served an internship at Elektra Records in the public relations department. When an employee heard his college recording project, she was impressed and encouraged him to return to engineering. The employee arranged an introduction to Gene Eichelberger, who in turn alerted him to an assistant's job at a newly opened sound studio. Initially standoffish, the studio manager changed his mind when Harding stated that Eichelberger had sent him, and he was hired for the position.

With free run of the studio when it was not in use on weekends, Harding started bringing in rock bands from around town to play while he practiced the effects he had seen the engineers do. One of the engineers was Ed Seay, who began handing off demo sessions to Harding, giving him the chance to operate in the first engineer position. When Intruder, one of the weekend bands, was signed to a label, he produced three of their albums, and won eight of the 1991 Nashville Music Awards, including Producer of the Year and Album of the Year.

Harding went on to produce recordings for Kennedy Rose, BB King, Etta James, Buddy Guy, and Cissy Houston, and engineered for ZZ Top. In 1995, he and a friend looked at a studio that was for rent, and the two decided to go into business together. They leased space on Music Row, bought a load of used equipment, and set up Tombstone Recording. Three months later, the tape machines broke down and had to be replaced. When the landlord raised the rent, Harding found another building, bought it, and began remodeling. During the process, his partner dropped out and he continued on alone. Since that time, numerous record labels and publishing companies, as well as artists like Burt Bacharach, Brooks & Dunn, and Pam Tillis, have made Tombstone their studio of choice. *www.tombstonerecording.com*

GENERAL MANAGER • MANAGER • OWNER

JOB OVERVIEW

The manager or owner manages and books the recording studio's rooms, acts as the liaison with the clients to ensure their needs are met when working at the facility, and solicits new business. "I'm like the concierge at a fine hotel," says Ocean Way manager Kelly Erwin. "I make sure that everything is running smoothly and that our clients are extremely happy."

PREREQUISITES

To succeed, you need good organization and problem solving skills, attention to detail, patience, and a pleasant phone manner. A friendly personality and the ability to get along well with people are essential.

A DAY IN THE LIFE

Upon her morning arrival, Erwin checks through e-mail and reviews the previous day's work orders. Throughout the day her focus is on booking the studio. "Doing the booking for so many rooms is like a puzzle. A producer could call and say, 'I want to book five days starting Monday.' It could take three days to receive the PO [purchase order] from the label because they don't know the producer and artist have decided to book time. There are several calls going back and forth between the label and the producer and finally you get the days all set. Then, late Friday or early Saturday, I'm at

CAREER TIPS

"When you finally figure out what you really want to do, it is so important to put it out there and have confidence in what you want. A person can really manifest that conviction. It's getting through the mind blocks that say, 'I can't,' and believing I can."

"It is impossible to know about all the recording equipment available, but the more you do know so you can answer clients' questions, is a big asset."

THE LEAST FAVORITE THING ABOUT THIS JOB:

"When I have rooms booked, someone cancels, and I have to scramble at the last minute to try and fill the time."

THE BEST THING ABOUT THIS JOB:

"When I've really tried to help somebody with a rate or tried to figure out a way to make it work so they can come in, and it happens. When I see that the client is really happy and excited to come in, I'm excited."

home and I get a call that they have to cancel everything because the artist has to do a show in Canada. I have to scramble and find someone else to book that time."

POINTERS FOR THE JOB SEARCH

"Find out all you can about the industry and how the recording process works. Become familiar with names of producers, engineers, and artists. Get an overall view of what is happening today in the recording scene, then start trying to just get your foot in the door and see where that takes you."

CASE STUDY:

KELLY ERWIN, MANAGER, OCEAN WAY RECORDING

Music has been a part of Kelly Erwin's life since she was a very young child, and she begged her brother to play his Beach Boys records. But it wasn't until years later that she would consider a career in the industry. After four years working as operations manager at an animation production house in Los Angeles, she found herself laid off and re-examining her career path. "I started to think about what it was I really loved and it was music." Not knowing exactly how to go about getting into the business, she began by telling everyone she knew about her dream. Over the next year several leads failed to produce a job, until a long-time friend of her mother's offered to introduce Erwin to a neighbor who worked in the business. The neighbor turned out to be Jack Woltz, general manger of Ocean Way Recording studios, who offered her a receptionist job at smaller sister studio, Record One.

Beginning as a receptionist in 1992, Erwin set her mind to learning everything she could about the facility and its equipment. After six months, she switched places with the receptionist at the larger Ocean Way studios, and sought out additional ways to keep busy. She started handling the studio's collections then took on accounts payable for Ocean Way Nashville. After proving her ability to handle multiple operations functions, she was taken off the front desk to book the studio rooms, and gained the title of manager. Paul McCartney, Black Crows, Black Eyed Peas, Eric Clapton, Diana

Kroll, John Mayer, and Janet Jackson are but a few of the artists who have recorded at Ocean Way. *www.oceanwayrecording.com*

PRO-AUDIO RENTAL COMPANY

Pro-Audio companies rent equipment to recording studios. Items for rent may include tape machines, microphones, and outboard gear such as delays and effects. Recording tape is available for purchase. Top of the line equipment can be very expensive and because recording technology is constantly improving and changing, it is often more cost-effective to rent special gear on a need-to-use basis.

GENERAL MANAGER • MANAGER

DUTIES

The manager handles the daily operation of the company, including customer relations, sales and service, contract negotiation, and management of staff. A thorough knowledge of current and cutting edge recording technology is essential.

PREREQUISITES

A background in electronics and experience with recording equipment is essential. "Being able to talk to people on the phone is a big plus with Dreamhire," says Jeff Altheide. "You've got to be able to convince them [potential clients] that you're going to be able to give them the equipment that they need and make sure that it works."

A DAY IN THE LIFE

Altheide arrives at the office at about 8:30 A.M. and gets the computer system up and running. (The company has a complex computer system that keeps track of the gear and prints out all of the contracts.) Throughout the day he handles phone orders and quotes prices for rentals. As manager, he is responsible for time cards, payroll, and other managerial duties. Because many of the company's clients are in Atlanta, Austin, Orlando, and other major cities with recording studios, the end of the day is devoted to filling orders and packing them for Federal Express pickup. "I keep track of every rental, what gear is going where, if the client calling already has billing set up with us, or if we need to get credit card information and set up an account. I delegate the authority to the other employees to

"Develop people skills: being able to talk with people and work with people."

"Stay updated with the equipment that is coming out and where the technology is going—that is very important."

THE LEAST FAVORITE THING ABOUT THE JOB:

"It's time consuming at times; being on call, keeping the phone around, but it gets easier. I'm the manager and responsible for the amount of business that we do, so I'm happy to see the phone calls come in."

THE BEST THING ABOUT THIS JOB:

"Being around the equipment and learning about a lot of different aspects of the recording industry. The whole idea of rentals got started because technology started growing so fast, with so many different pieces of equipment coming out, that there is no way a studio could afford to keep up. I get to go to trade shows and meet people from all over the country that have new pieces of equipment—gear that all of those studios can't afford to buy. We go out and buy all those pieces of gear and rent them to the studios. And, we get to use the gear whenever it's not being rented. That's always a plus if you're a musician and getting your own recording projects going."

get the gear delivered or packed up." When he leaves the office at the end of the day, he is still on-call 24 hours a day.

POINTERS FOR THE JOB SEARCH

Working for a studio rental company is a good beginning job for those interested in becoming studio engineers and producers, because you get an opportunity to become familiar with, and use, cutting edge equipment. When delivering equipment, you meet individuals who work at recording studios. A basic knowledge of equipment is required and can be gained through taking recording or electronics classes, reading and studying about equipment, or interning at a recording studio or rental company.

CASE STUDY:

JEFF ALTHEIDE, MANAGER, DREAMHIRE

Jeff Altheide grew up in Evansville, Indiana where he learned to play the guitar when he was eight, later switched to bass, and played in local bands throughout his junior and senior high school years. After high school, he continued to play music for a few years until he heard of a recording engineer class offered by Recording Workshop in Chillicothe, Ohio. After completing the six-week crash course, he returned to Evansville to find a job. "It's a good-size town, but not overloaded with recording studios," Altheide recalls. "In 1989, I decided to move to Nashville because it wasn't far from my home town. I figured if I got down there and couldn't make any money, it wasn't too far of a crawl back home."

Altheide found work at a tee-shirt printing company that supplied merchandise for country artists Hank Williams, Jr., Randy Travis, and Brooks & Dunn. He decided that a greater knowledge of electronics might help his chances of landing a studio job, and he enrolled in courses at ITT. "I was ten years out of high school, so I was a little more serious about college." Altheide graduated with honors, earning a 3.9 grade point average, and was offered a job at the school. "I had real long hair at the time and I didn't want to cut it. The school didn't want to hire an instructor that had hair down to his waist, so I went out and bought a wig. Every morning I would get up and ball my hair up, tie it up, and put this wig on over the top." A year later, Altheide was ready for a change. One of his students worked at Dreamhire as a tech repairing gear, something Altheide yearned to do. He telephoned the general manager of Dreamhire USA and landed a job, negotiating a pay raise from his teaching job. When the manager position became available, Altheide initially turned it down. "I was playing in bands and wasn't interested." He later became assistant manager and a couple of years later, when the manager position opened up again, he accepted. In 2003, parent company Zomba closed the Nashville office of Dreamhire, but the company was reopened later that year as Dreamhire LLC and continues to thrive in its New York City location. *www.dreamhire.com*

OFFICE MANAGER • STUDIO MANAGER

JOB OVERVIEW

These managers are responsible for scheduling sessions, booking sessions for staff engineers, overseeing the production schedule, accounting, payroll, and other administrative duties.

PREREQUISITES

Marketing skills, an understanding of the recording process, and a college education are assets, but not required. "You need to be a people person, friendly and outgoing. I'm organized and able to multi-task. My experience as an administrative assistant helped."

A DAY IN THE LIFE

"The first thing I do in the morning is check to see that everything on the

CAREER TIPS

"Do your job to the best of your ability and other doors will open up for you." Once you are working in the industry, most advancement opportunities come by referral from someone you previously worked with.

production schedule was done last night," says Lee. "When somebody comes in and masters an album, they usually need some type of part the next morning. I check through all of those requests and make sure that all of it is done. Then I usually confirm sessions for the next day or two. I do the accounting, recording checks and paying bills. Throughout the day people call me to schedule sessions or to approve a mix so parts can be sent to the manufacturing plants. I make sure those parts are going out on time to meet the deadline. I make sure that all the tapes that come in to us for a session—it may be one DAT or six boxes of tapes—are returned to the right person."

POINTERS FOR THE JOB SEARCH

"You almost need to have a connection in the music business. Many positions are filled by word of mouth; someone recommends someone they know."

CASE STUDY:

SANDY LEE, STUDIO MANAGER, MASTER MIX

Sandy Lee's inability to sing, or even hum on key, precluded any childhood aspiration for a career in music. After doing administrative work in an orthodontist's office for seven years, she quit to get married. When her husband lost his job unexpectedly in 1995, she needed to find work in a hurry. Through a friend who worked at Benson Records, Lee heard that the label's president was looking for an office administrator. She got an interview and was hired, but after just six months on the job, the label president was fired. Lee found a position as assistant to the president of Warner Alliance Records, but two years later she was laid off during label restructuring.

Lee heard about an opening at Jeff Roberts and Associates booking agency, and was hired as office manager to handle scheduling and contracts. A year later, Hank

THE LEAST FAVORITE THING ABOUT THIS JOB:

"I love everything about my job except when we make a human error and I have a manufacturing plant or an artist calling me to say there is a dropout in the production tape. Consequently, the plant can't manufacture the CD and we're up against a deadline. One of the bad things is record labels wait to the last minute to master an album and they've got a deadline of when CDs have to be duplicated, and they don't allow themselves enough time for any type of error, whether it's ours or theirs."

VOICES OF EXPERIENCE

Williams, whom she had met while working at Warner Alliance, asked if she would manage his recording studio. After checking out the position, Lee was hired as studio manager in 1999. *www.mastermix.com*

PRODUCTION ASSISTANTS AND COMPANIES

GENERAL MANAGER • MANAGER

JOB OVERVIEW

At Hamstein Productions, Ginny Johnson oversees the daily operations of the company in its three areas of focus: coordinating projects for producers and artists, managing producers, and developing artists with the goal of landing a major recording contract.

PREREQUISITES

To succeed, you should have an ear for great songs, an understanding of the A&R and recording process, strong contacts within the industry, and people skills. "You have to really listen and be aware of everything that is going on in the industry in general and with your clients. The ability to find great songs is invaluable because that is where the whole process starts. It all starts with the music and in order to be successful, you've got to have hit songs."

A DAY IN THE LIFE

"On Mondays we start the day off with a staff meeting to discuss all of the projects that we're coordinating," says Johnson. "We go over our signed artists in detail and converse about what needs to be done on their projects. We have an A&R meeting that is solely to listen to songs for our artists. In between meetings I'm constantly on the phone, coordinating various projects, talking to song pluggers, putting songs on hold, and taking them off hold. Because we're always looking for new artists, I'm constantly asking publishers about writer/artists. Throughout the day I talk with label A&R staff and managers about the different projects we're working on. I might be looking for a manager for one of our artists, dropping by a studio to

CAREER TIPS

"You have to be dedicated, work very, very hard, and be willing to work long hours. That is what enabled me to move up as quickly as I did. I put in long days, worked hard, and I always went the extra mile. It paid off for me."

Read liner notes and learn credits for producers, songwriters, and publishers.

THE LEAST FAVORITE THING ABOUT THIS JOB:

"The accounting and paperwork. When we coordinate albums, we have to track budgets, and even though it's as important as the music, it's not the most fun part."

THE BEST THING ABOUT THIS JOB:

"What I love most is working with all the people that are involved in this business; they're very interesting, intelligent, artistic, and gifted people. It's fun to be in the studio when their music is going down. It's fun to have the writers come in and play you great songs. Those are fun experiences that you get every day in this business."

check in on a project, or pitching one of our producers to a label to work with a particular artist. My day starts about 9 A.M. and ends around 9 P.M. every night."

POINTERS FOR THE JOB SEARCH

A position, or internship, in A&R or A&R administration is a great way to gain the skills necessary to manage producers and handle production coordination.

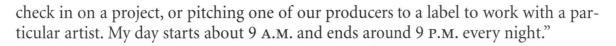

GINNY JOHNSON, GENERAL MANAGER, HAMSTEIN PRODUCTIONS

"I knew I wanted to be in the music business from a young age," says Ginny Johnson. "I had friends that were in the business; some were artists and some were family members of artists." Johnson moved to Nashville from High Point, North Carolina when she was 19, entered the music business program at Belmont College, and landed an A&R department internship at Capitol Records. The internship, with label executive vice president Jerry Crutchfield, lasted 18 months and ended when he hired her as his personal assistant. Johnson's duties included managing the A&R department, coordinating the label's videos, and acting as production assistant to her boss. "Jerry was producing eight or nine acts a year. It was a busy time and a great learning process because I was involved in so many different areas."

Johnson continued her duties through the transition of Capitol Records into Liberty Records and the installation of a new label head. Several years later, when Crutchfield was hired as president of MCA Music Publishing, he took her along as his assistant. Along with coordinating album projects, she was introduced to the many facets of the publishing world. After three years on the job, she decided to go out on her own as an independent production assistant.

After renting an office in 1994, Johnson quickly began working with some of country music's leading producers, among them, Buddy Cannon, Scott Hendricks, Blake Mevis, Billy Joe Walker, Jr., and Paul Worley. In 1998, she met with Bill Hamm and Richard Perna, and three days later was brought in as general manager to set up the project coordination division of Hamstein Productions. Within six weeks, business had grown so much that she hired two staff members.

PRODUCTION ASSISTANT • PROJECT COORDINATOR

JOB OVERVIEW

Production assistants and project coordinators work for a record producer and handle the business side of recording. This includes formulating a budget, scheduling the studio, hiring the engineers, musicians, arrangers, and mixers, making arrangement for any necessary travel, tracking the costs, approving and paying bills, and overseeing the project until it is completed.

PREREQUISITES

To succeed, you should have organizational skills, self-motivation, a friendly personality, knowledge of the recording process and administration, and sensitivity.

A DAY IN THE LIFE

"At the beginning of a project, I may be sitting in front of the computer writing the budget," says Ivy Skoff. "If it's crazy and there is a lot going on, I'll be writing the budget very, very early in the morning, maybe at 4 A.M., so I can do it before the phones start ringing. There are always AFM contracts to process, budgets to write, billing for reimbursements and billing the client, and other administrative tasks. Then

CAREER TIPS

"If someone wants to be a project coordinator, they really need to be aware that it's not the creative side of A&R, it's the administrative processing."

"Print up business cards that say 'Production Project Coordinator.' If you see it in writing, whatever it is, you'll believe it and you'll start doing it."

Study liner notes and learn what musicians played on each track and who produced it. Learn about the recording process and who does what. Try to land an internship in A&R at a record company.

I send my paperwork off to the administrative people at the label. Sometimes there might be an emotional problem with a client. You're sort of a friend and sort of a shrink. Throughout the day you're juggling paper, and there are days I want to throw my computer out my window and light a match to my desk. Some days are crazy and some aren't."

POINTERS FOR THE JOB SEARCH

Jobs in which you can gain the necessary skills, experience, and contacts are found in the A&R administration department of a record label, and in administration at a publishing company, where the staff processes demo recording paperwork.

CASE STUDY:

IVY SKOFF, PRODUCTION PROJECT COORDINATOR

When Ivy Skoff was laid off from her job as a Girl Friday to Mel Blanc, legendary voice of the Warner Brothers cartoon characters, she quickly found a job at the personal management company next door, as secretary to two of the managers. "I used to run into people from BNB [Associates] in the hallway. One day I saw this man I thought was Sherwin Bash, one of the principals in the company. We talked and he said 'If you ever need a job, come in.' When I was laid off, I marched into BNB and told the office manager that Sherwin Bash said that if I ever needed a job I should come in." Later, Skoff learned it was not Bash she had met in the hall, but another manager. Still, her friendly manner in the hallway led them to offer her a position. "When I started, I didn't even know what a personal manager was, but working in the music industry just felt right. I had found my niche and started learning everything I could about the business."

THE LEAST FAVORITE THING ABOUT THIS JOB:

"The bad part of my job is that when someone hasn't gotten paid, it's my fault. If an airplane is delayed, it's my fault. Anything that goes wrong is the production coordinator's fault."

THE BEST THING ABOUT THIS JOB:

"The best part of my job is the relationships you build. When you work with somebody for a long time you feel that camaraderie. You feel like you're on the same team. Sometimes I go to my clients' concerts and I watch them on stage. At the end of the show everyone is applauding and I get choked up and teary-eyed."

VOICES OF EXPERIENCE

One of the firm's clients was a record producer. Seeing an opportunity to learn more, Skoff began handling the business aspects of recording, and coordinated the project for the producer. Before long, she was earning extra money doing the same for other clients. Never one to admit that she didn't know how to do something, when Skoff was asked if she had completed the AFM contracts, she lied and said, "'Sure!' Then I walked up to my desk and got on the phone with a friend of mine who was a bass player and said, 'Help.' He came over with a stack of AFM contracts and showed me how to do them."

When heavyweight management firm Fitzgerald Hartley Company was created, Skoff came in as administrative assistant, handled all the company's paperwork and continued to coordinate projects for clients. After six years, she felt that she had reached her potential with the company and was looking for a new challenge. She came up with the title of Production Project Coordinator, had business cards and letterhead printed, and set up her own business.

With referrals from her previous employer and those from record companies, Skoff's client roster quickly grew by word of mouth. Over the years, her resume grew to include work with artist/producers like Baby Face, Michael Jackson, Kenny Loggins, Madonna, Manhattan Transfer, Randy Newman, Lionel Richie, TLC, and many more. Skoff also worked on the soundtracks for *Waiting to Exhale, Cold Mountain,* and *The Ladykillers,* and served as the music contractor for *Dreamgirls.*

MUSICIANS

MUSICIAN • SINGER

JOB OVERVIEW

Session musicians are hired to create the music that is recorded.

SPECIAL SKILLS

Tammy Rogers says important skills are, "Having a lot of experience improvising and being able to play by ear; to hear things once and turn around and play them back. Being very technically proficient on your instrument. For me, also being able to play mandolin has helped. Being able to bring a couple of different things [instruments] to the table has been a definite asset. I think having a particular style helps. I also think it helps to have a pretty easygoing personality that doesn't make people uptight or worried. When I show up, they know I'm going to be able to cover my part."

A DAY IN THE LIFE

"Most sessions are booked 10 to 1, 2 to 5, or 6 to 9," explains Tammy Rogers. "If you're booked for a 10, you show up before 10 and get your gear set up. Recording demos, people are trying to squeeze five tracks in three hours. On master sessions, people usually take a lot more time getting the sounds exactly right. The engineers are making sure everything is going to tape exactly right and that the sound quality is the best you can get. The producer is making sure the arrangement works and the tempo is right. Time is spent figuring out parts for different instruments. It can be a real creative time. It's not unusual for a musician to have some input. It depends on the tone that the producer and the artist set in the studio; if they're open to getting the input from the players, or if they say, 'Here is what we're going for; this is what we want.' Most of the time it's a pretty relaxed atmosphere."

"Demos can be a lot of fun. It's not as stressful as making records, but you have to work really quickly. That seems to amaze people when they come to Nashville and realize that musicians are used to walking in, hearing a song, and immediately playing it. We use the Nashville Numbers System so there is nothing notated except the chord changes and time fills. The parts are not mapped out. Occasionally a lick will be written out, but not very often. You have to be lightning fast, otherwise you slow down the whole session and that costs the songwriter a lot of money. Then the publisher is screaming at them that their demos cost $1200 apiece. You won't be hired again."

When tracking, Harry Stinson arrives a half hour before the session is scheduled to start. "Drums require the most mikes and are the first instrument checked, so I'm there a little earlier than the other players. I go in and make sure I'm comfortable and clear with the engineer as to what I need. If I need a line for a quick drag or whatever, then we'll bang through the drums and make sure everything sounds good. When the session starts, you listen to the song and play them down. You go back and do them

"Commit yourself to being the best and then stand in line and wait your turn. If your skills are far enough along when your time comes, then you'll move on to the next step, but you have to be ready."—HS

Practice, practice, practice your instrument. Learn to play more than one instrument and/or become good at vocal harmony. Take every opportunity you can find to play with other musicians, whether in clubs or just jamming at someone's house. It teaches you how to work with a lot of different personalities and skills levels.

CAREER TIPS

again if you have to. Yesterday, for instance, I did a demo session at 10 A.M. We did five songs in three hours and then I went over to another studio where we're recording a Del Beatles album. I went in and did vocals and then some tambourine work. I had a bite to eat and then I went back to the studio where I played on the demos and sang background vocals on the five tunes. I left my house around 9 in the morning and got home around 10 that night."

POINTERS FOR THE JOB SEARCH

"I think you are called to be a musician; it's not something you just decide to do. There is a burning desire that's down inside and you have to feed it. If you have that, then surround yourself with the best musicians and learn as much as you can."—HS

CASE STUDY:

HARRY STINSON, MUSICIAN, SINGER, MUSICAL DIRECTOR, CO-OWNER, DEAD RECKONING RECORDS

"I wanted to be a drummer from the time I was in fourth grade," says Harry Stinson. "My parents started me on piano, but drums were my passion." Growing up in Music City, he played in bands during grammar school and continued through high school, eventually ending up in a band with the eldest son of country singer Dottie West. Since none of the other members could sing, he was chosen by default. "It was the best training I ever got because being a singing drummer has been my greatest asset. It's the core of my success over the years."

VOICES OF EXPERIENCE

THE LEAST FAVORITE THING ABOUT THIS JOB:

"When you're the session leader you have the responsibility of making sure that everybody is there and everything is lined up. That wears me out because I have to be on the phone so much."—HS

THE BEST THING ABOUT THIS JOB:

"I love the creative process. That is what keeps me going. The money is great, but I love making music."—HS

"Seeing a song take shape, then it's preserved on record or CD, and knowing that I was a part of it; that I put my stamp on it and helped be a part of what the person wanted. I'm proud when I get hired to do something and they hire me over someone else because they want what I have. That is the thing that attracts me to recording."—Billy Thomas

Stinson's first professional gig was not as a drummer, but as a rhythm guitar player on a tour with Dottie West during the summer after he graduated high school. He attended college in Nashville for several years, but was an indifferent student, preferring to play in local bands. He left school in 1973 to tour the Southeast with a lounge band, but ended up back in Nashville a year later not knowing what to do next. In the right place at the right time, he got an emergency call to replace a drummer who had broken his hand and could not complete his tour with America. Stinson scrambled to find the band's albums, tried to learn their music, and met up with them in Muscle Shoals, Alabama the next day. "We did a two and a half hour sound check where I played the whole show, and then I went back to the hotel and listened to a tape of the live show they had made a couple of nights earlier. I was able to hear their arrangements and I studied that tape all the way up until show time. I went out on stage and played the show with the bass player yelling cues in my ear and the drummer with his hand in a cast, holding a flashlight on my charts. They were so happy by the time we got to the encore, they were just giggling on stage." After a month on the road, he returned home and wondered what to do next.

The next move was to join a band in Buffalo, New York, playing in the city's showrooms. A year later, Stinson got a call from America's manager to go out to Los Angeles to work with another band. When the gig fell apart after four months, he fell in with another group that toured as the opening act for the Beach Boys and the Doobie Brothers. Beginning in 1978, Stinson landed a series of extended tours as a sideman with Al Stewart, Jay Ferguson, and Etta James, before recording with Peter Frampton and going on tour with him. When Stinson finally returned to Los Angeles in 1983, the music scene had changed to the point that he felt like he no longer fit in. The final blow came the following year with the introduction of the drum machine. Suddenly all the session work that he counted on between tours dried up. He turned to his singing skills and recorded with Juice Newton and also began to write songs.

On a weekend trip to Nashville to visit industry friends, Stinson decided it was time to move back. That weekend, he landed session gigs to record as a backup singer to Jimmy Buffet and Pam Tillis that more than paid for the trip. After making the move, he worked as a drummer on tour with Nicolette Larson and recorded with Steve Earle, then joined his band. Two years on the road convinced Stinson it was time to settle down. He recorded with Lyle Lovett, did a lot of session work, and landed a publishing contract that got a couple of his songs recorded by Patty Loveless and Steve Earle. After a few tour dates with Rodney Crowell, he quit road trips for good.

The next phase of Stinson's career began when he got a call to put together a band for *American Music Shop*. During the second of four years that the series aired, he was hired as musical director for *Live at the Roundup* with Ricky Scaggs, which lasted two seasons. He went on to act as musical director of a number of programs, including *The Dove Awards, Music City News Awards* show, Trisha Yearwood's CBS pilot *XXX's and OOO's*, and two of Kathie Lee Gifford's Christmas specials. Over the years, Stinson has recorded with some of the most successful artists, including Brooks & Dunn, Jimmy Buffett, George Jones, Vince Gill, Faith Hill, Lyle Lovett, Reba McEntire, Bette Midler, and Johnny Cash. He co-produced the 2007 Grammy-nominated album *Live at the Ryman* by Marty Stuart and his Fabulous Superlatives. Stinson is also co-founder of Dead Reckoning Records. *www.myspace.com/harrystinson*

SESSION SINGER • SINGER • VOCALIST

JOB OVERVIEW

A session singer is hired to sing the lyric melody, harmony, or both.

SPECIAL SKILLS

"The two things that have served me best are having a good ear and a versatile instrument," says Gene Miller. "I'm able to sing a lot of different styles. Another thing for me is my range, which is three and a half octaves, and I have a first tenor voice. If you can sing extremely high or extremely low, where most people can't sing, it helps."

A DAY IN THE LIFE

"On the way to the session I vocalize and get my instrument warmed up," says Miller. "I'm not like a guitar player where you can plug in and play. A lot of times I have to sing pretty high, so if I go in with a cold voice it's the equivalent of a sprinter walking up to the starting blocks and running without stretching his legs first. You're going to end up hurting yourself. You need to come out of the block strong. I generally get the material beforehand, if I'm singing a demo in Nashville. In Los Angeles, you walk in cold and learn the song in fifteen or twenty minutes and sing. That is kind of a neat challenge to learn it that quickly and then sing it like you've known it all your life."

CAREER TIPS

"Singing is like acting. When you're singing, you're playing a role. The greatest singers to me are people who can really come from the heart and make you believe the story they are telling you. It comes from way deep inside of you. Anybody can learn the mechanics of how to sing, but unless you have heart, the ability to draw up from the center of who you are, people are going to hear a mechanical performance."—GM

"I spent a lot of time in my bedroom when I was a kid learning how to play [guitar] and singing; emulating people and listening to harmony."—GM

"Musicians work in three-hour blocks, tens, twos, and sixes, with one hour breaks between," explains Harry Stinson. "If you're the singer, you can be called in at any time. You might go in at 11 A.M. or 12:30 P.M., whatever works for the producer. They might bring in two or three other co-singers for different sounds. We usually work for about an hour and a half to two hours on one song, getting the parts right and making sure the intonation is good. When you're the singer, you're in the studio working throughout the session. You get your water, hit the bathroom, and work some more. I've sung all day many times."

POINTERS FOR THE JOB SEARCH

"When you get involved in the arts, music, painting or whatever, I think it chooses you; you don't choose it. I think you need to have a sense of the business and then have a real frank conversation with yourself. For someone starting out I would advise, 'preparation, preparation, preparation.' You've got to have a good ear and be able to sight-read music. Most session singers are good enough that when someone tells you to take the bottom or top part, you just know what to sing. You can listen to the melody and you just know how to harmonize. You've got to develop those abilities. Session work is very competitive. There are thousands of people that want the same job that you want. The more you're prepared and the more you have developed your craft and artistry, the better your chances of getting a job."—GM

CASE STUDY:

GENE MILLER, SINGER

Shy about his voice, Nashville native Gene Miller had never performed publicly until a friend coerced him into singing at a high school function. "I performed about ten songs, just my guitar and me, for about 300 people. I was hooked from that moment on." He sang and played guitar in bands and got involved in high school

THE LEAST FAVORITE THING ABOUT THIS JOB:

"Certain producers expect you to be a chameleon. Sometimes their interpretation doesn't feel right. Most people I work with allow me to be not just a singer, but an artist. They allow me to bring in my own heart and my own interpretation to the session."—GM

THE BEST THING ABOUT THIS JOB:

"The diversity of things that I get to do. The part I like about being in the studio is that you're not tied down to one specific style of music. If I had been an artist making records, I would have to do a specific style. Instead, I've gotten to do a broad range of things and I really love that."—GM

VOICES OF EXPERIENCE

theater productions. Following graduation, he landed a gig performing in a musical revue at Opryland theme park. Miller progressed from job to job until he was hired as a backup singer for Barbara Mandrell on her tours and television show. In between, he learned studio technique by singing jingles and doing sound-alike vocals for an advertising agency.

In the mid-1980s, Miller moved to Los Angeles to tour with Donna Summer and break into West Coast studio work. "L.A. was a harder nut to crack. People have work wrapped up and you have to really network." It took some time to build up a reputation through word of mouth, but eventually he had steady session work. "I sang everything: sound tracks for film, television commercials, cartoon scenes, records, song demos, and live television performances." When he moved back to Nashville in the mid-1990s, he quickly established himself as a session singer with artists like Faith Hill, Tim McGraw, Phil Collins, Jewel, and Martina McBride. In addition to song demos and his session work in Nashville, Miller also continues to do periodic work in Los Angeles and New York. He added "actor" to his credits, when he performed on Broadway in the musical *The Civil War*, and sang on the album sound track.

CHAPTER

MANAGEMENT

Managers function like air traffic controllers, keeping things in the air, routing things in and out safely and on schedule. They are constantly on the hot seat to make decisions and keep things on course. Great managers are those who share their client's vision and passion, and who work diligently to help them achieve their goals. This chapter is divided into two sections: Personal Managers and Management Staff.

PERSONAL MANAGERS

ARTIST MANAGER • MANAGER • PERSONAL MANAGER

JOB OVERVIEW

Managers direct all aspects of an artist's career, including record company issues, publishing, touring, marketing, publicity, business management, film and sound track work, sponsorships, endorsements, and other opportunities. Some managers secure recording and/or publishing contracts and are involved in the negotiations, either handling it themselves or, in most cases, working with the artist's attorney.

PREREQUISITES

To succeed, you should have a well-rounded understanding of how the entire music industry works, and allies within its ranks. Generally, managers have one or two particular strengths, such as touring, publicity, publishing, recording, or legal backgrounds, and they then surround themselves with a team that has strengths where their own knowledge is weakest.

SPECIAL SKILLS

"A gift for communication and an ability to work with people on all different levels" facilitated Dixie Carter's success. "I have a creative mind and an ability to see opportunities. When things aren't going well for a client or for myself, I try to take what has happened and turn it around and make it an opportunity."

"I think communication is without a doubt one of the strongest allies of anybody wanting to be a manager," says Terry Elam. "It also takes determination: the ability to have your [butt] handed to you and not leave and never come back. Instead, go reattach your [butt] and come back the next day and go to work."

A DAY IN THE LIFE

Managers begin their day checking on the e-mail and incoming faxes that require a timely response. Throughout the day they talk with the artist's booking agency to discuss tour details, and field offers from the publicist for interviews and television appearances. They meet with the record company to strategize a marketing plan for an upcoming album, or to approve artwork for a CD or promotional piece. Some managers speak with radio stations to help move a record up the charts. They may work to secure a sponsorship deal, place a song in a film, or negotiate a new publishing deal. A manager is on call 24/7.

CAREER TIPS

"If you're just starting out in the music business, find something that you're passionate about; something that excites you to where you're driving into work and you can't wait to get there. That's what a job is supposed to be."
—DC

"I set goals for myself all the time: goals for the week, goals for the month, for the quarter, the year, and where I want to be in five years. I think that helps you reward yourself on a weekly basis. You can see what you accomplished and what you need to go back and finish. It gives you points of reference for the year and sets standards for you to strive to achieve."—TE

"Without growing up in the business, the most effective way to break into the industry is with a good education, good communication skills, and strong people skills."—TE

POINTERS FOR THE JOB SEARCH

"Expose yourself to as much about the industry as you can. Research your job. Research the people that you're interviewing with. Immerse yourself in trade publications and just soak up as much knowledge as possible."—DC

"I'm a very, very strong believer in internships. I was a marketing major and a Spanish minor and didn't really know what I wanted to do. I interned for two years during college and was offered a job in an industry I love."—DC

"My advice is to stay in school and get a college education. That is one thing I regret to this day, that I didn't finish and get my degree. Make a point of developing strong people skills, communication skills, math skills, and persevere. There is not a lot of money for many years in most service jobs. You have to be willing to sacrifice a great deal to get to a point where you're comfortable. You have to work really long hours. Stay in school, get your education, and come into the job as prepared as possible."—TE

CASE STUDY:

DIXIE CARTER, PRESIDENT, TRIFECTA ENTERTAINMENT

Dallas native Dixie Carter was a marketing major at Mississippi State University, unsure of what she wanted to do professionally, when a chance meeting set the direction of her future. The mother of a home town acquaintance recognized her name in

VOICES OF EXPERIENCE

THE LEAST FAVORITE THING ABOUT THIS JOB:

"The hours are long; it would be nice to get home a little earlier, but I really don't dislike any part of my job. I enjoy the people, I enjoy the musicians, I enjoy the artists, I enjoy the whole creative process."—TE

THE BEST THING ABOUT THIS JOB:

"I love when I'm able to not only gain success for my clients, which is a tremendous feeling of satisfaction, but when I'm able to take their celebrity and use it to help people, to really touch their hearts and do a lot of good things for people. A small gesture might make a sick kid's year, week, or life happier. To me, that is one of the greatest pleasures of this job."—DC

"Without a doubt, what I love most about my job is the music. Being able to hang with the musicians and artists, to see the world from their point of view. They can take an emotion or a thought and turn it into a piece of music. That is the reason I'm here."—TE

the school newspaper. After finding out that Carter had promoted campus events and concerts, she suggested that Carter take an internship at the advertising agency where the woman worked. That agency turned out to be Levenson and Hill, Dallas' largest advertising and public relations firm, where Carter interned during summers and Christmas breaks for two years. She was hired upon graduation in 1985.

"My first day on the job was working with Tom Hanks, Jackie Gleason, and Gary Marshall for the movie *Nothing in Common.*" Initially assigned to a variety of corporate and film accounts, she found her greatest satisfaction came from her involvement with the major marketing campaigns of music artists such as ZZ Top, Merle Haggard, and Tanya Tucker. Eventually, she was promoted to vice president and director of client services.

In 1993, Carter was approached to run PLA Media, which had offices in Los Angeles and Nashville. After much debate about leaving behind a great job, great salary, her family, her husband's employment, and a new home, she accepted. Just as she had severed her Dallas connections, the deal fell through and she was left hanging. Trusting in fate, she made the move to Nashville. "Tanya Tucker called me up and said, 'I'll be your first client. You can handle my publicity and marketing.' I didn't give myself time to think. I just packed up the U-Haul and moved to Nashville—it sounds a little like a bad country song—I started my company and hoped for success." Within three months she picked up several new clients, hired three employees, and opened her own full-service promotion/publicity/marketing company: Trifecta Entertainment.

Through the course of building up a client list that included corporate accounts like CMT and Sony Music/Nashville, and artists like Naomi Judd and Tanya Tucker, Carter became aware of the need to include management among the services her firm offered. Hiring Andy Barton away from Chief Talent Agency in 1996 provided her with a partner in her management company. Together, the two have built a management roster that includes Take 6, Doug Stone, Michael English, and The Lynns. Carter and her company expanded into the world of professional wrestling and became TNA Entertainment LLC.

CASE STUDY:

TERRY ELAM, MANAGER, FITZGERALD HARTLEY COMPANY

Terry Elam's musical career began on trumpet. After years of struggling to master the instrument—"I quickly found all the flat notes in that instrument"—at age 15 he switched to drums and joined a band. "It was a garage band. We worked at sock hops, the YMCA shows, and high school dances." He continued to play in bands while attending the University of Tennessee Memphis. One of these groups landed a contract with Mercury Records and moved to New York City, but it fell apart a few years later. Back home in Memphis, Elam got a call from a friend who played guitar for singer Roy Orbison, and traveled to Nashville to audition for the band.

Hired as Orbison's percussionist in 1972, Elam spent the next four years observing the mistakes of a series of inept road managers. By 1976, he felt he could do a better job and, allowed the opportunity, took over the duties of road manager in addition to his role as musician. During Orbison's career slump, Elam also took on the responsibilities of working with the booking agency, something that a personal manager would ordinarily handle. He continued his dual roles throughout the artist's mid-1980s career resurgence, and worked with the estate following Orbison's death in 1988.

In 1989 an offer came for Elam to road manage fledgling country artist Vince Gill. Following a meeting with Gill's management team in Los Angeles, Elam set out on a tour bus in early 1990 with a seven-piece band, a skeleton road crew, and a then-struggling and almost unknown singer. Gill spent the beginning of the year working small club dates and opening for artists like Reba, Clint Black, and Randy Travis. His career took off when the single "When I Call Your Name" shot to number one, and he ended the year as a headliner. When Gill's management re-opened its Nashville office in 1995, Elam was brought in-house with both personal and road management responsibilities.

Elam shares management responsibilities of Gill with Larry Fitzgerald and Oliva Newton John with Mark Hartley and has previously managed Sherri Austin and Pam Tillis. The Fitzgerald Hartley roster includes Dwight Yoakam, Lee Ann Rimes, Brad Paisley, Kellie Pickler, Big Bad VooDoo Daddy, and Los Lobos. *www.fitzhart.com*

MANAGER OF PRODUCERS, ENGINEERS, AND MIXERS

JOB OVERVIEW

These managers direct and oversee clients' careers, including looking for production opportunities, publicizing achievements, negotiating contracts, and other business functions.

"You've got to be able to get along with people. At the end of the day you can be the smartest person in the room, but if you anger people or alienate them, you'll fail."

Working at a recording studio or in the A&R department at a record label is good training for managing producers and engineers. Read recording updates in the music trades and study the liner notes of albums to become familiar with who produced, engineered, and mixed what records.

SPECIAL SKILLS

"Being organized and able to solve problems as they arise. Problem solving is a big part of what I do," says Frank McDonough. "My particular gig is very service oriented. My clients are providing a service to people and I have to be accommodating to people when representing them."

A DAY IN THE LIFE

McDonough is up early and in the office by 7 A.M. Throughout the day he listens to music, but his attention is focused on answering e-mail and working the phones. "For instance, RCA just signed a new band and they're looking for a record producer. They want 'the guy' who produced whatever band sold ten million records last year, or they want 'the guy' who mixed Santana's 'Smooth' record, or whoever. I represent some of those people and others who don't have those credits, but are creatively similar. I act as a matchmaker by saying, 'Have you considered this producer? They might be someone you'd want to talk to.' I know it's hard to imagine how that would consume 12 hours a day, but it does."

POINTERS FOR THE JOB SEARCH

"My job is an out-of-the-way niche in the music business. I'd be surprised if there were a hundred people in the whole country who did this job. My advice is to find someone who does this work and work for them. That's about the only way to gain the knowledge you need. A&R is about the only other job where you would learn the skills and make the connections you need to represent producers and engineers."

VOICES OF EXPERIENCE

THE LEAST FAVORITE THING ABOUT THIS JOB:

"There is potential for a lot of conflict and arguing, and that's not why I got into the record business. Some people enjoy a good argument. I don't. It's my nature to want everyone to come away feeling good and that they got a fair shake."

THE BEST THING ABOUT THIS JOB:

"What I love the most is being exposed to new music. I like being involved with people who are creating that music. However tiny my role is, I like that I have a part in bringing that music to fruition."

CASE STUDY:

FRANK McDONOUGH, PRESIDENT AND MANAGER, McDONOUGH MANAGEMENT LLC

Frank McDonough credits his career in the music business to being a failed rock star. After playing guitar in bands during high school in St. Louis, sure that one day he would be a star, he appeased his father by enrolling at Loyola Marymount University in Los Angeles. Although college was just a cover for playing in bands and trying to land a record deal, he still managed to graduate before a contract materialized. Needing a temporary job to pay the bills until he got signed to a label, he found work in the aerospace industry.

After three years, McDonough says, "I realized that working for a living might not be as temporary as I first thought." He decided that if he had to work while waiting to be a rock star, it should at least be in the music industry. He got a job in A&R administration at Arista Records in 1988 on the strength of his aerospace computer skills. "At the time, they were keeping track of quarter-million dollar recording budgets on giant ledger sheets. I think I got there just after they graduated from using quills to actual ballpoint pens," he laughs. "I had experience with computers and spreadsheets. That is why they hired me. At Arista I got a good sense of what each department did, and I knew I didn't want to work in promotion or retail and I didn't want to work in publicity." That knowledge was an asset when an offer to manage record producers came in 1992.

Thinking that management might be interesting, he took the job. When the owner of the company he was working for made a career change in 1995, McDonough and a group of his clients moved to Moir Marie Entertainment. Together, McDonough's diverse and talented roster of producers, engineers, and mixers have worked on recordings for AC/DC, Aerosmith, Black Crows, Paula Cole, Shawn Colvin, Def Leppard, Goo Goo Dolls, Loudmouth, Madonna, Sarah McLachlan, John Mellencamp, Pearl Jam, Rage Against the Machine, Lou Reed, R.E.M., Santana, Stone Temple Pilots, and Shania Twain.

After six years with Moir/Marie, McDonough decided to form his own company and established McDonough Management LLC in 2000. His new roster of clients have produced recordings for Babyface, Tool, Live, and Switchfoot. *www.mcdman.com*

MANAGEMENT STAFF

ARTIST MANAGER • DIRECTOR OR MANAGER (ADVERTISING, PUBLICITY, AND INTERNET TOOLS)

JOB OVERVIEW

The focus of Stephanie Green's responsibilities is to coordinate label, independent, and in-house forces to maximize advertising, publicity, and marketing campaigns in all media forms, including the Internet and new technology.

SPECIAL SKILLS

"There are no set rules in this business, so you are constantly challenging yourself to be creative. You set up an album one way for one artist and set up an album a different way for another artist. You have to be able to keep track of paper and be detail oriented. I'm tenacious and persistent. I like to go after things and think big. If it doesn't work, I try to find another way to go about it."

A DAY IN THE LIFE

The first thing Stephanie Green does each day is check her e-mail and read the daily faxes. She tries to carve out some time in the morning to read trade magazines and then hops on the Internet and starts surfing. "I do a fair amount of research and marketing on the Web. I work closely with our graphic and multimedia design folks to maintain our artists' sites. On any given day, I could be answering a phone call from an independent publicist or the record label asking me to coordinate an interview with an artist, handling a request for an autographed auction item, or tracking down an artist to get an autograph, or to have them do a phone-in interview. This afternoon I'm mapping out an itinerary."

POINTERS FOR THE JOB SEARCH

"There aren't any rules to finding a job in the music industry. Sometimes you know somebody; sometimes you fall into a job; sometimes you start as an

CAREER TIPS

"Ask questions. If you don't understand something, ask. I always try to find new ways to go about accomplishing things."

"The highs are very high and the lows can be very trying, but if you stay at it and go for it, management can be just wonderful."

While in college, take marketing and writing classes. Both will help you land a job and be successful in it.

VOICES OF EXPERIENCE

THE LEAST FAVORITE THING ABOUT THIS JOB:

"The politics, and probably a close tie with politics is the disappointments. It hurts when I see a client of ours who is disappointed. That breaks my heart."

THE BEST THING ABOUT THIS JOB:

"My reward comes from knowing that I was a part of something. If I can contribute in some way and accomplish something, do it successfully and see the reward, it really means something to me. When I see a client achieving a level of success and they're shining, there is no better feeling in the world."

intern. I know people who have interned through school at publishing companies, at record labels, and at a management office. You couldn't ask for a more well-rounded, hands-on education for becoming a manager."

CASE STUDY:

STEPHANIE GREEN, DIRECTOR OF PUBLIC RELATIONS, SEA RECORDS/STERLING ENTERTAINMENT ASSOCIATES, LLC

"I was raised around music," says Stephanie Green. "My family were all musicians; some were recording artists." Ironically, it was working in a restaurant during high school that led her to the music business. Beginning at the take-out window at 15 years old, she worked her way through every position, before becoming the bookkeeper at age 18. While taking business and accounting classes at a junior college, her previous bookkeeping experience landed her a part-time job in the business management office of Glenn Campbell Enterprises. Finding that she enjoyed the work, she soon abandoned her studies to carry a full workload.

In 1994, Green took over the position of personal secretary to Glenn Campbell. In addition to handling Campbell's own accounts, she interfaced with his personal manager and road manager. As Campbell's Nashville business interests experienced success, particularly in launching an unknown writer/artist named Alan Jackson into superstardom, the company expanded to include an artist management division based in Nashville. Green found that a significant part of her time involved in the West Coast operation of the new venture, and she got hooked on the excitement of seeing new talent being developed.

When the opportunity arose in 1997, she left behind the business side of the music industry and moved to Nashville to work in a more creative capacity. While

"If you're nice to people, there is not much that you ask of them that they won't do. I treat people like I want to be treated."

"In the music business, there is no security and no guarantee that you're going to have a job tomorrow. Every day you have to do the best you can and have no regrets about how you treated somebody or how you did your job."

Skills learned working for an agent who books artists' tours or a travel agent translate well into a tour assistant.

officially in charge of advertising, publicity, and finance, Green quickly discovered the truth about working at a young company: you end up pitching in wherever you are needed. As the careers of the company's roster have taken off, especially the phenomenal rise of client Bryan White, Green found herself juggling many duties, and loving every minute of it.

In late 2003, Green joined SEA Records/Sterling Entertainment Associates, as director of public relations. Green was given responsibility for all media relations for the company's entities, including SEA Records, music and book publishing divisions, and the concert division.

TOUR ASSISTANT • MANAGEMENT ASSISTANT • PRODUCTION COORDINATOR

JOB OVERVIEW

Staff in these positions assist and provide office support to the artist, tour manager, band, and crew. Duties include travel arrangements, such as booking airfare, hotels, and ground transportation, or scheduling tour buses and drivers; confirming catering specifications; handling meet and greets, and other issues related to the tour.

SPECIAL SKILLS

To succeed, you need organizational skills, attention to detail, patience, problem solving skills, a friendly personality, and self-motivation. "Honesty. Not telling people what they want to hear, but what they need to hear. Being a people person."

THE LEAST FAVORITE THING ABOUT THIS JOB:

"What I like least are the constant changes. Once you get things all set, something is thrown in and you have to change everything you've done. You spend more time undoing and redoing than originally setting things up, but that's just part of the job when you're dealing with artists."

THE BEST THING ABOUT THIS JOB:

"Taking care of 22 people and knowing they're happy; knowing that I can take care of that much responsibility from the start of the tour until it's over, and that everything goes well between."

A DAY IN THE LIFE

On one particular day, Debbie Cross arrived at the office to find a voice mail from a band member who needed to have his travel arrangements changed from flying to driving, so her first call was to the travel agent. Next, she made arrangements for the support act to be picked up at the airport and taken to the venue. "I don't have a routine. I can come in and think I'm going to read contracts all day, but come five o'clock, I haven't even looked at them because something has come up I have to take care of right away. For instance, I'm working on May travel and had it almost complete, but they just added a few dates and that means I have to rearrange flights and other travel arrangements. Often you don't just do, you redo." Throughout the day, Cross may set up an interview for Kenny Rogers, field calls from the road from the tour manager, talk with building managers and promoters about catering for upcoming shows, and then try to return to reviewing those contracts. "Kenny [Rogers] works mostly weekends, so if the crew needs to discuss something I've done, they call me at home. That's just part of the job. It's not a Monday through Friday, 9 to 5 gig. If you want that kind of job, don't get in the music business."

POINTERS FOR THE JOB SEARCH

A receptionist position is one of the best ways to get a foot in the door, learn about the company, and then offer to take on more responsibilities. An internship, or an assistant's job, is another way in.

CASE STUDY:

DEBBIE CROSS, TOUR ASSISTANT, KENNY ROGERS PRODUCTIONS AND DREAM FACTORY

Debbie Cross was introduced to the music business when she answered a blind want ad in her local newspaper. Bored after several years of being a stay-at-home mom, she just wanted something to do that she liked. The job turned out to be as a receptionist for the firm that booked and promoted Kenny Rogers' touring interests. After two days on the job, she was already bored, and asked for additional duties. Soon she was checking on tour routing, availabilities for potential support artists, issuing contracts, talking with promoters about dates, advancing production, and handling just about everything to do with Rogers' tours, except for accounting and payroll. She worked with Rogers' organization for 13 years and advanced to event/production coordinator.

In 1994, Cross was hired away by Real World Tours to work for Alan Jackson. As tour assistant, her job was to provide backup assistance to the production manager, tour manager, lead bus driver, and everyone who worked under them, as well as review tour contracts and handle personal errands for Jackson. As Jackson gradually cut his touring schedule back from 110 to 40 dates a year, Cross' position became redundant and she was let go in 1999. Several job offers were immediately forthcoming, but she didn't feel that any of them were a good fit. After about two and a half months, she was called back to work at Kenny Rogers Productions, this time as tour assistant in charge of scheduling and co-ordinating air and ground transportation, accommodations, and any associated special events. *www.kennyrogers.com*

EXECUTIVE ASSISTANT • ASSISTANT

JOB OVERVIEW

These assistants handle a variety of paperwork, answer phone calls and e-mail, order concert tickets, and interface with record label, management team, publicists and agents.

SPECIAL SKILLS

"Being anal; being meticulous," are skills that helped Beth Barnett become successful. "You're getting information and paperwork from all different directions and if you're not organized, then it gets a little crazy. You're dealing with

CAREER TIPS

"It's a lot easier to communicate with people if you're a little laid back and easy to talk to, rather than someone who is rigid and uptight."

"You definitely have to do the grunt work at the beginning and feel okay about it."

THE LEAST FAVORITE THING ABOUT THE JOB:

"I think the worst thing is dealing with new artists' unsolicited material. You just get bombarded. The fans can be a little hard; somebody calling and saying, 'Hi, I'd like to have R.E.M. play at my cookout in July.'"

THE BEST THING ABOUT THIS JOB:

"Being able to stand on stage behind them [Widespread Panic] and see what they see—the expressions on people's faces—being able to see that perspective at a live show is cool. Whenever I get frustrated with my job, I will put in a bootleg of Widespread Panic and go for a drive and listen to them—I love that band."

contractual agreements, so you have to be meticulous and orderly. Communication skills."

A DAY IN THE LIFE

"When I arrive, I go through e-mail—I'm the computer person at our company, so if there are any computer glitches, I deal with those first. Take calls that come in for Buck [Williams, her boss] and I arrange a time for them to talk. Most of those I speak with are people at Widespread Panic's management company. I schedule any trips that Buck needs to take. I'm the go-between person sometimes, passing words between Buck and his bands or anybody else. I talk to the record labels. Anything that needs to get done here in the office, I take care of."

POINTERS FOR THE JOB SEARCH

Gain strong clerical skills and organizational skills so that you are an asset to an organization. Be willing to start as a receptionist, an intern, in the mail room, as part-time or temporary help to gain experience and get a foot in the door.

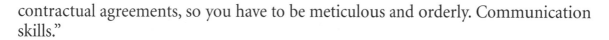

BETH BARNETT, EXECUTIVE ASSISTANT TO BUCK WILLIAMS, PROGRESSIVE GLOBAL AGENCY

Virginia native Beth Barnett was living in Colorado when the urge to work in the music business struck. "I was hanging out with people who ran a lot of the bars that had live music, and with the publicity people from Fox Theater. One of my Colorado friends had worked for Buck [Williams] in New York and when he decided to start this company, he called her. She knew I really wanted to be involved in the music

CAREER TIPS

"This business is a business of networking. That is the key." In the music industry, there is a lot of truth in the adages *"it's who you know"* and *"being in the right place at the right time."*

"Be willing to help people and they'll help you in return."

business, so as the company grew and she needed an assistant, she called and asked if I'd like to move to Nashville." When her friend left the firm, Barnett took over her duties and became Williams' executive assistant, becoming less involved in the agency side of the company, and devoting much of her time to artist management issues. Some of the agency's clients include Widespread Panic, Tyler James, R.E.M., Tortured Soul, and DJ Logic. *www.pgamusic.com/agency*

PERSONAL ASSISTANT • OPERATIONS MANAGER

JOB OVERVIEW

Like all personal assistants, Mandy KenKnight handles personal errands for the artists she works for, namely Faith Hill and Tim McGraw. Additionally, she is responsible for maintaining the artists' web sites and overseeing fan club operations, including newsletters, and club merchandise design, creation, and sales.

SPECIAL SKILLS

To succeed, you should possess discretion, people skills, and follow through. "You have to be able to work well with people and have a positive attitude. Certainly you need basic computer and organizational skills."

A DAY IN THE LIFE

VOICES OF EXPERIENCE

THE BEST THING ABOUT THIS JOB:

"What I like the most is that Faith and Tim are wonderful people to work with. They are very generous and respectful of my personal life."

Before she leaves home for the office, Mandy KenKnight starts her day with a phone call. "I generally touch base with Faith [Hill] first thing in the morning to see if she needs anything, which could be having photos developed, returning clothing to her stylist and working with him, or organizing her home office. I'm also the liaison between the management company, the record label, and Faith. If something needs to be done between them, generally I'm the one who is making that happen and running between their offices." KenKnight works with Hill and McGraw's fan club presidents to write and lay out each artist's newsletter. She meets with merchandisers to design a new tee shirt or hat, and spends time with the webmaster to put up new information on both artists' web sites. Although she is on call 24 hours a day, 7 days a week, KenKnight says, "Faith is very respectful of typical business hours and she doesn't usually call me on the weekend."

POINTERS FOR THE JOB SEARCH

"Be aggressive and make connections in the industry. I got my job through someone that I met working on a school project."

CASE STUDY:

MANDY KENKNIGHT, PERSONAL ASSISTANT AND OPERATIONS MANAGER, FAITH HILL AND TIM MCGRAW

From the age of five, Mandy KenKnight loved to sing, and participated in church and school choirs all the way through high school. "I grew up in a small town south of Atlanta. Music had always been part of my life, so when it came to deciding on a college major, there was no question that music was what I wanted to do." She earned her associate degree in music entertainment management at the Art Institute of Atlanta, and transferred to Belmont University in Nashville to complete her studies. As part of her student activities, she organized campus artist showcases, and progressed to co-producing one in 1995. Through that experience, she met Faith Hill's personal assistant, who told her that a position was open to oversee Hill's fan club. KenKnight was interviewed and hired for the job. Hill later took a year-long hiatus and her personal assistant moved on to another job. When Hill resumed her career, KenKnight was promoted to that position. Having worked for Hill for more than a decade, KenKnight says, "Working with Faith has given me the opportunity to see this industry from the inside out, and to learn from one of the most successful women in the business." With that knowledge of the industry, KenKnight is also pursuing performing and her own vocal interests. *www.mandykenknight.com*

PROFESSIONAL

Lawyers and accountants have diverse opportunities open to them in the music industry. Some have become managers, record label executives, publishers, songwriters, tour accountants, and producers. Those profiled in this chapter work for legal and business management firms and represent music clients.

LEGAL

ATTORNEY • LAWYER • LEGAL COUNSEL • LEGAL AFFAIRS

JOB OVERVIEW

Lawyers in the music industry provide legal counsel, negotiate contracts and other agreements, and defend the rights of music clients. Many attorneys are involved in the overall strategic planning of their artist, writer, producer, and other clients. "Our goal is to get them a team to put together and structure their management, record, publishing, merchandising, and other agreements," says Debra Wagnon.

PREREQUISITES

In this field, you need a law degree and experience in the music industry.

POINTERS FOR THE JOB SEARCH

"Entertainment is changing drastically with the advent of new technology; it's a great time to be practicing [law]." Wagnon advises those interested in the music industry to "gain experience in the entertainment field long before they're in law school. If you're genuinely excited about the industry, you'll work in the mail room or do a summer undergraduate internship and be passionate about it. Be willing to work for free, delivering paper clips or whatever it takes to get inside the entertainment

"I believe the best entertainment lawyers are those who have experience in the arts," says Debra Wagnon. "You cannot treat the business the same as a civil litigator or criminal attorney would. As an attorney for an artist, you may need to say some negative things in order to get your client on the straight and narrow road to success. It may set them back emotionally and hurt their work product, unless you can word the message in such a way that it doesn't deliver an arrow to their heart."

"You've got to make a decision on what you are willing to accept and be prepared to walk if you don't get it. If you're not, you're not that good a negotiator."

Gain international experience. "You will not have a career if your whole focus is the United States market. You can't survive."

"You have to be content to work alone. You'll see people before you start, after you finish, and to have discussions in the process, but you're alone with your work."

field. Get the best solid law education you can. If you have a choice between one of the best law schools, versus one devoted to entertainment matters, I would choose the former, because your education is with you forever and is the structure for your entire career. It's not what you learn in law school that will make you a great entertainment attorney; it is what you learn in the field. In the summer get an internship at a record label, a music publisher, a management company, with a promoter, a radio station, or an Internet company. If you have hands-on experience, it is the very thing that will advertise and advise people about you. The second year of law school I would advise they do an internship as a paralegal or a legal secretary in a law firm that specializes in the area you want. Work on a pro bono basis for an artist. Volunteer to work for an organization. Gain some experience beyond just having a law degree."

THE BEST THING ABOUT THIS JOB:

"What I love most is making friends and forming relationships. I love closure."

DEBORAH WAGNON, CHIEF OPERATING OFFICER, PORTIA ENTERTAINMENT GROUP LLC

"Driven" is the only word to describe Deborah Wagnon. With the idea of using a law degree to empower her planned entertainment career, she entered law school at Stanford University, sang three shows a night—every night—from San Francisco to Lake Tahoe, built up 100 hours of studio production time, and competed in the Miss California Pageant. Following graduation, she worked a year at a large Los Angeles legal firm, hated it, and decided to return to music as a singer/songwriter. She put together a band, went to Tokyo, Japan, spent her nights performing and her days making contacts within the Asian music industry. After six months, Wagnon returned to Los Angeles. The day of her arrival in 1988, she saw an ad in *The Hollywood Reporter* for a producer's position with Landmark Entertainment Group for a project at Universal Studios Japan. Without mentioning her legal degree, she landed the job within 24 hours, based solely upon her musical ability, studio experience, and Asian contacts.

Wagnon lined up some valuable male mentors and quickly filled in the gaps in her skills. Within a month, she was back in Tokyo producing recording sessions for the project. More projects followed until in 1991, she decided it was time for a new challenge. She revealed her law degree and put together a proposal to become senior vice president of music business affairs at Landmark. Once hired, she set about establishing a publishing company and moved the company into the recording industry. Soon she was promoted to corporate general legal counsel.

In 1994, Wagnon felt she had drifted too far from her love of music and made a move to Nashville. She took a professorship in the music program at Middle Tennessee State University, and within months partnered with John Mason in opening John Mason Partners Ltd., a private practice specializing in music industry law. She began teaching one day a week at the music school of Georgia State University at Atlanta in 1999, and early in 2000, joined the prestigious Greenberg, Traurig firm as the first female partner.

Wagnon returned to Nashville in 2001 to serve as counsel for the firm of Cornelius & Collins, which specializes in litigation and corporate law. Her primary duty was to act as counsel to the firm in all matters relating to entertainment law. She was offered a partnership and to be head of the entertainment practice at Hunter Maclean Exley & Dunn, P.C., which took her to Savannah, Georgia. Missing Nashville, she returned and opened her own international entertainment representation firm, Portia Entertainment Group LLC. In 2007, Wagnon's historical novel *Great and Wide Sea* was published. *www.portiaentertainment.com* and *www. deborahwagnon.com*

BUSINESS MANAGEMENT

CERTIFIED PUBLIC ACCOUNTANT (CPA) • BUSINESS MANAGER • DIRECTOR OF ENTERTAINMENT SERVICES

JOB OVERVIEW

These professionals provide music clients with accounting and financial services including royalty accounting and examination, budgets, financial and investment planning, bills payable, purchasing of homes, cars and buses, and tax work.

PREREQUISITES

In these areas, you need a degree in accounting or finance, a knowledge of tax law, and a well-rounded understanding of the music business.

A DAY IN THE LIFE

"We have 50 people that work at this accounting firm and only about 15 of us work in the music area," says Mike Vaden. "Those who work in other areas can plan their days and tell you what they're going to be doing three months from now. I can't tell you what I'm going to be doing tomorrow. I can be working on anything from financial planning and estate work, to helping people with their divorces, paying bills, royalty work, you name it—buying farms and equipment, bailing someone's kid out of jail."

POINTERS FOR THE JOB SEARCH

Supplement your education in accounting and taxes with courses in music business to gain a basic knowledge of publishing, record company contracts and royalties, touring, and merchandising. "Find someone who is already doing entertainment accounting and work for them. You just have to come up through the ropes."

"Get a heavy background in tax work and be ready to work long hours."

CAREER TIPS

CASE STUDY:

MIKE VADEN, CPA, DIRECTOR OF ENTERTAINMENT SERVICES, CROSSLIN AND VADEN & ASSOCIATES, CPAs

Mike Vaden grew up in Nashville and was already established as a CPA in the audit department at a large accounting firm when one of the firm's partners asked for

THE LEAST FAVORITE THING ABOUT THIS JOB:

"You work a lot of weird hours, but I don't really mind that."

THE BEST THING ABOUT THIS JOB:

"What I like most are the clients I work with that appreciate what I do in helping them—saving them money on their taxes. It's a personal business. That is why I like it better than working for a big company or conglomerate. I like the interaction with people."

a volunteer to handle a music client. Everybody but Vaden ran for cover. "I'd grown up listening to The Opry. I enjoyed listening to music, but I never thought accounting was a viable career in the music industry." Bored with what he was doing and ready for a new challenge, he took on the project, found that he liked the personal interaction, and recognized a need for his services in the music community. Vaden switched his focus from auditing to tax accounting, and built a full-fledged business management service that specializes in the needs of music industry clients. "Accountants are typically boring people. This [music business] makes accounting interesting." Vaden's specialized services to music professionals include concert tour accounting, royalty examinations, tax planning and compliance, investment analysis, business management assistance, and catalog valuation. *www.crosslinvaden.com*

CHAPTER 8

CREATIVE SERVICES AND VIDEO

Creative services comprise the artistic individuals involved in artist imaging. They imagine, conceive, design, devise, groom, photograph, and create images in print and on video that tell the consumer about the artists and their music, enticing the public to want to know more, and ultimately to buy the product.

ART DIRECTOR AND GRAPHIC DESIGNER • CREATIVE DIRECTOR

JOB OVERVIEW

These creative people design and direct the creative process that brings an advertising piece, such as the artwork for a CD, cassette, video, ad or other promotional piece, to realization. Art directors sometimes have complete freedom to design, and at other times must realize the concept of the client. Most projects are a combination of gathering ideas from the client and then creating an original design.

SPECIAL SKILLS

To succeed, you should have an education or experience in design, creativity, and strong people skills.

A DAY IN THE LIFE

Like many freelance creative types, Brunt has no typical day. He may be art directing a photo shoot, which will take him away from the office from early in the morning until late into the evening. Other days he meets with his staff to review completed work and give new assignments. He may take final comps (mock-ups of a

"Developing concepts; that is the first part of art direction. If you're good with concepts and you're good with people, you might make a good art director."

"I'm not convinced you can be taught to be an art director. I think you have to inherently be an art director. I know a lot of people that are talented graphic designers that aren't good art directors, and I know a lot of good art directors that are not graphic designers."

CD) to a client for review and approval, stop off elsewhere to see proofs from a photo shoot, then meet with a new client about creative direction for the design of a CD package. Because Brunt deals with about ten different record companies, he is constantly juggling a variety of projects in all different stages of completion.

When art directing a photo shoot, Brunt generally is involved in the initial planning stage of selecting location, clothes, lighting, and giving other creative input. Sometimes he is involved in selecting the photographer, stylist, and makeup artist. On the day of the shoot, he arrives at the location early and is there throughout the day to offer creative input on lighting, angles, setup, and props.

THE LEAST FAVORITE THING ABOUT THIS JOB:

"In country music, there is a certain framework that is forced on you. They won't let you go beyond a certain kind of type and size and color and image. It is very restrictive."

THE BEST THING ABOUT THIS JOB:

"I like the challenge of creating something definitive."

POINTERS FOR THE JOB SEARCH

"There are schools that teach art direction, which is just a matter of developing concepts. Another good way to become an art director is to start out in a studio or an advertising agency and work your way up to the responsibility of having to develop, define, and take concepts all the way through to completion. That is what an art director does."

CASE STUDY:

BILL BRUNT, ART DIRECTOR AND GRAPHIC DESIGNER/OWNER, BILL BRUNT DESIGNS

On the way to becoming an architect, Bill Brunt combined his love of music with a vocation and became an art director. He grew up in Chicago and, although he earned a bachelor's degree in anthropology, was intent on becoming an architect. In 1977, with his undergraduate work behind him, he took time off from school to go on the road as a lighting director for a rock band, with the idea of returning to school later for a master's degree in architecture. Drawing upon his background in architectural rendering, he designed the cover art for the band's first album. "Whether you're in architecture, lighting design, or graphic design, it's really all the same structure. You're dealing with space and moving things around in relationship to one another." When the band later signed a contract with Mercury/Polygram Records, he continued to do their album covers, and was soon doing the same for other Polygram artists.

When Mercury/Polygram closed their Chicago office in 1982, Brunt knew he would have to move to New York, Los Angeles, or Nashville to continue his career in art direction and design. He began commuting to Nashville twice a month to build up a clientele. He landed a 15-cover greatest hits package for CBS Records that financed his move and enabled him to open his own business. Several of his subsequent projects include *Charlie Daniels' Decadent Hits*, and pieces for Garth Brooks, Vince Gill, Roy Orbison, Wynonna, and many others. Over the years, Brunt has won numerous national and regional awards for album, video, and advertising design. In 2000, he finally found time to return to school to pursue that master's degree.

DESIGNER • OWNER OF A GRAPHIC DESIGN COMPANY

SPECIAL SKILLS

To succeed, you should have skill in computer graphic design, artistic flair, creativity, and people skills. Knowledge of the music business and commercial printing is helpful.

JOB DESCRIPTION

The designer's primary job is to bring to realization the concept of the art director or client. The level of creative input from the designer varies from job to job depending on how concrete the concept is. Some art directors sketch in detail what they expect. In other cases, the clients may have a vague idea of what they want to achieve and look to the designer to present options. A business owner, or freelance designer, is also responsible for landing new accounts, invoicing, and all paperwork involved with running a company.

"Remember that it's business—it's not just art."

You must be able to take direction from others and accept sometimes harsh criticism. You may have a great idea, but if the artists or their managers don't love it, or the marketing team thinks it's the wrong image, you have to put on a smile and go back to work on another concept.

A DAY IN THE LIFE

"If it's really busy," says Kimberly Levitan, "I'll spend 12 hours a day designing. All I can do is stare at the computer and go as fast as I can. If it's slow, I'll spend six hours doing office work like billing and paying bills, organizing and filing, and I make a lot of calls and try to drum up business. It's one or the other—it's like a roller coaster."

POINTERS FOR THE JOB SEARCH

Build a portfolio that is representative of your best work. Design CD packages for local bands or redesign a current release using scanned images. Design fictitious ads or flyers.

CASE STUDY:

KIMBERLY LEVITAN, DESIGNER AND OWNER OF GOOD AND EVIL DESIGN

Kimberly Levitan grew up in Nashville, the daughter of a successful entertainment attorney/artist manager Ken Levitan who also served as a label head. Yet music business was not a natural progression for her. Instead, she enrolled in design courses at the prestigious Pratt Institute in New York for a year, then transferred to CalArts in Los Angeles to finish up. After graduation, she worked as a designer for a printing company in Atlanta. She realized, "the music industry would be fun and I could move home." Unable to land a paying job, she acted as in-house designer for upstart label

THE LEAST FAVORITE THING ABOUT THE JOB:

"The hardest part of my job is there are many hands in the pie. You have a creative idea, but there are 15 people at the label, that have 15 different ideas, and you have to take your idea and incorporate it with all those other ideas. It's hard to keep a good solid design when you've got so many different opinions, but it's part of the job."

THE BEST THING ABOUT THIS JOB:

"I have a chance to be creative and I get paid for it. That's a dream come true."

Rising Tide, for free. "It was like a really long internship," she laughs, "but it was the smartest thing I ever did because I knew nothing about the industry. Being at the label, actually inside, I learned what everybody's job was and how it functioned together as a whole." At Rising Tide, Levitan designed ads and promotional pieces for the label roster, in addition to promotional CDs and singles.

Eventually she found part-time work with Bill Brunt Designs and when Rising Tide closed, she moved into a full-time position. Under Brunt's art direction, the company designed CD and promotional pieces for Atlantic Records, MCA, Orbison Records, Orby Records, RCA, and others. With a few years of experience under her belt, Levitan made the decision to start her own firm, Good and Evil Designs. "It was very scary. I had saved up a lot of money, though, so if all else failed, I could live for three months until I got another job." After spending part of her savings to purchase needed equipment for the new venture, she began to wonder if anyone would hire her—and they did. At first they were small projects, then she landed design work for indie labels Eminent Records and Blue Hat Records, and the work has continued to snowball. Some of her design work includes John Hiatt's *The Tiki Bar Is Open* and the cover of Brooks & Dunn's *Cowboy Town*.

PHOTOGRAPHER

JOB OVERVIEW

The photographer photographs music artists in live performance and in pre-arranged settings.

PREREQUISITES

To succeed, you should compile a portfolio with both live and studio setting photographs of artists. You should be friendly and have an outgoing personality, and contacts within the industry.

A DAY IN THE LIFE

"People often say, 'Man, you have the coolest job in the world. You just lay around and watch TV all day and then go out to concerts at night.' If it were only so," laughs photographer Paul Natkin. "I put in ten hours a day, every day. Then I go out and shoot concerts at night. I've been up in my office since eight this

CAREER TIPS

"There are a lot of webzines—startup web magazines—that are getting access to concerts on a fairly regular basis. Find one of them that needs a staff photographer in your region, to gain experience."

Talk with a local band or two and offer to shoot their performances for free in order to gain more experience photographing a live concert.

VOICES OF EXPERIENCE

THE LEAST FAVORITE THING ABOUT THIS JOB:

"Up-and-coming bands that believe all their own publicity. I find it amazing that managers don't tell bands that they should act in a more respectable manner. This is the only business I know of where you can be in it for 25 years and be treated [badly] by somebody who is not even 19 years old and has been in the business for about six months."

THE BEST THING ABOUT THIS JOB:

"When people are nice to me; when people have respect for me. It proves that what I've worked at all my life is actually worth something. When a band like the Dixie Chicks personally requests that I come out and photograph them, that's pretty darn cool."

morning making duplicate slides for The Judds. I just shot them over the weekend. I'm making prints for Natalie from the Dixie Chicks. Brian Wilson is working on a live album in Los Angeles and I'm in the middle of organizing for that. Between all of that, I'm making phone calls and invoicing people. Around four this afternoon I'll have to go and shoot Peter Murphy, which means I have to lug four cases of camera equipment over to the venue, shoot him, bring that gear back home, grab some dinner, and then go back tonight and shoot his show. That's a pretty normal day."

POINTERS FOR THE JOB SEARCH

"It's a bit like catch-22: you can't shoot concerts unless you've already shot concerts. The first thing you're asked is, 'Who have you shot in the past?' If you say you're just starting out, they're going to say, 'Go start with somebody else.' They may ask what magazines that you've worked for. You've got to come with experience, but how do you get that experience? You've got to have someone who will vouch for you." Approach local bands and hone your skills shooting them. When you have the beginnings of a portfolio, talk with club and theater owners to see if you can shoot a show for their use to further your experience in shooting bigger shows. Once you have a good book, then approach magazines, artist managers, and record label representatives.

CASE STUDY:

PAUL NATKIN, PHOTOGRAPHER/PRESIDENT, PHOTO RESERVE, INC.

Paul Natkin decided to become a photographer in 1971 for the sole reason that it provided free admission to sporting events. He learned the basics from his father. "I was in college at the University of Illinois and had no idea what I wanted to do with my life," recalls Natkin. "My father came home one day and said he had gotten a job photographing the Chicago Bulls. As a photographer, you get the best seat in the house, right at courtside." When Natkin discovered in 1975 that the same held true for concerts, he combined his work with his love of music to become a music photographer. "I was coming home from photographing a tennis match and was listening to the radio. They were talking about a concert on the Northwestern campus with a woman named Bonnie Raitt. I had all my equipment with me and figured if I could [talk] my way into a sporting event, I could [talk] my way into a concert. The guy at the door saw my equipment and before I could say anything he said, 'You can do anything you want, just don't walk onstage.' That was my introduction to music photography. I had always been a music fan and went to concerts from the time I was 12. I basically figured out a way to get into them for free," he laughs. Although it took some time to learn the technical aspects of photographing a live concert, he began to get photos published in local newspapers and magazines. "I learned by trial and error and spent a lot of time sitting in the darkroom watching my father."

At a concert in Chicago, Natkin met the art director of *Cream* magazine and at his invitation, began calling the magazine's editor every day about selling his photos. After two weeks, the editor finally accepted his call and ended up buying a photograph. "I think he finally took my call just to get rid of me," Natkin says, "If you're going after something, you go for it and don't give up." The editor was soon calling Natkin every month, and eventually he shot 20 covers for the magazine. He was able to do the same thing at other magazines, including *Rolling Stone* and *Playboy*. Soon his ability to get photos published in such prestigious international magazines made him in demand with artists and publicists alike.

During a photo shoot with Keith Richards in 1988, Natkin heard the artist say he was going out on a solo tour. Natkin wrote a letter to Richards' manager offering his services as a tour photographer, was accepted, and spent three weeks on the road with the artist. He did the same thing a few weeks later with the Rolling Stones, and ended up spending three and a half months with the band on their record-breaking Steel Wheels Tour. Since that time, he has covered all the subsequent Rolling Stones tours, as well as Bruce Springsteen's Born in the USA Tour, which got his photo on the cover of *Newsweek* magazine, and Prince's Purple Rain Tour. During his 25 year career, Natkin has photographed more than 3,000 different bands and individual artists, spanning almost every style of music. In addition to his ongoing career photographing musical talent, Natkin signed on as tour manager of former Beach Boy Brian Wilson's comeback bid. *www.natkin.net*

MARKETING AND PUBLICITY

Marketing and publicity people are an artist's link to the media. They fulfill many of the same functions as their record company counterparts. However, they are generally able to focus their energy on a specific artist or project because they have smaller rosters of clients and fewer corporate business tasks. Being independent also allows marketers to specialize in areas. This chapter covers two main areas: the more traditional role of independent Publicity and some of the diverse possibilities of Alternative Marketing.

PUBLICITY

INDEPENDENT PUBLICIST • PRESS AGENT • PUBLICIST • PUBLIC RELATIONS

JOB OVERVIEW

The publicity staff strategizes campaigns and coordinates all publicity efforts, including national media, television, syndicated radio, and tour press.

SPECIAL SKILLS

To succeed, you should have good phone and organizational skills, an outgoing personality, enthusiasm, self-motivation, creativity, and the ability to write.

"Creativity is the most important part of the job," says Sarah McMullen. "It is manifest in the ability to write a great pitch letter and the ability to verbally sell and inspire the journalist, who thinks he's heard every kind of angle known to man, into writing about your artist."

Mark Pucci says, "To be a good publicist, you've got to have the gift of gab and know what you're talking about. You've got to know what the person on the other end of the phone wants to hear in order to get them to be interested in what you're working on. You've got to be a good researcher. The fact that I was a music writer was helpful to me, not just knowing the mechanics of writing, but having been on the other side of the phone with people pitching stories to me taught me a lot."

"I found as my career moved forward, if I didn't love the person for whom I was doing the work, it meant nothing. I was blessed by loving the two main people for whom I did most of my work: Elton John and Roy Orbison."—SM

"It's all about your relationship with press people, who tolerate us as long as we have a creative thought."—SM

"Understand early in your career the importance of stress management. When the day comes that you can't turn your head to the right or left, understand that you are the only person responsible for your massage and acupuncture appointments. I say that with humor, but know that I'm serious. The publicist is the person who has to keep the eight plates spinning in the air, like the guy in the circus—you can't drop a plate."—SM

"When I start working with an artist, I try to read everything that has been written about them already and I try to see them perform as many times as I can. I listen to their music a lot and try to pick up things about the artist that make them special and different from other artists; things I think make them unique. Then my job is to try and convey that information to the people that I work with."—MP

"You've got to have a passion for music above everything. There are going to be so many things that come up against you—obstacles—unless you love it, you're not going to be able to hang in there and put up with the discouragement."—MP

"Learn as much as you can. Don't be afraid to find out about other areas of the business so you can become a more complete person."—MP

POINTERS FOR THE JOB SEARCH

Many colleges and universities offer a degree in publicity and marketing. Make sure the school you select has an internship program affiliated with music businesses, where they can place you to gain experience. "There is no substitute for actual experience. I would suggest that people get into some music company as an intern and learn as much as you can about the business. Even if it isn't the particular area you want, the more you know how publicity fits into promotion, marketing, sales, A&R, and all the other aspects that make up the big picture, the better you're going to be able to do your job."—MP

CASE STUDY:

SARAH McMULLEN, PUBLICIST/PRESIDENT/OWNER, McMULLEN & COMPANY

With interests in music, acting, and writing, Los Angeles seemed an obvious destination for Sarah McMullen to seek her fame and fortune. "My cousin was already in L.A. working in the music business and she said, 'Come out to the wealth of creative opportunities in California. You won't be alone. I'll help you.'" McMullen recently had graduated from the University of Texas at Austin with a degree in English and

THE LEAST FAVORITE THING ABOUT THIS JOB:

"When I start drowning in the administrative side. It happens if you own your own business, but it is my least favorite task."—SM

"The only thing I don't like about my job, and fortunately it has never really been bad, is to chase people to get paid."—MP

THE BEST THING ABOUT THIS JOB:

"The thing I love the very most about what I do is that it is creative and hands-on."—SM

"This is not a 9 to 5 job; you put in a lot of hours and work weekends and holidays, so you've got to love what you do. I love listening to music. I love seeing people perform music, and I love to be around people that are creative. For me there is a real joy in starting out with someone at the beginning of their career, when they are virtually unknown. When that whole thing sort of takes off and happens, there is no feeling like it in the world."—MP

speech. She had postgraduate writing courses in creative, feature and non-fiction genres, and had done a brief stint at a Dallas advertising agency. She felt ready to take on the world. McMullen started out as an actress. She showcased in little theater productions, then graduated to spokesperson in a long-running television commercial series for a local nursing school, and finally appeared in an American Film Institute production. Eventually, she grew tired of the "struggling" part of being a "struggling actress." When faced with the choice between waiting tables and a job offer at BMI, she chose the latter. As assistant to a department head, she faked her way through many of her duties. "I had no training in dictation, but I had been memorizing scripts for plays. So when my boss dictated letters, I would pretend to be writing it down in shorthand, but I would memorize them. Of course it didn't always work; I could never remember the important figures he gave me, but because I was a writer, his letters were always beautifully composed." After a year on the job, her boss retired and McMullen became assistant to the directors of writer relations, where she learned about the business of songwriting and publishing. After three years at BMI, she was recommended for an assistant's job at Planet Records, which proved to be short-lived.

Out of work when her boss was let go, McMullen's business contacts rallied to help her find a job. One of the interviews they secured for her was in the publicity department at RSO Records. On the strength of her friends' glowing recommendations, and the college writing portfolio she brought along, she was hired as assistant to the vice president of publicity. She learned her craft publicizing the label's monster sound track album *Saturday Night Fever* and the subsequent career relaunch of the Bee Gees. After being promoted to director of public relations, she found herself out of work once again, when the label closed in 1979. This time, it was her boss that recommended her for a job in the music division of publicists Rogers and Cohen.

Now the account executive over more sedate corporate and theatrical events, she was surprised when rock acts like Wham and Rod Stewart began requesting her services. In 1983, she took on her biggest project to date as publicist for Elton John. Encouraged by the managers of artists she had worked for, McMullen went out on her own in 1985, but when the dust settled, she was left with Elton John as her sole client. Once again, a business contact stepped forward to help. While the two were planning a strategy over lunch, the contact introduced her to an attorney who had worked with Wham. He recommended client Roy Orbison and set up a meeting for that afternoon. Borrowing the contact's office, and quickly making it appear she had been in business there for years, McMullen signed her second client, and landed two more the following week.

For the next few years, McMullen devoted herself to re-establishing Orbison's career; mounting a successful Grammy Award campaign for Jefferson Starship that won album and song of the year honors; publicizing the ongoing career of Elton John, and taking on special fundraising events for clients from her days at Rogers and Cohen. In 1990, McMullen began producing the fundraising events for the Elton John AIDS Foundation, the first year in conjunction with World Team Tennis, and the second year as an alternative Oscar Awards night party. At that point, devoting nearly all her time to John's career and foundation, she effectively closed her doors to all but a few long-term clients.

In 1998, McMullen took stock of her life and starting dividing time between Los Angeles and Austin while making plans to eventually relocate. She and John amicably parted ways professionally the following year, but she maintained her position on the executive board of his foundation. She was retained as a consultant to the college of communications for the University of Texas at Austin. In 1999, she returned to her earliest interest in music publishing when she joined the Internet entity Supertrack, which protects the interests of songwriters, publishers, and artists by providing secure solutions for the digital downloading of recorded music.

CASE STUDY:

MARK PUCCI, PUBLICIST, PRESIDENT/OWNER, PUCCI MEDIA

In high school, Mark Pucci pursued his three major interests—music, playing basketball, and writing—and dreamed of being a sports journalist. After graduation, he worked for an insurance company by day and took business courses at night, saving up enough money to attend college full time. He earned a degree in personnel administration from the University of Tennessee at Memphis, hung around the city's music scene, and wrote articles for fanzines and various underground publications. A job as music editor for *River City Review* led to writing and producing radio advertising for regional promoter Mid-South Concerts. He also submitted articles on speculation to national magazines, two of which were published in *Rolling Stone*.

Through writing local music reviews, Pucci got to know the head of publicity at Capricorn Records, then the home of bands like Wet Willie, Marshall Tucker, and the Allman Brothers. A huge fan of the music, he accepted the job of tour publicist at the label's Macon, Georgia home office in 1974. As the label expanded, he was handling up to 20 bands on the road. He was promoted to department head in 1978, but found himself out of work the following year when the label filed for bankruptcy.

Wanting to remain in the area, Pucci opened Mark Pucci Associates in Atlanta in 1979. Initially he worked out of the offices of a music publisher client, and within two years his business grew and he moved into his own location. Gaining clients through word of mouth, he worked with some of the great alternative bands emerging out of Athens, Georgia in the mid-1980s: R.E.M., Guadalcanal Diary, and Love Tractor, as well as roots and blues musicians like Delbert McClinton, Elvin Bishop, Charlie Musclewhite, and Jimmy Dale Gilmore.

Late in 1991, Capricorn Records had reopened in Nashville, and Pucci was brought in as vice president of publicity. He worked with such artists as Hank Williams, Jr., Kenny Chesney, Widespread Panic, and Lynyrd Skynyrd. He rose to the position of vice president/general manager of the label, but six months after being promoted, he was let go when Capricorn began having financial difficulties. The same afternoon, he called HighTone Records, with whom he had a long-standing relationship, and secured his first publicity client. He returned to Atlanta in January 1996 and formed Mark Pucci Media. Pucci's firm has handled publicity for HighTone Records, Trainwreck Records, and Blue Bella Records, as well as individual artists on BNA and Columbia labels. His clients reflect his own musical tastes, running the gamut of blues, jazz, R&B, rock, alternative rock, rock-a-billy, hillbilly, country, and alternative country. *www.markpuccimedia.com*

DIRECTOR OR FAN CLUB PRESIDENT

JOB OVERVIEW

The director or president manages and oversees client's fan club activities and marketing efforts through the fan base.

SPECIAL SKILLS

"You have to have good grammar both in speaking and writing. You have to be a nice person with a good deal of patience so you can deal with the calls from fans. You are an extension of the artist you work for. You have to be willing to go the extra mile for people."

A DAY IN THE LIFE

"What keeps me interested in my job is that there is no typical day," says Sharon Eaves. "I have a staff that sorts through the mail and they handle each request, whether it is to purchase merchandise, request an autograph, or they have a question. We answer them all. We send thank you notes for any gifts that are received. We handle all requests for 'meet and greet' passes the day they come in. I have ten different artists' newsletters to get out two or four times a year, so I spend a lot of time writing all the content, editing, and working on the layout. I have meetings with management to plan events and how we can best use the fan base to market the artist's record. I oversee the design and planning

"If you make a promise, you have to keep it. If you make a mistake, and we all do, admit it and then work to resolve the problem as best you can. Own up to your mistakes and people will respect you for it."

"Treat everyone the way you would want to be treated." One minute you are dealing with an artist's manager or someone from their record label and the next you're taking a phone call from a fan with an outrageous request. You have to treat each of them with the same level of respect.

CAREER TIPS

of the fan club merchandise, and meet with the artist or management to get approvals."

POINTERS FOR THE JOB SEARCH

Learn as much as you can about the music industry and how it works, then apply to work as an assistant or intern for a fan club company. Once you have some experience, and an understanding of how the business operates, then contact managers of artists you respect and find out if they have a fan club president.

CASE STUDY:

SHARON EAVES, OWNER, FAN CLUB HOUSE

While attending college in Bowling Green, Kentucky, Sharon Eaves got involved with a community access television channel as a talk show host, interviewing people involved in the local music scene. Intrigued by her brush with the music business, she was soon booking talent for local shows and finding up-and-coming bands to manage. She moved to Nashville in 1983 to pursue her interest and landed a job as a receptionist at a recording studio, and worked her way up to manager.

When Paul Worley, a record producer Eaves had met at the studio, became a senior vice president at Sony Tree publishing, he brought her in as his assistant. By the late 1980s, she also began managing Wild Rose, the first all-female country band, which eventually became a full-time job. Able to run the group's fan club at a profit, she received offers from other artists to do the same for them. Initially reluctant—"I was focused on building my management business and didn't want to be labeled a fan club company"—she finally agreed to take on another club. As word of mouth spread, Eaves soon found herself running the fan clubs of four groups. Eventually putting aside her plan to be an artist manager, she opened her own business, Fan Club House, and today creates merchandise lines and operates fan clubs for artists like Bryan White and Wynonna. To understand the volume of business generated, Eaves confides that one of her clients grossed more than $500,000 in annual club sales in one year. Eaves has expanded the companies' services to include publicity, merchandise, fulfillment, and fan marketing services for the entertainment industry. *www.fan-clubhouse.com*

AGENT

The primary function of an agent is to secure work for the client. Many agents carve out their own niche by specializing in international tours or representing clients for film, television, and advertising work. At a large company, agents usually focus on a particular region of the country and work with fellow agents to book cross-country tours.

AGENT • BOOKING AGENT • INTERNATIONAL AGENT

JOB OVERVIEW

The agent routes tours, and negotiates fees and contractual obligations for musical artists' live performances.

PREREQUISITES

"You've got to have a very strong work ethic," says Buck Williams. "This is not a 9 to 5 job. You've got to be willing to work seven days a week. Whatever hours it takes to get the job done. You have many shows to attend and there is a lot of travel. You have to have good phone skills; be able to talk with people. You have to be a good people person in order to not only sign talent and get people to believe in you, but also to get along with the people you're selling to. You have to be able to negotiate, not just demand, but negotiate."

A DAY IN THE LIFE

Williams begins his day by organizing his phone list and resolving leftover tasks from the previous day. Then he works from the East Coast to the West Coast, because of the time differences. Throughout the afternoon he may route a tour, negotiate fees and other contractual obligations, or get confirmations for dates. Every Tuesday Williams has a strategy meeting with his entire staff to plan tours and go over routing. "When we route a tour we find out what traffic and competition is in the market and even though we're set and ready to go, we may turn around and reroute the tour to avoid traffic. The bigger the artist, the more you have to do that. We make sure the ticket prices are right, that there is a specific marketing plan for the market. I make sure all my people do those things every time on every level, clubs and all. The most important thing is to do sell-out business."

Due to the fact that Chris Dalston is focused on international touring, he begins his day early, arriving at the office by 7:30 A.M. "I try to get calls to Europe out of the way in the first three to four hours. Then I start responding to my faxes and e-mail.

CAREER TIPS

"The older I get, the more I realize success is about how you get along with people. People have got to trust and like you—there is a great comfort factor in that for managers. If you like someone, you're going to work with him more than if you don't like somebody."—CD

"You've got to be able to listen and hear other people's side of the story. You may not ultimately agree with them, but you've got to be able to listen and see what they have to say."—CD

"It's not easy being an agent. If you're not serious about doing it, don't get into it."—CD

"A lot of agents look at success by how much money they make for their artists. They don't care about the other side [the promoter]. You want to get the best deal for your artists, but not one that runs the person you're selling to out of business."—BW

"The odds are against you no matter what you want to do, but the job is going to be done by someone and that someone can be you, if you have the dream, the perseverance, and the wherewithal to get it done." —BW

"Learn everything you can about what is current today and a little bit of history of the music business. Know about the genre of music you want to be involved in. If you're going to be in pop music, know a lot about pop music; know what is happening in England and in Australia; know what is up and coming. Try to learn what the third track on the last record of an artist is."—BW

By mid-afternoon, when Australia and Japan open up, I'm focused there. I try to go home by 7:30 P.M. I then will either go to a show or my day continues at night, at home, because in Japan and Australia it is the middle of their day. My job actually starts Sunday afternoon because that's Monday morning in Asia. My home phone is available at all times."

POINTERS FOR THE JOB SEARCH

The mail room or an internship is one way to get in the door at an agency. "We have a very good system at CAA," says Dalston, "where we reward people that work internally. There have been three assistants that have been made agents in the last year. My assistant is now being put in the position of trainee and the next step up for him is agent. When you work in a team environment, you learn how the team operates. It's a continuation of passing the torch so that the team stays in place, as opposed to hiring somebody to bring in a big act to make a bit of money, which could ruin the chemistry of the whole department."

Sharpen your clerical, organizational, and phone skills and apply to be an assistant or an intern. At larger agencies, the mail room or temporary work are other ways to get into the company. Once inside, after you've completed your assigned work, offer to help agents or their assistants getting building avails or performing other tasks. "I find some of the best people come off the concert committees from schools," says Williams. "Those kids know a lot about music. They have studied it; they love it."

THE LEAST FAVORITE THING ABOUT THIS JOB:

"Basically, the agent is always wrong. It doesn't matter what happens, some way, somehow, people figure out a way to blame the agent."—CD

"It's not fun when an artist or manager makes you do something that you know is wrong [for their career], but you have to do it anyway."—BW

THE BEST THING ABOUT THIS JOB:

"I love the people. I love the clients. I love the way we're treated here [at CAA]."—CD

"What I really like is being able to take something and see success come of it; to take a small act and build it to a big act. That's incredibly rewarding, not only to see the success that the individuals in the band have, but the promoters and everybody making money. One of the most exciting things is being able to take a band like R.E.M. and go from a club to a stadium."—BW

VOICES OF EXPERIENCE

CHRISTOPHER DALSTON, INTERNATIONAL AGENT, CREATIVE ARTISTS AGENCY

Christopher Dalston was a photographer on the European golf circuit, working for a small photography company in Leeds, England when he decided that he needed a change. "I'd been to America and I really liked it," he recalls. He moved to Miami, Florida and signed on as ship's photographer aboard the *SS Norway* for three years. During that time, he became friendly with Phyllis Diller's road manager, and the comedienne offered to help him find a job if he was interested in getting into the entertainment industry. "I was pretty naive. One day, I just gave her a call and she ended up getting me a job working for The Amazing Kreskin." Dalston relocated to New Jersey and for the next two years he saw every corner of the United States, serving as road manager for the mentalist. At a show in Los Angeles, Dalston met three agents from the newly formed Triad Artists Agency. "They said, 'If you ever want to get off the road and get a proper job, give us a call.'" Dalston made the call.

"I started answering the phone, 'Good morning, Triad Artists,' and I was promoted to receptionist, to floater, and to assistant. Then, they made me a club agent." When his boss walked out to take a job at rival William Morris Agency, Dalston inherited his workload, in true trial-by-fire style and organized international tours for George Michael and Whitney Houston. Later, when William Morris bought Triad Artists, Dalston finished out the remaining two years of his contract, then moved to Creative Artists Agency (CAA) in 1995. *www.caa.com*

CASE STUDY:

BUCK WILLIAMS, PRESIDENT/OWNER, PROGRESSIVE GLOBAL AGENCY

Music was a driving force in Buck Williams' life from a young age. He grew up in Chapel Hill, North Carolina and became part of a band in high school. "Eventually, it had James Taylor in it and his older brother, Alex Taylor, was the lead singer." Following graduation, Williams served a stint in the army. When he returned to North Carolina, he discovered a band and decided to call James Taylor, now a major star, for advice on how to proceed working with the group. Taylor suggested a New York contact, and thus began William's learning curve, talking to people already in the business. He got a job with an independent booking agency in North Carolina, selling talent to colleges and clubs, as well as managing and road managing small acts signed to the agency. "Then I went on the road with Alex Taylor and toured with him as a roadie, gopher, harmonica player, and sidekick. I later ended up managing Alex and I booked all of his dates. From managing Alex, I learned a lot about promoting shows. I learned about negotiating and I learned about riders."

The skills he gained working with Taylor were an asset when Williams moved to Washington D.C. and began promoting concerts. "Mostly I promoted jazz concerts at Kennedy Center," and later worked into the Raleigh, North Carolina area with acts like Chick Corea, Little Feat, Weather Report, and Bonnie Raitt. In 1975, he moved to Macon, Georgia to work as an agent at Paragon, representing artists like the Allman Brothers, Charlie Daniels, and Lynyrd Skynyrd. Ian Copeland joined the agency during that time, bringing in the Police and Squeeze.

When Paragon folded in 1980, Copeland went to New York and, with John Huey, formed Frontier Booking International (FBI). A year later Williams joined the agency and became a partner. "I worked there until we merged with Intertalent," a Los Angeles film talent agency. Not wanting to move to the West Coast, Williams instead joined Monterey Artists, but differing business philosophies soon prompted him to open his own agency. In 1994, he formed Progressive Global Agency, representing acts such as R.E.M. and Widespread Panic. Two years later Williams became co-manager of Widespread Panic. *www.pgamusic.com/agency*

AGENT TRAINEE • ASSISTANT • EXECUTIVE ASSISTANT

JOB OVERVIEW

Assistants issue deal memos and contracts, handle a variety of paperwork, answer phone calls and e-mail, order concert tickets, track building avails, and perform other secretarial functions.

PREREQUISITES

Some agencies require a four-year college degree to be accepted into their agent training program. Computer skills, ability to handle multiple tasks and follow directions, attention to detail, and a professional phone manner are important skills for success.

POINTERS FOR THE JOB SEARCH

Mail room, receptionist, and temporary jobs are good ways to get your foot in the door of a company. Temporary positions, in particular, give you an opportunity to present your skills, showcase your work ethic, and prove yourself indispensable to a potential employer.

ON TOUR

It takes a diverse group of individuals to form the team whose common goal it is to put on a great show. This chapter discusses jobs involved in the rehearsal and design of a tour, individuals whose task it is to promote concerts, and the people who travel on the road to make it all happen. The chapter covers five areas: Rehearsal and Storage Facility; Production; Promoter and Venue; Crew; and Musicians.

REHEARSAL AND STORAGE FACILITY

Spacious rooms in rehearsal facilities are generally rented for recording artists to use in the staging and rehearsing of live shows. Space might also be rented to audition new band members, or to stage a showcase or private performance. Most facilities also rent lockers where touring and studio musicians can store gear; provide cartage service, and rent back-line equipment.

GENERAL MANAGER • OFFICE MANAGER • OPERATIONS MANAGER

JOB OVERVIEW

These managers oversee all aspects of the company operation including invoicing, bookkeeping, taxes, trouble-shooting, and hiring, firing, and scheduling of employees.

PREREQUISITES

To succeed, you need clerical and bookkeeping skills. You must be able to work well with a variety of people such as artist managers, road managers, musicians, technical staff, production assistants, producers and engineers, and record label and business managers. You should be able to manage a staff and negotiate pricing.

CAREER TIPS

"I've only got one year of college behind me. Now you've got to go to school—you've got to—before anybody considers you." The music industry has become so competitive that some companies require a four-year degree to be considered for employment or acceptance into their training program.

"Listen. Don't be afraid to be quiet and learn from someone else."

A DAY IN THE LIFE

SIR's Laura Ford Bartschi's day begins around 9 A.M. "I come in and go through the invoices for the previous day. At any given time, I could be paying bills, doing taxes, and booking rehearsals. We get a lot of large tour rentals and I help the staff with pricing and delivery fees. We travel all over the country delivering gear."

POINTERS FOR THE JOB SEARCH

Bartschi sees working at a rehearsal facility as "a great stepping stone, if you're a musician or studying the music business, because you meet a lot of people. You can learn so much from people coming into the building. That's one great thing about Nashville: there are so many good people around that are willing to teach."

THE LEAST FAVORITE THING ABOUT THE JOB:

"There is a lot of negotiating in prices and many times people think we make money hand over fist, but we don't. It takes a lot of money to run a company like this. There is a lot of overhead. People don't realize that. That's the part I hate."

THE BEST THING ABOUT THIS JOB:

"I love the rehearsals more than anything else. It's fun to have people in the building enjoying the employees and everything about the facility."

VOICES OF EXPERIENCE

CASE STUDY:

LAURA FORD BARTSCHI, GENERAL MANAGER, STUDIO INSTRUMENT RENTAL (SIR)

Bartschi's introduction to the entertainment industry was as a receptionist at a talent/modeling agency, where she later became an agent. Born and raised in Detroit, she moved to Nashville in the early 1980s. "I don't write, I don't sing, I don't play," she says, but she did possess good organizational skills and was good at working with people—strong assets to any employer. After the agency downsized, she landed a job working for producer/label head/publisher Harold Shedd at the Music Mill. There she met the general manager of SIR and learned the company was looking for an office manager. After she interviewed with the owner in New York and completed a series of tests, she was offered the job. As office manager she learned all she could about every aspect of the company, and was rewarded with more responsibility. When her boss left the company, she was offered the position of general manager, a title she has held since 1993. *www.sirtn.com*

PRODUCTION

PRODUCTION DESIGNER AND DIRECTOR • SET AND LIGHTING DESIGNER

JOB OVERVIEW

The designers formulate a concept for artists' live performance and either create or oversee the design of the stage, lighting, special effects, and choreography. They are involved in song selection, the pace of the show, and the direction of the overall performance.

PREREQUISITES

To succeed, you should have a background in set or lighting design, or both, and the ability to create unique show presentations that are feasible to construct and transport. Willie Williams was once told that he possessed "'a rare combination of eccentricity and common sense.' When you're designing a rock show, you're trying to show people something that they've never seen before. Obviously, you need a lot of imagination. It really requires both your right brain and your left brain; it is a crucial combination because if you can't turn something you've dreamed up into something that that will work, and that will travel, the tour will be a disaster."

"The worst technicians are people who really want to be designers. If you have a choice of being a technician on a big tour, or designing a show on a much smaller scale, it's much more important to be doing what you want to do."

"You have a real relationship with the road, when you're doing this job. It's the nearest you can come these days to running away and joining the circus."

Classes in theatrical set design and lighting are an asset.

A DAY IN THE LIFE

Much of Williams' job begins long before the artist goes on tour. "The real job for me is conceiving the show, designing it, having it built, and most importantly, getting it through rehearsals. When you install the show, normally it's in the first venue that you're going to be playing. You'll go in a week early and put the show together. You put the set up for the first time and the band will come in and rehearse. That's when I make my money, when I've really got to perform, because quite often I'm the only person that understands the big picture of what is supposed to happen. That is the hardest part and in some ways, it's the most exhilarating too." Throughout the process, Williams confers with the artist and oversees the installation of the stage, lighting, and other effects. "I can't tell you the amount of time I've sat in darkened buildings, staring at stages, programming lighting and effects, and just running through things. That's a very big part of the job."

On a show day, the crew begins loading in around 7 A.M. and Williams arrives around noon to ensure everything is running smoothly. At 3 P.M., the band does a sound check. Afterward, unless some effect or equipment needs attention, there is downtime until the opening act is finished. "During the show, I'm usually on the intercom system talking to the follow spot operators and the lighting operators, giving cues and instructions throughout the show. If there are video cues, I might cover those, and often I'll operate one of the lighting consoles, too." After the performance, the crew tears down the stage and lighting, stores it on trucks, and the group travels through the night to the next venue.

POINTERS FOR THE JOB SEARCH

"There are many different places to go and learn about the music industry. A lot of people who want to design shows or events will do some associated technical job on a tour. Someone who really wants to be a lighting designer will go out and tour as a lighting technician, just to get a foot in the business. There are some lighting and equipment companies that are always looking for crew people."

CASE STUDY:

WILLIE WILLIAMS, PRODUCTION DESIGNER AND DIRECTOR

"I always loved music, but it never occurred to me that it was something I could do for a living," says Willie Williams. Growing up in Sheffield, England, Williams was an excellent student who had every intention of attending university and becoming an electronics engineer. He fell in love with theatrical design as a teenage extra with the local opera company, but never considered it as a possible career. "Both my father and my grandfather sang opera. My father didn't make a living out of singing opera; he always had a day job as well. Subconsciously, I guess, I just assumed you couldn't

THE LEAST FAVORITE THING ABOUT THIS JOB:

"I dislike not always getting my way. Everything that I do is a collaboration. The thing that hurts me most is when I have a great idea or vision for something, and either I can't describe it well enough to persuade them to do it, they just don't get it, or they disagree. There have been ideas that I absolutely believe in which never see the light of day. You're always dependent on other people to approve your ideas."

"I think of travel as the best and worst part of the job. You get to see some great places, but constantly traveling is exhausting on a level unknown by most human beings."

THE BEST THING ABOUT THIS JOB:

"I love the live event. I love that fact that there is no such word as 'cut' once the show starts. I love the moment before the video picture comes up, or before the stage does something, because I know what is going to happen and the audience doesn't. There is that moment of anticipation. It's a real thrill for me to hear the audience have this communal thrill of seeing something that they love."

make a living out of working in the arts." That notion was about to change. During the long summer vacation between high school graduation and university, Williams attended a music festival where he met groups of musicians from London and Liverpool. "It was the height of punk rock in England. It was an exciting time when you believed anybody could do anything." Williams decided to defer university for a year and beginning in 1976, crisscrossed England in a van, working as a roadie for several punk rock bands. Enthralled with the visual and lighting effects possible with live events, he quickly lost all interest in engineering.

With no lighting design or stage production courses available to him at the time, Williams had to learn his chosen craft where he could. In between working with small bands on the road, he found jobs with lighting and equipment contractors, all the while soaking up as much information and experience as he could. After five years, the band he worked with most frequently, broke up and he found himself looking for another gig. "There was this young band from Ireland called U2 that had just put out their first record, which I thought was great. I knew they were about my age. I was 22 at the time. I set out to find them." Locating the manager's phone number, Williams called from a pay phone, described his experience, and offered to send more details. "He said, 'Actually we're looking for someone to do lighting,' at which point I just about dropped the phone." Williams met the band members when they came to London the following week for a radio interview. "We just got along like a house afire." Beginning in 1982, and for the next 18 years, Williams and U2 literally grew up together. "When I first got on board, they were doing colleges and small places. In a way it was the completion of my education and the way I was able to gain the confidence to take really big projects. The first time we did an arena show, it was the first time any of us had done one. The first time we did a stadium, it was a first for all of us."

Between U2 tours, Williams has designed and directed major tours for many legendary rock acts. A fan of David Bowie since his early teens, it was particularly rewarding when Williams began an association with the artist in 1989, on his Tin Machine Tour. In 1995, Williams heard that R.E.M. was planning to tour again after more than a half dozen years off the road, and he telephoned the band's management. Once again, everyone clicked, and he began yet another continuing working relationship. Over the years, Williams' family has often teased, "You're having fun, but when are you going to get a proper job?" To which he replies, "No sign of a proper job as of yet."

FRONT OF HOUSE ENGINEER • SOUND ENGINEER • SOUND MAN

JOB OVERVIEW

The front house engineer is the main sound engineer for live performances. These technicians gather all the sound information being played and sung on stage, and mix it to achieve optimal volumes and blends. That is the version the audience hears.

PREREQUISITES

To succeed, you should be well-versed in how to set up and operate sound equipment and have a basic understanding of music. You need an ear for pitch and overall sound quality. "If you have a guitar player that is a whole step or a half step flat or sharp, you don't want to put that on the mix as much," explains Fernando Alvarez, Jr. "You want the end result to sound good, so you have to control certain things like that. Knowing every aspect of the electronic side helps out a lot: what a console does, what an amplifier does, what the speakers are supposed to be doing."

A DAY IN THE LIFE

Most bands and crew travel by bus through the night, arriving at a hotel or venue in the early hours of the morning. The crew then wakes up at the venue, where breakfast is catered and shower facilities are made available. Smaller bands might rent a hotel room for members of the crew to shower and change clothes, and then eat breakfast at a local diner. "The first thing that is done is unloading the trucks," says Fernando Alvarez, Jr. "Every venue has stagehands [usually members of a local union]. Everything is put into its proper place and uncased, uncovered, and so forth." Each crew member is ultimately responsible for setting up the gear he uses. The front house engineer's equipment may be some of the last to be unloaded and set up. The lighting generally goes up first and comes down last, and then stage set pieces are added. (Usually the venue provides the actual stage, although some large touring artists carry their own.) Sound equipment and gear complete the set-up.

The sound engineer does everything in his power to ensure that the gear and equipment are working and in place, so that when the band comes in to sound check, things will run smoothly. Sound check is the time each band member and singer tests the microphones and amplifiers to ensure proper sound is achieved. They also work with the monitor man at this time to get proper mixes for each individual. The front house engineer then is free until show time (which may be in just a few hours) and often uses the time to eat dinner, take a nap, or watch a movie on the bus. After the show is over, the equipment is broken down by the stagehands and loaded onto the trucks, and the crew is off to the next city.

The crew rarely, if ever, sees a hotel room, opting to stay at the venue until show time and then loading out afterward to hit the road. Sometimes set-up might be done

"There is something my dad told me when I was young: 'The minute you think you're too good to sweep the floor is the minute you need to be handed a broom, in order to sweep the floor.' "—FA

"I'm always trying to be on top of things so that they [the artist] are not having to ask for something or wondering why I didn't take the initiative to get something done. In this business, I think, it's almost 75 percent networking and marketing yourself, and the other 25 percent is technical. The schooling will help, but we're looking for someone that is able to represent our company and themselves in a proper manner."—FA

"People who ask questions and are interested in learning more, and who will actually go out of their way to get things done, are the people that I spend my time with. I don't like working with people who just sit and wait to be told what to do."—RO

"Don't give yourself a backup plan. If you don't give yourself another choice, then you have to stick to it and make it work, one way or another."—RO

in time for a quick excursion to a music store, an outside restaurant, or a point of interest in the city, but this is rare. Generally the crew spends their day at the venue.

POINTERS FOR THE JOB SEARCH

Take classes in sound engineering or contact local clubs and see if there is a house sound person that you can assist for free, to learn the basics. Next, find a local band or club that needs help with sound, and offer your services to get some experience. As you become more experienced, give a business card to bands coming into the venue, or others you see out performing, and let them know you're available. Even if you work for free in the beginning, get experience. No one wants to pay someone with no experience.

CASE STUDY:

FERNANDO ALVAREZ, JR., FRONT HOUSE ENGINEER, DIXIE CHICKS

Fernando Alvarez, Jr. was studying architecture at the University of Texas at San Antonio (UTSA) when an opportunity to work in music presented itself. The San Antonio native's brother was playing in a local group that needed crew assistance and Alvarez got the call. "I started with the group as lighting engineer, and then moved to

VOICES OF EXPERIENCE

THE LEAST FAVORITE THING ABOUT THE JOB:

"What I hate the most is exactly what I love most: having to overcome challenges. At times it's a little stressful."—FA

"This last summer I probably worked between 90 to 98 hours a week. This past March I did 70 to 80 hours, with only a day off each week. The long hours start to get to you."—RO

THE BEST THING ABOUT THIS JOB:

"It's a different scene every day out there [on the road] in the sound business. Different faces, venues, cities—that's the best part of it. Seeing a lot of different things and trying to overcome the challenges."—FA

"It is exciting to realize some of the people I've worked with: Loretta Lynn, Michael Bolton, Ray Charles, Spyro Gyra, Roberta Flack. Because I was a piano player, Billy Joel has been an idol of mine since high school. Working with him—standing three feet from him while he played for 45 minutes—that was probably the biggest moment in my career so far."—RO

monitors, and eventually became the front of house guy. I liked every position and started seeing that music is something I wanted to do." Mostly self-taught, Alvarez later enrolled in a course at the Audio Engineering Institute in San Antonio. "I would sit in that course to just gather information on how things are done in a basic form so that I knew what was going on—so I used the right terms and lingo when I was hanging out with the real dudes. I learned a lot, but most was self-taught. To a certain degree, it's all about your own ears. Hearing everything exactly, or trying to hear it, the way it's supposed to be heard."

After a year at UTSA, he set aside architecture for a full-time career in music, and landed a gig with Century Music Systems, a full-line production company. Over the next six years, Alvarez continued to hone his skills, working with artists like Robert Earl Keen. Along the way he met steel guitar player/producer Lloyd Mains. Impressed with Alvarez's skill mixing Keen, Mains asked if he would be interested in mixing the Dixie Chicks, his daughter Natalie's band. "I had heard about them. Their first single had just come out, so I gave him my business card and said, 'Sure, call me if they ever need someone.' I really didn't think much about it." Three months later, Senior Management's Simon Renshaw telephoned and offered Alvarez the job. He joined up in June 1998 and says of the experience, "It's been incredible. I've learned quite a bit, seen a lot, and done a lot." *www.gsdpro.com*

CASE STUDY:

ROB OWENS, SOUND ENGINEER, GLENN SCOTT DAVIS PRODUCTIONS (GSD)

Rob Owens' future was cast in eighth grade when he saw a local high school theater production. "As soon as I saw that play, I knew I wanted to do this [production]," he says. By the time he reached high school, he was playing piano in the pit band and running sound for his classmates' theatrical productions. After graduation, he attended Nassau Community College and got further production experience with the Nassau Concerts series at a 600-seat venue, working with such artists as Jeff Healey, Meatloaf, and Melissa Etheridge. At the time, he was studying to be an accountant, until a guidance counselor asked him the question that changed his life: "Do you want to wear a suit and work at a desk, or wear a tee shirt and meet famous people?" It was an easy choice. "From that point on I devoted myself to music."

Accompanying his piano teacher to an Aerosmith concert, Owens got to hang out backstage, where he struck up a conversation with the sound contractor. This chance meeting led to a job as a laborer at Eastern Stage Productions. As is typical with New York production companies, new employees have to prove themselves by working their way up the ladder from the bottom. "I started out just pushing cases. I always carried the attitude—I still do—that I'll do whatever has to be done to make sure the show starts on time and that everybody is happy." Over time, Owens built a reputation for his work ethic and reliability, such that artists asked for him by name.

In 1990, he returned to his roots, running sound for a small Long Island theater company for two years. While there, he met his future employer, who was handling the theater's lighting. Owens worked freelance jobs for the company for six months before joining Glenn Scott Davis Productions full time in 1992 as a sound engineer. He assembled and operated the sound system for touring artists' gigs at major venues and coliseums. While working, he continued to attend college, and graduated in 1993 with a degree in music business with a concentration in audio recording technology.

JOB OVERVIEW

During a live show, the vocalists and musicians require different mixes of music in order to achieve the best overall sound. For instance, the rhythm section may want the drums and bass mixed hotter so they can hear one another to keep the beat tight, while the background vocalists may require the lead vocals and guitar mixed louder so they can harmonize and stay on pitch. The band's overall sound would be distorted if they heard only the feedback from their live performance, with no monitor playing a mix back to them. The monitor engineer gathers all the sound produced onstage, mixes it to each performer's specification, and feeds it back through their respective monitors. This enables the performers to hear the sounds each needs to achieve the best performance.

PROMOTER AND VENUE

BOOKER • BUILDING MANAGER • CHIEF OPERATING OFFICER • GENERAL MANAGER • OWNER • PRESIDENT • PROMOTER • TALENT BUYER

JOB OVERVIEW

These individuals are responsible for the overall direction and operation of the company. They contact talent, negotiate deals, oversee marketing and promotion strategy, and other details associated with promoting concerts and other events.

PREREQUISITES

To succeed, you need a strong knowledge of the touring and promotion aspects of the business; the ability to read a financial statement; marketing skills and salesmanship; honesty and integrity. "I took accounting in college and that, as it turns out, was very important," says Jon Stoll.

A DAY IN THE LIFE

Bill Bachand usually gets into his office between 9 and 9:30 A.M. and begins going through the 20 to 25 phone messages from the previous late afternoon and evening. If the theater had a show the night before, much of his day is spent doing accounting tasks for that event. He is very involved with promotion and meets twice weekly with his staff to go over marketing, advertising, radio events, and ticket sales for upcoming shows. He will check in with his bar, box office, and sponsorship managers. He talks with talent agents and negotiates deals to book artists into the venue, and works closely with his executive director, who also handles bookings. He talks with radio station and newspaper representatives about marketing opportunities. Because he is responsible for the fiscal aspects of the operations, he also spends time working on reports and forecasts.

The first things on the agenda when Jon Stoll arrives at his office is to check his e-mail, sort through phone messages, and find out what is going on around the office. "I try to get in early so that I have time to deal with office administration, advertising plans, and other business. The majority of the work is either in Nashville or California, which are in different time zones. Because of the time difference, our office is open from 9 A.M. to 7 P.M. every day. By the time I finish my other work, agents and building managers are just getting into their offices and I can begin talking with them."

"Listen to the radio, what program directors say. Do your research. If a radio station isn't playing an act, it is going to be hard to sell tickets to see that artist. In fact, it is impossible."—BB

"Pay your bills. Make sure that you always have enough money when the artist arrives to pay them, even if the show stiffs. Otherwise you'll get blackballed and people won't work with you. Do the job right, do the best you can, and make sure everybody gets paid."—BB

"I'm sort of like a doctor, in that I'm on call all the time to bands, managers, and agents. They are on different time zones, whether it be Europe or California, so I'm dealing with things night and day. I tell people when I'm about to hire them, 'You live this job.' "—JS

POINTERS FOR THE JOB SEARCH

Look for opportunities to book and promote bands in local clubs. Get involved with your college concert promotion organization. With that experience, apply to work with a local or regional promoter, or for a building manager that promotes some in-house concerts.

"It is becoming increasingly difficult to become a promoter because of all the national tours going on. It takes a lot of money."—BB

"My best advice is to make allegiances with certain artists and promoters. Try to get yourself a job with a promoter or venue and learn before you go out on your own. You need to be very well financed, too."—JS

CASE STUDY:

BILL BACHAND, GENERAL MANAGER AND CHIEF OPERATING MANAGER, CELEBRITY THEATER, AND PRESIDENT OF MR. BILL PRESENTS

Between graduating from the University of Michigan in 1968 and opening a country nightclub in 1984, the closest Bill Bachand had come to a career in the music business was a short stint selling guitars. In the intervening years, he also sold cars, assembled an apartment and duplex conglomerate, and operated a real estate brokerage company in Arizona. One of those pieces of real estate, a Phoenix dive bar named Toolies, was on the verge of bankruptcy when Bachand took it over. With a little cleaning and some judicious advertising on the local country radio station, the club was turning a profit within 90 days. A year later, the club tripled in size at its new

THE LEAST FAVORITE THING ABOUT THIS JOB:

"My heart lies in the promotion and booking, but I find myself having to spend more time on the administration and paperwork involved in running a large venue, than what I did in a club atmosphere."—BB

"I don't like the fact that there is so much stress and tension, and so many people are insecure in this business today because of a lack of ethics. I don't like the fact that the numbers [cost to book an artist] are so out of sight, that the new entrepreneurs in this world are limited in the concert business."—JS

THE BEST THING ABOUT THIS JOB:

"First, the variety of acts. Second, the fact that in a theater setting, the show is over by 11:00, so rather than getting home at 2 or 3 a.m., like I did at the club, I'm now getting home at midnight. Third, I love the progress we've made at this venue compared with three or five years ago. I love the reaction from people who come to the theater and see the difference we've made in it. I love seeing people smile and having a good time."—BB

"I love the music and I like learning. I like the fact that I discover new artists. I still like putting on shows and feeling the rush when the show starts and seeing new artists."—JS

location and soon became the region's hottest country nightspot. Now attracting top name acts, Toolies played host to everyone from Clint Black and Garth Brooks to Vince Gill and the Dixie Chicks. The success of Toolies brought opportunities to book the entertainment for the Arizona State Fair and promote a few festivals in the area. In 1994, Toolies won the Academy of Country Music (ACM) award for Best Nightclub of the Year, and Bachand won the first ever ACM award for Talent Buyer/Promoter of the Year.

That same year, Bachand began looking for the next challenge. He bought the ailing Celebrity Theater in 1995 and spent more than $1 million renovating and improving the facility. It took a year just to overcome the former owner's bad reputation with both artist management and the public, but by 1998 the theater was successfully hosting concerts for major national acts. Bachand sold Toolies the following year to concentrate on his other ventures. One of those ventures, Mr. Bill Presents, opened in 1991 as an outside talent buying and production company. Through it,

Bachand brokers talent and produces concerts for the Arizona State Fair, as well as corporate and private clients. *www.celebritytheatre.com*

CASE STUDY:

JON STOLL, PRESIDENT/OWNER, FANTASMA PRODUCTIONS

Jon Stoll grew up with music all around him. His mother sang opera and his sister was also a vocalist. At age 15, when all his friends were forming rock and roll bands in their garages, he was organizing those same groups into "battle of the bands" concerts to raise funds for his New York City high school. Soon he was putting together small shows around town and in upstate New York. He watched location film shoots to gain production pointers, which led to his starting a lighting company to do technical production for the shows he organized. In his senior year of high school, Stoll got the opportunity to produce a touring summer concert series in conjunction with a rock radio station, and a friend who owned drive-in theaters. He worked with up-and-coming artists like Bob Seger and Ted Nugent, and earned nearly $100,000 that summer, which provided the start-up capital for his own independent promotion company.

While studying accounting in college, Stoll continued to produce shows in the New York area, but grew tired of New York winters. "It was very cold and gray, and I hated that." He moved to Florida to complete his degree and opened Fantasma Productions. "In the beginning, we did everything from arts and crafts festivals to theater concerts and an occasional area show." Stoll continues to promote live events, including national concert tours, Broadway shows, and events at his company's own theater, nightclub, and restaurant. *www.fantasma.com*

INTERNATIONAL FESTIVAL AND TOUR PROMOTER • INTERNATIONAL PROMOTER

JOB OVERVIEW

Promoters route tours, promote festivals, negotiate contracts, and arrange other details for music artists to perform outside the United States.

PREREQUISITES

To succeed, you need a background in touring and promoting concerts or festivals, and an understanding of the European or other foreign markets. Fluency in a second or third language is

> *"International touring is very detail oriented. If you forget one detail before an artist leaves, they're going to end up paying for it."*
>
> *Learn a second or third language; foreign travel experience is an advantage.*

THE LEAST FAVORITE THING ABOUT THIS JOB:

"Dishonest people: people that say they are going to do an event and cancel it, artists that don't honor their commitments."

THE BEST THING ABOUT THIS JOB:

"Being fortunate enough to have a God-given gift for picking artists that I know will work in Europe, and then they go onstage and they do their show and people go berserk—the audience just goes nuts. That is probably the most satisfying part of my job: knowing that I played a part in bringing those people an evening of happiness."

an asset, as well as experience and contacts in the music industry. Trisha Walker Cunningham cites "a love of people, a love of music, and a love of Europe" as being keys to her success. "There is nothing more satisfying than choosing an artist, based on your gut feeling and ear for music, who you think will work in Europe, and they do."

POINTERS FOR THE JOB SEARCH

A position as an international agent or promoter, and touring internationally with an artist as a road manager, are helpful in learning some of the skills, and making the contacts necessary for this job.

CASE STUDY:

TRISHA WALKER CUNNINGHAM, INTERNATIONAL FESTIVAL AND TOUR PROMOTER, TRISHA WALKER INTERNATIONAL

Born in Singapore, raised in Cyprus and London, an international upbringing proved to be the perfect background for Trisha Walker Cunningham to one day become a global concert promoter. During a short stint at Radio Luxembourg in London, she answered a newspaper ad for an assistant to a concert promoter, who turned out to be the driving force behind the prestigious Wimbledon Country Music Festival. She worked on nine of the annual festivals and was eventually put in charge of the event. "I organized every detail. I did the contracts, the work permits, the musician exchanges. I handled television and press and organized a pre-festival banquet for 600 people, including booking the entertainment." Working with American country artists proved so enjoyable that she decided to move to Nashville in 1978. "I had five hundred dollars in my pocket, a suitcase of summer clothes, and no job. I had never been to Nashville before. I knew three people well enough to call them at home, and all three were out of town. I never felt so lonely. I cried myself to sleep thinking, 'It's got to get better than this.' "

A week later, one of her contacts gave her a backstage pass to Fan Fair, the annual meeting of country artists and their fans, where she met someone who led her to work with a local film company. The company soon went broke, but not before she had made enough contacts to start up her own freelance international promotion office. Her first client was Buddy Lee Attractions, for whom she also handled television and radio bookings of the agency's artist roster. Business continued to build, with Walker Cunningham booking talent for *Nashville Now* and other programming when The Nashville Network (TNN) went on the air in the early 1980s. In 1985, George Strait asked her to handle his in-house publicity, which she did for two years, adding press and public relations to her skills.

In 1987, Walker Cunningham was approached by some of her foreign contacts to handle the promotion of country music festivals in England, Ireland, and Switzerland. She was the first to introduce Reba to Europe in 1989, and over the years has done the same for Emmylou Harris, the Mavericks, Kenny Rogers, Trisha Yearwood, and many more. A short-lived position as head of the international department at the Jim Halsey Company in 1988 convinced her that she was better off working for herself. From then on she has worked for others only on a consulting basis, as with her 1993–1997 association with MCA International. In 1995, Walker Cunningham was honored with the CMA's first International Achievement Award. In 2005, Walker Cunningham took on management duties for Koch Records artist Eric Heatherly.

CREW

ROAD MANAGER • TOUR MANAGER

JOB OVERVIEW

Road managers are responsible for making sure the touring artist is properly represented and that the performance runs smoothly from start to finish. Depending on the size of the tour, the road manager may also oversee travel arrangements and advancement of each performance date. Road managers also act as liaisons between the publicist and the media to ensure that artist interviews and other events run smoothly. They manage the road crew and musicians, reconcile and collect performance fees owed to the artist, and distribute per diems.

PREREQUISITES

"You've got to be able to communicate effectively with people, from the guys unloading your bus, to the promoter and the general public," says Jeff Jackson.

"You've got to be detail oriented so you can keep your road report, and have math skills to handle the money."

A DAY IN THE LIFE

On the road, Jeff Jackson begins the day waking up on the tour bus in the parking lot of a hotel. His first chore is to check into the hotel and distribute the keys and room assignments to the band and crew. "I make sure everyone has a map of where their room is and let them know what time they need to be back on the bus to go to load-in and sound check. If there are scheduled interviews, I might put my artist on the phone for those. I check in with the agency, call the manager, and basically take care of necessary business." After lunch, the band and crew are back on the bus and taken to the venue. "I'll ride the bus down to load-in to meet the promoter or the venue representative while my crew is off-loading the bus, and meet with the box office and set up my tickets. I find out where we're going to have a 'meet and greet' before the show, reconfirm the show times, and check that our catering requests were fulfilled. Usually, I'll ride back to the hotel with the venue runner to pick up my artist for sound check. Once sound check starts, I'll check with our merchandise person, and continue to oversee sound check until the doors open." While the audience arrives, the group eats and relaxes before show time. "Depending on the situation, I typically settle my shows before the performance and if there are any bonuses, I'll do that and the actual ticket count after the show. During this time, the band and crew are loading out. Then we get everybody on the bus and leave for our next destination. We roll through the night and in the morning it starts all over again."

"Although our management office has the capabilities to advance our dates, I prefer to advance my own shows when I'm home. I get deal memos and contracts, once they are fully executed, from the agency. First, I sit down and read the contracts and see what has been agreed to, provision-wise. Then I call the contractor and we literally go through the contract page by page and make sure that we're on the same page as far as what he has agreed to. When I'm home off the road, I also set up hotel rooms and I do the itineraries, and fax them out to my artist, management, the band, and crew. The day before we go back out on the road, I call everyone who will be on the bus and make sure they are aware of our leave times and other details. I call the driver and the bus

CAREER TIPS

"*Remember that everything you and your entourage do reflects upon the artist's image. People aren't going to remember the road manager was impolite; they'll say the artist was rude.*"

"*Surround yourself with people that are better than you because it elevates you, it sort of makes you rise to their level of achievement.*"

company, too. While I'm home, I'm also talking with management and our agency on a daily basis."

POINTERS FOR THE JOB SEARCH

"If you want to be a road manager, you need to get out on the road at any level—whether that's selling tee shirts, as a sideman, or a member of the crew—so you can learn how everything works and have a handle on the political structure of being on the road."

CASE STUDY:

JEFF JACKSON, ROAD MANAGER

Jeff Jackson knew from the time he was in grade school that he wanted to work in a band. At age 15, he and some friends put together a group to play for their Grand Junction, Colorado high school dance. They were terrible, but bass player Jackson felt like a rock star. Moving on to more talented groups as the years passed, in 1989 he played for an artist that got some label attention, and went to Nashville to showcase for Warner Brothers Records. The deal never happened, but Jackson felt at home among the area's musicians and decided to stay.

Planning to land a job as a sideman with a major country artist, Jackson began showing up at all the late night jam sessions where that city's leading players hung out. Doing so allowed him to play with, and learn from, musicians of a caliber he had not been exposed to before. He picked up whatever gigs he could find to support himself and auditioned for various artists, but never made it into a major group. In 1993, through a friend who knew the co-manager of a new country artist, Jackson got another audition. While not hired for the band, his friendly, outgoing personality led management to offer him the position of road manager. The career change did not

THE LEAST FAVORITE THING ABOUT THIS JOB:

"It's a bit like the military, being on the road: you have to hurry, hurry, hurry, and then you end up waiting for two or three hours. The waiting is the worst part. It's not like that every day, but when you're dependent on other people to stay on time, you often end up waiting."

THE BEST THING ABOUT THIS JOB:

"I really enjoy the travel and being in a different place every day."

VOICES OF EXPERIENCE

prove much of a stretch, since Jackson had always been the one to handle business for the regional bands he played in. But, he did have to adjust to the differences of traveling on a national level.

When the artist downsized his organization at the end of the year, Jackson was faced with the choice of returning to the role of musician, or continuing to work as a road manager. He turned down an offer to play bass with a band in order to road manage singer David Ball. Since that time, Jackson has been out on the road almost continuously with artists like Hal Ketchum, Buffalo Club, David Kersch, and Gary Allan.

GUITAR TECH • INSTRUMENT TECH • STRINGED INSTRUMENT TECHNICIAN

JOB OVERVIEW

These technicians ensure that all stringed instruments are in good repair and are on stage for the live performance. This includes electronic repairs, changing strings, and overall upkeep of the instruments. They also clean, polish, tune, and setup the stringed instruments on stage prior to each performance. They are available during the show to change broken strings and handle any other problems, and oversee the packing and transportation of instruments to the next gig.

PREREQUISITES

"Without a doubt, my basic hands-on knowledge of stringed instruments and how they function is the reason for my success. There is a lot of electronics involved. It's knowing how the instrument functions—all the parts that come together to make that whole—knowing how to take care of instruments. I'm kind of a doctor and guitars are my patients. They come to me when they're sick, and I make them well."

A DAY IN THE LIFE

"When you're the headline act, you get everything packed up after the show and get on the bus that night and roll to the next venue. There could be as little as 150 to 200 miles, all the way up to 600 to 700 mile runs overnight. You wake up on the bus at the venue the next morning, stagger into catering and get yourself some breakfast, and start taking care of your individual job. 'Building your world,' as we call it. I build guitar world, the monitor engineer builds monitor world, and so forth."

"You normally start loading-in rigging around 8 A.M., sometimes earlier. The techs are usually the last off the bus because we can't start building our world while the production crew is putting up lights and sound. You don't want to have the guitars sitting out and have a speaker cabinet or lighting tower fall on one of them. Typically, I'm in the building from 10 A.M. and, except for a quick lunch break, I'll work nonstop through sound check. We do a line check before sound check, which means that we technically check everything out before the band comes in to do sound check. Then the band comes in and does sound check, and after that the artist comes in and does another sound check. Everyone has a certain time they arrive at the venue. Once sound check is over, I'll shower, change clothes, and get ready for the show. The technical and production crew doesn't see a hotel at all. Most of the venues have a pro sports team of some sort and we use their showers and lockers as dressing rooms."

"You have to be self-motivated to be a tech, because of the long hours and lack of sleep. It's hard to get out of bed and face another 18-hour day when you've already had three of them in a row."

"I might get an hour to relax, sit on the bus, and watch some television before the show starts. About the time the opening act goes on, I'm back in the building re-tweaking the instruments and making sure everything is fine-tuned. I'll work through the show, and afterward get everything packed up and ready to go on the truck. I take another shower and get back on the bus. That's normally about midnight or 1 A.M. I'll relax a bit and then try and get some sleep while we roll on to the next venue."

POINTERS FOR THE JOB SEARCH

One of the best training grounds for a guitar and instrument tech is to work for an instrument manufacturer where you can learn how to perform basic repairs. Then you are able to offer a prospective employer more skills than just being able to tune the instrument. "Learn the technical aspects of instruments, inside and out. Instruments

THE LEAST FAVORITE THING ABOUT THIS JOB:

"Probably the long hours, in conjunction with not being able to rest very soundly because you're bouncing down the road at 80 miles an hour in a bunk that sometimes feels more like a coffin than a bed. You don't get the real good sleep that your body needs. At the end of a three or four-day run, you come home exhausted."

THE BEST THING ABOUT THIS JOB:

"I really enjoy the camaraderie on the road. It's wild to see so many individualists—the technicians, engineers, musicians, and others—who put aside their differences and come together to make a show happen. When it's show time, there is electricity, a certain vibe, like a switch that turns on. It's really exciting."

are organic by nature because, of course, they are for the most part made of wood. They fluctuate with different temperatures, humidity, and such. They are always contracting and expanding. They can change in 15 minutes. You have to understand that to make them play like they're supposed to."

CASE STUDY:

KEITH PILKINGTON, STRINGED INSTRUMENT TECHNICIAN, THE DIXIE CHICKS

"I was kind of born into pursuing music," says Keith Pilkington, who grew up in a family of guitar pickers in Shelbyville, Tennessee. "On Sunday we used to go to my grandparents' house. My grandfather would play banjo and my grandmother played guitar. They would sit around and pick gospel songs and everybody would sing along." Pilkington became an accomplished player himself, adding his guitar prowess to rock bands before becoming interested in the technical aspects of the instrument. He got a job with acoustic bluegrass guitar manufacturer, Gallagher and Sons, and learned how to build instruments by hand. During that time, he earned a degree in electronics engineering at a local technical school.

In 1990, Pilkington combined his acoustic and electronic expertise at Gibson Guitar in Nashville, doing repairs and custom modifications for two years, until being promoted to the artist relations department. For a year, he networked with the artists who endorsed Gibson guitars, making custom modifications and building relationships. Wanting a new challenge, he left in 1993 to spend three years on the road as a guitar tech with Alan Jackson. The ability to repair acoustic and electric stringed instruments including guitar, mandolin, dobro, banjo, and fiddle—beyond merely tuning and changing strings—is what sets Pilkington apart from the vast majority of other guitar techs.

Looking for a different challenge, he became merchandise manager for Trace Adkins, touring and learning another aspect of the music business. After 18 months, Pilkington needed a break from the road. He sold guitars in a small retail outlet until 1999 when he went to work for the Dixie Chicks. On the road since then, he accompanied the Dixie Chicks on their 2000 tour, the largest production touring out of Nashville that year.

MUSICIANS

MUSICIAN • SINGER • GROUND VOCALIST

JOB OVERVIEW

A road musician is hired to travel with an artist and recreate the music on his album and other material as directed.

PREREQUISITES

To succeed, you should possess musicianship, a friendly and positive personality, and be dependable.

A DAY IN THE LIFE

"I always thought being on the road was like working the second shift," says Tammy Rogers. "Typically, you've rolled into town overnight on the bus, and you don't have to show up anywhere until the middle of the afternoon for sound check, and you don't play until somewhere between eight and midnight. By the time you've done the show and loaded everything back up on the bus, you're rolling to the next

"There is a lot of hurry up and wait, but you have to stay mentally prepared to play. I usually try and get a set list as early as I can and make my notes about what I want to do on it, so I can be as prepared as possible when I step onstage, so I can give the best performance."—BT

"If the lights are down low and you're reading charts, make sure that you have a stand and lights so that you can see."—BT

"Being an employee, a sideman employee, there are certain rules of etiquette. You need to keep your comments to yourself unless someone asks your opinion. Don't be negative. A good positive attitude is part of being a professional."—BT

"So much of this business is people calling people they like to be around. It is personality oriented. People don't just say, 'Get me a guitar player.' They know the players and they know what their personalities are like. If your personality works for you, that's going to be a big plus. Then, you've got to be able to stand there and deliver. I was able to come up through the ranks quickly because when people called me, they knew I would deliver."—TR

"Try to be an easygoing, accommodating person, because out on the road that can be tough when you're cooped up on the bus with six to eight other people for a week at a time."—TR

town around one or two in the morning. You don't get to sleep until three or four o'clock, like the second shift.

"Depending on how far the drive is, you roll into town and you might get there early, and have to wait until your clean-up room is ready, or you might just have time to take a shower and go to sound check. Most of the time, tours are planned to where it's a six or eight-hour drive between the venues, so you usually have time to get up and work out or take a walk, read a book. I used to try to get out and see if I was in an interesting town. Go hit some antique stores, junk shops, or music stores—whatever was local. Then show up at sound check ready to play. There are usually a few hours of downtime before the actual show. That is what you've waited for the whole day: those few moments on stage. That time arrives and you get all dolled up to perform. You play, and when it's over you're back in your sweat pants, tee shirt, and sneakers, and you hop on the bus and roll on to the next town."

"There are no typical days," says Billy Thomas. "Artists like to do sound check at different times of the day. They like to eat at different times of the day. Basically, if you're traveling on a bus, you wake up on the bus and go have some breakfast, which is a social time with all the other players. Then you go to your room and rest for awhile, depending on how much rest you got the night before on the bus. Then you shower and get ready. With Vince [Gill], we have a sound check at 3 P.M. every day. Sometimes he'll sound check for two hours, playing and jamming. He loves to play. We use it as a rehearsal time, try out new songs and just play over the top. If you're the headliner, you get that time available to you. It's stipulated in the contract that you want the stage with all the production from 3 to 5 P.M. Then the opening act comes on after us and sound checks. We eat our dinner and then we have downtime until around nine, when we go on. We stay at the venue during that time. With McBride & The Ride, we played sound check and then went back to the hotel, showered and changed clothes, and then came back for the gig. It varies from artist to artist."

"After the show with Vince, we get back on the bus and change out of our stage clothes, hang out, maybe eat a little something and then travel on to the next city, arriving early in the morning around three or four. We would continue to sleep on the bus until ten or eleven, and go into the hotel and then eat. That was our day. With some artists they want to get off the bus early, when they get in, check into a room and sleep in a bed. Every artist has a different set of rules."

POINTERS FOR THE JOB SEARCH

"Make sure that you know your instrument. That's the bottom line. Try to get out and meet other players. Try to get as much performing experience as you can, preferably before you even get to town, so that when you get an opportunity, you're ready to step up to the plate. Listen to records. Hear what is current so you kind of know the musical vocabulary."—TR

"There is no substitute for moving to where the industry is. Technology is bringing us closer all the time, but you still need to be in the city where music happens. The three main cities are Los Angeles, Nashville, and New York. Pick your poison and go after it."—BT

"It's a real competitive world when it comes to studio or road playing. My advice is to learn to play and sing so you have that competitive edge over someone else that might be good at just one thing."—BT

THE LEAST FAVORITE THING ABOUT THIS JOB:

"The downside of this job is the stress related to being self-employed. Your employment is based on the phone ringing. Sometimes that can be kind of stressful. When the phone is ringing, you feel good and when it's not, you feel bad."—TR

"The actual physical part of traveling, I'm not real crazy about. Now that I've seen all 50 states, mostly by bus, I don't need to do that much anymore. I like to stick around town a little more. I'm a dad and a husband and I'd like to spend more time at home. The road can definitely take its toll, family-wise. I've missed so much in my kids' lives."—BT

THE BEST THING ABOUT THIS JOB:

"Just playing music. Living here in this town [Nashville] we kind of forget how many players there are out there in the world that don't get to support themselves playing music for a living. Quite honestly, I wasn't able to support myself solely from music until I moved to town. I try to never forget that: how fortunate I am to have the opportunities I've had."—TR

"I love the other players in the community. I've been doing this for a long time now, and I feel like the guys [male players] are like brothers to me. It's always a great time to walk into the studio and see half dozen friends sitting there. It's just fun."—TR

"What I like best about performing live is you have an audience's involvement. Also, there is something about playing drums; it's a very physical instrument. I really enjoy that."—BT

CASE STUDY:

TAMMY ROGERS, MUSICIAN, CO-OWNER OF DEAD RECKONING RECORDS

The Texas home where Tammy Rogers grew up was filled with musical instruments and sounds. "My dad always had bunches of instruments lying around the house," she recalls. "My earliest memories are of my parents singing Porter [Wagoner] and Dolly [Parton] songs." Piano was the first instrument she learned, later adding mandolin to her repertoire. But at age ten, the violin became her passion. "It became what I was all about. It was almost second nature, in a sense." She spent her teen years performing around Texas in her father's bluegrass band, and won a full scholarship to Southern Methodist University in Dallas as a classical violin major. She later transferred to Belmont University in Nashville to finish her degree. After graduation, she moved to east Tennessee and played in a bluegrass band for a couple of years.

When a friend recommended her for a job playing fiddle and mandolin, and singing harmony with Patty Loveless, Rogers was sure she would never be considered. To her amazement, she was hired in 1990 and spent the next 14 months on the road. "I was totally green. I had never played in a band with a drummer, never played in an electric band. I had either played classical music or bluegrass." Ready for a new challenge, when Rogers was offered a gig with Trisha Yearwood, she accepted and spent another 15 months on the road. Despite her enjoyment at working with both artists, Rogers felt disappointed at not being asked to play on their records. (Nashville draws a distinction between road and studio musicians.) She decided she wanted to have her own work documented on recordings.

Once Rogers made the decision to actively pursue studio work, the calls started coming in and she was quickly able to make the transition from road musician to studio player. She spent much of her time in Los Angeles for the next two years, playing on pop and alternative country recording sessions with artists like Maria McKee, Victoria Williams, and Rosie Flores. Just when she was about to permanently move to California in 1995, she began getting more work in Nashville, and was soon recording with artists like Pam Tillis, Matraca Berg, and Neil Diamond. That same year, Rogers and several musician friends formed the independent record label, Dead Reckoning, to release music considered outside the Nashville mainstream. Since that time, she has remained in demand for session work both in Nashville and Los Angeles. *www.deadreckoners.com/artists/tammy_rogers.html*

CASE STUDY:

BILLY THOMAS, MUSICIAN, SINGER

"I started my first band when I was 12," recalls Billy Thomas, whose first drum set was a discard from his older brother. "I got the drum set out of the attic and started playing it when I was 11." Thomas taught himself by playing along to Beatles and Gene Krupa records, and learned to read music in the school band. Encouraged by his father, he entered talent contests, and his band played at teen dances in the Fort Meyers, Florida area. He progressed in skill from band to band, finally opening locally for touring groups like the Allman Brothers.

After chasing jobs back and forth between Florida and southern California, with little success, Thomas realized he had to live where the work was, and settled in Los Angeles. "My wife and I drove out with the promise of two weeks worth of work at a little place in Marina Del Rey; that was it. Luckily, she found work and helped support us for a year. I couldn't find work, though, and we moved back to Florida with my tail between my legs." The lack of opportunity in Florida soon convinced the Thomases to take another shot at making it in Los Angeles. Thomas worked with some groups that didn't pan out, struggled to find session work, and ended up driving a furniture delivery truck. Finally, an audition with the Hudson Brothers led to a touring gig. Between session work and his sideman gig, Thomas learned the importance of professionalism: responsibility, punctuality, preparedness, and the ability to convincingly play different styles of music. After several years of touring and recording with the Hudsons, he put in several more years with Rick Nelson's Stone Canyon Band, and then with Mac Davis.

Realizing that Los Angeles was no place to raise children, Thomas moved his family to Nashville, where he quickly found work. "Our furniture had not arrived from Los Angeles. We were living in a little rental and I got a call from a guy in Los Angeles who was looking for me to sing on a record. I got to the session and the other singer was Vince Gill. We sang together for two days, hit it off, and on the second day he asked if I played any instruments." As it turned out, Gill was looking for a drummer and Thomas ended up filling the slot. He performed on the road with Gill, and did session work with Marty Stuart, Emmylou Harris, and others. Thomas went out on the road with Harris before being signed as an artist with the band McBride & the Ride.

When his five-year contract with McBride was up, Thomas left the group to return to recording and touring with Vince Gill. Between gigs with Gill, Thomas is in constant demand, both as a studio drummer and as a backup singer. "The thing that has always given me a little edge when it came down to getting jobs is that I have two talents I can bring to the table: singing and playing drums." Thomas has become a triple threat adding songwriting to his list of talents. He and Gill co-wrote "Nothin' Left To Say," which was released on Gill's four-CD set *These Days*. Thomas also makes time to play with the 1970s pop group The Little River Band.

12

MUSIC FOR FILM, TELEVISION, ADVERTISING, AND NEW MEDIA

What would films like *Forrest Gump*, *The Big Chill*, *Saturday Night Fever*, or *Star Wars* be without music? In the late 1990s, music became increasingly important to television, with programs like *Ally McBeal*, *Felicity*, *Malcolm in the Middle*, and *Melrose Place* featuring music, on-air artist performances, and issuing sound tracks. How many theme songs can you sing? Music is also an intricate part of advertising. Remember The Gap ad featuring khaki-clad swing enthusiasts tossing one another through the air to the sounds of Louis Prima's "Jump, Jive an' Wail?" This chapter profiles some of the people who work behind the scenes of your favorite films, television programs, and advertising campaigns, to ensure there is music to enhance the picture.

For convenience only, this chapter is divided into three categories: Creative, Business Affairs, and Technical. Frequently, those working in a creative capacity also perform business affairs functions and vice versa.

CREATIVE

VICE PRESIDENT • SENIOR VICE PRESIDENT OF MUSIC (FILM STUDIO)

JOB OVERVIEW

At DreamWorks, Todd Homme is responsible for all live action film and television music matters. He works closely with filmmakers to determine music needs, and coordinates with his staff to fulfill their requests by contracting a composer, securing a previously recorded or original song, or procuring a sound track deal. He is also involved in the financial aspects of music use.

PREREQUISITES AND SPECIAL SKILLS

To succeed, you should have a broad knowledge of music, music composition and publishing, and an understanding of how the film industry works. You need diligence in learning about the industry, who the important players are, and staying abreast of new music. The ability to negotiate is important. "You have to be able to get along with people," says Homme, "and it helps to have a sense of humor."

A DAY IN THE LIFE

On any given day, Todd Homme negotiates a fee to hire a composer for a film, or talks through logistics of score production with the composer and producers. He meets with directors and producers throughout the filmmaking process to determine their music needs, such as which composer is desired, specific songs they are interested in licensing, artists they want for recording, and whether there will be a sound track album. At any given time, he usually has eight to ten pictures in various stages of production. He may be on the phone with a record company representative discussing sound track issues, or arranging for the label to receive artwork and marketing materials. "At any moment I might be called to handle paying a guitar player, hire a world-class composer or a superstar artist, book a studio, or establish a music budget for a film." Throughout the day, he attends a screening of a film, meets with other department employees to

"Don't be phony or overstate what you can deliver. Don't run your mouth off about what you can do, just do it. That will be conspicuous enough."

"Do your homework and be diligent about learning." An important part of the job is to know composers and songs—both current and older catalog music—and to be informed about events in both the film and music industry.

CAREER TIPS

ensure they have the information and tools they need, or listens to music for song ideas to pitch to a director.

POINTERS FOR THE JOB SEARCH

Become a member of industry organizations and volunteer to work at seminars and other events so that you are in a situation to meet people and develop contacts. Learn all you can about the industry, such as the names of important players. Become familiar with a variety of musical styles, songwriters, and recording artists. Once you have gained a good base of knowledge, then apply for an internship or assistant position to get a foot in the door.

CASE STUDY:

TODD HOMME, DREAMWORKS

Todd Homme grew up in Saskatchewan, Canada "where everybody freezes and every boy learns to play hockey." As a boy, Homme was torn between dreaming of a

VOICES OF EXPERIENCE

THE LEAST FAVORITE THING ABOUT THIS JOB:

"*Arguing about money. That is a short sentence about a big subject. I work for very conspicuous people in this business, and we're riding the crest of our recent success. We've had Steven's [Spielberg] picture,* Saving Private Ryan, *win several Oscars, including Best Director. Then most recently,* American Beauty, *which was a small film, done for a modest budget with a first-time director and a first-time writer (both of whom won Oscars), together with a young cast. In many respects, it was a small project. The fact that there are three guys that run this company [David Geffen, Jeffrey Katzenberg, Steven Spielberg], that are very big in the industry, doesn't mean every project has an enormous budget. Sometimes you get tired of explaining that we have budgets and limits we have to live within.*"

THE BEST THING ABOUT THIS JOB:

"*Variety. There are all kinds of commingling of people, ideas, attitudes, and challenges. There is always something new. I like working with the people in creative disciplines that are the best in their given field. You get to talk with them and ask questions about their own journey. That is pretty wonderful.*"

career as a hockey player, or as a guitarist. Little did he know that hockey would one day be the key that would open the door to a job in the music business.

Homme attended Berklee College of Music in Boston, then kicked around in a few bands and gained some recording experience, before heading west in 1989. In Los Angeles, he quickly discovered the city already had too many great studio musicians. He found a job to make ends meet and began coaching and playing amateur hockey. "I ended up on a team with some agents and other entertainment people. I was hating my job and asked if anyone knew anyone in the music business." A teammate gave him the name of Bill Schrank, vice president of music production at Warner Brothers Studios, and suggested that he write a letter, since Schrank was too busy to talk on the phone. Soon afterward, Homme was unemployed and beginning to worry about his lack of prospects. About a week after he had sent the letter, he decided to try to reach Schrank by telephone. "I was walking downstairs to make the call and the phone rang, and it was him on the other end of the line." Homme was invited to come by the studio to talk, where he learned about jobs he never knew existed, including one he thought he would be perfect for: the one Schrank held. "He said, 'Good luck! There are about seven of these jobs in the business, one per studio.'"

Over the next eight months, Homme was only able to get three or four interviews in unrelated fields. He even offered to work for free, just to gain experience, but was turned down for insurance reasons. At the point when things looked desperate, Schrank Homme was hired as manager of music production at Disney Studios. Unaware of his status at his new job, Homme recalls, "I was taken to my office by my assistant (I would have taken the job as my own assistant) and she said, 'You've got a meeting tomorrow morning at eight.' I said, 'Will there be any executives there?' She said, 'Duh. You are an executive.' It was really kind of wacky and unbelievable, because I got the job I dreamt about."

Determined not to lose this opportunity, Homme learned his duties while working on the 11 films and sound tracks then in production. Over the next four years, he worked on a total of 75 films. A few months after DreamWorks was formed, he came on board as the equivalent of vice president of film music (there are no titles at DreamWorks), working on such box office hits as *Gladiator, Almost Famous*, and Academy Award winning films *Saving Private Ryan, American Beauty, Catch Me If You Can, Road to Perdition*, and *Collateral*. Homme still plays on a hockey team, which includes some of the industry's most successful actors, agents, producers, and directors, and credits it as being the single most important networking tool he has ever discovered. *www.dreamworks.com*

PRESIDENT OR VICE PRESIDENT OF MUSIC

JOB OVERVIEW

These executives are charged with supervision of the music in both production and post-production phases, with an emphasis on pre-existing music. Some also supervise the scoring and mixing process.

SPECIAL SKILLS

"Being organized, responding properly, and keeping my word," are skills Celest Ray cites as keys to her success. "Knowledge of the music business and a good business sense is important, and an understanding of music publishing, and how record companies work is essential."

A DAY IN THE LIFE

During her hour-long commute to work, Ray listens to music. "I might be picking music for a bar mitzvah in one show and the opening credits for another." Once she arrives at the office, her first task is to confirm arrangements for an artist appearance on a show, make sure the poster art has arrived, and finalize any necessary approvals. Twice monthly, she attends spotting sessions with a television show's executive producer, associate producer, composer, and music editor to pick out scenes where music, whether songs or score, are needed. On any given day she talks with songwriters, publishers, record company representatives, and artist managers, or she may work up a music budget to present to a producer. Charged with overseeing the licensing of masters and publishing owned by Spelling Productions, she provides quotes and approves their use.

POINTERS FOR THE JOB SEARCH

"The best advice that I can give to somebody who wants to be a music supervisor is to find somebody that you respect that you can model," says Ray. Work hard and look for opportunities to prove yourself. "When I was working in business affairs and I wanted to do a

"When we put our fears first, we always lose. I hope that I grow old in the business and that I'll grow to drop my fears, believe in myself, and be a guide for truth. Know that you can be who you are and still succeed."

Be constantly listening to music so that you have a vast library of music in your head to pull from. Write down notes about songs that resonate with you as a quick reference for when you're looking for music.

more creative job, I stood up to the plate and asked for the opportunity. Then, I would stay late to do the work, over and above my business affairs work. Instead of being resentful that nobody was letting me try to be a creative person, I took that on in addition to my other work, and people came to rely on me more and more for my creative input."

CASE STUDY:

CELEST RAY, VICE PRESIDENT OF MUSIC, AARON SPELLING PRODUCTIONS

A job meant to supplement her income while in college changed Celest Ray's career path from nursery school teacher to music executive. "I fell in love with the music business. I always loved music and I really liked the mix of the business aspect with the creative aspect." As secretary at an independent record label and music publishing company, owned by artist Johnny Rivers, Ray gained experience in every conceivable aspect of the business and was eventually promoted to general manager. After ten years working for Rivers, she was ready for a new challenge. In 1983 she accepted an offer from producers Norman Lear and Jerry Perrenchio to be director of music for Embassy Pictures. During her tenure, Ray supervised such films and sound track albums as *This Is Spinal Tap*, *Stand By Me*, and *A Chorus Line*. When Embassy's theatrical division was sold to Dino DeLaurentis in 1987, she stayed on, working on *Crimes of the Heart* and *Bill and Ted's Excellent Adventure*, among others.

Embassy went bankrupt in 1992, but Ray already had been operating her own company, Music in Motion, since 1988. As a contractor, she cleared music rights for *Seinfeld*, numerous projects with MGM and Universal film studios, and a series of film sound track albums for Big Screen Records. Hired part time by Ken Miller to clear music rights for the first season of *Beverly Hills 90210*, she was then asked to supervise music for *Melrose Place* the following year. Ray took a position at

THE LEAST FAVORITE THING ABOUT THIS JOB:

"The politics—I don't like it when deals should happen, but they don't because there is a personal interest in conflict. Or, when one executive won't talk to another executive because they don't want to admit that they have to ask a question."

THE BEST THING ABOUT THIS JOB:

"Picking music and seeing that what I've selected tickles the fancy of whomever I'm pitching it to. Then, seeing it on screen, seeing that it really works. That's what I love most about my job."

VOICES OF EXPERIENCE

Paramount Studios in 1994, but after six months was hired full time by Spelling Entertainment Group as director of music coordination and continued to supervise music for *Melrose Place*. Promoted to vice president of music, today Ray is involved in numerous Spelling television productions, including *Charmed*, *Kindred*, and *Any Day Now*. Ray also served as music coordinator for the television series *7th Heaven*, from 1996 to 2007.

MUSIC SUPERVISOR

JOB OVERVIEW

A music supervisor is hired to oversee all the music that is used in a production, whether on film or television. The supervisor works closely with the director in selecting songs, choosing a composer (if one is used), and acquiring the rights for the production to use the songs. If there is a sound track, the supervisor secures the record deal and works with the appropriate parties to bring the album to release.

SPECIAL SKILLS

"The ultimate skill is sensitivity," says Barklie Griggs. "When they're looking at a scene in a film, you have to imagine how that character feels. What is happening in their life in this movie and what song could make that scene better; what music could enhance the feeling. Being perceptive about what the director is trying to convey. Also, knowing every kind of music and remembering songs."

Julie Houlihan says, "I think the number one thing that has made me successful is my passion for music. I love all different kinds of music. I think that a good music supervisor has both sides of their brain working. You have a budget that you stick to and clearances to get. You have to work with a lot of people—studio executives, directors, producers, the sound track company—with many different agendas. You have to learn to be a problem solver and to think through issues. You have to be strong on the business side and creative side."

A DAY IN THE LIFE

"I get to the office between 9:30 and 10 A.M.," says Griggs. "For two to three hours, I play songs to see if the music I've picked for a film fits appropriately into each scene. Between, I jump on my computer and check who wrote the song, who has the rights, and how much it will cost to use it." Once Griggs determines a song will fit into the film's budget, he places the appropriate CD into a pile that he will later play for the director. In the early afternoon, he makes calls to publishers, record company people, and directors. Between 2 and 4 P.M., he drops by the editing room and plays songs for the film's director. Afterward, Griggs makes calls to find music or to get more specific information about a song. He may be involved in negotiating a com-

"The most valuable asset that you can have in this business is trust."—BG

"Be straight with people and expect and demand the same from them, and you'll save a lot of time."—BG

"There are a lot of talented music supervisors, that are not musicians and don't know their way around the recording studio, that still do a good job. But, I think I have a little bit of an edge on them, being a musician, because I can talk to composers a little more specifically about things."—JH

Listen to all genres and time periods of music and take notes to remind yourself of songs you want to file away for future use.

poser deal, working to get a new song recorded by a specific artist, or putting together a sound track deal. In the evening, he often attends film screenings.

"When I'm working on a movie," explains Houlihan, "I might get up and go to the casting session in the morning. Then, around noon, I might have a pitch meeting at *Roswell*. I'll spend an hour to an hour and a half there and then go straight from there to the editor's suite and lay songs in with the music editor. Then I'll return to my office and give my assistant a list of songs we want to get clearances for. I'll cram in listening to songs, because I have a *Malcolm in the Middle* pitch meeting the next morning." Once a week she sits with the *Roswell* music editor and makes sure that the correct music has been cut in, and that it matches her clearance paperwork. If a song doesn't work, they may make a decision on the spot to change it. She listens to music whenever she can, in the car, while in the office; she even carries a DiscMan while taking a walk.

POINTERS FOR THE JOB SEARCH

"Do your homework. That means you have to know your music. It really helps when you're listening to the radio and you hear a song you like, if you stop and remember how it makes you feel. Did it make you feel sad or happy? What kind of scene could you see it in? Remember the feeling, the song title, and the album. Start compiling CDs and make a separate place for songs you love."—BG

"I would advise people who want to music supervise to get some type of assistant job. You're learning a craft, a trade, and it has its own specific language. You need to learn publishing and licensing, and who manages whom. My advice would be to get a

THE LEAST FAVORITE THING ABOUT THIS JOB:

"There is a certain amount of ego in the movie business, and some of those with bad egos, can ruin the business because they make everything so uncomfortable and limiting. You're not inspired by somebody trying to impose their will just because they can, not because that is the best creative choice."—BG

"The clearances and legal work."—JH

THE BEST THING ABOUT THIS JOB:

"Being able to have control over, or having a big part of, the emotion of a scene that makes people feel a certain way. There is nothing greater than sitting in a screening of a movie, and a scene comes on that you really know the music is going to start turning people inside out emotionally. They start to feel love or scared or conflicted, that's really the best part of this job. You get to have a creative impact on a movie."—BG

"I love being involved with the creation of new songs and new covers of songs."—JH

job with a music supervisor, a film studio, a television studio, or a record company, and just absorb as much as you can."—JH

CASE STUDY:

BARKLIE GRIGGS, MUSIC SUPERVISOR/OWNER, TILTED WORLD MUSIC

It would be hard to decide which Barklie Griggs loves more: films or music. As a teenager, the two consumed all his time and money. "I was always a music fan and a movie buff. I loved going to see movies and I loved listening to music. I paid attention to the music used in films. "I'm Alright" by Kenny Loggins in *Caddyshack*, Simple Minds' "Don't Forget About Me" in *The Breakfast Club*, "Get Into The Groove" by Madonna in *Desperately Seeking Susan*, the sound track to *Diner* was a favorite. I began to buy sound tracks and just started learning more and more about music."

After graduating from high school, Griggs left New York for Los Angeles, and worked as a waiter while trying to decide what to do with his life. In conversation with a regular customer one day, he discovered that the man was a music supervisor for films. The idea that someone actually did that for a living had never occurred to Griggs. But now that it had, he saw the way to combine his two great loves. Offering to quit his job on the spot and work for free to learn the business, he was politely turned down. Undaunted, he formulated a plan.

Griggs began going to a record store every day, reading album covers, and making a list of the names and titles of all the music people involved with film sound tracks. "I started to learn who all the players were." Through a friend who knew a theatrical director, he began supplying music for plays. He studied *The Hollywood Reporter*'s film and television music issue, learning everything he could about the people who held the job he wanted. After four months, he quit waiting tables and began telephoning everyone on his list.

The roommate of a friend, who had on a few occasions spoken to music supervisor Sharon Boyle, made an introductory call on Griggs' behalf, securing an opportunity for him to send a resume and cover letter. "I had zero on my resume. I had no record business experience, nothing. I had just worked in restaurants. So I sent a cover letter that basically said, 'I'm a record junky and I know a lot about music. I have over 800 records and I would die to work for you. And, I make really good coffee.' That was a lie. I couldn't make coffee for the life of me." After several follow-up calls trying to get a meeting with Boyle, Griggs was given an appointment. "It was Monday, the fourth of March, 1990. I threw myself at her. I said, 'Please, I'll do anything. I'll work for free. I'll work from midnight to 6 A.M.'" With no openings at the company, Griggs left the interview with only the assurance that Boyle would consider his offer. The very next day, one of Boyle's employees decided to go part time, and she decided to give Griggs a chance to come in on a temporary basis and see how things went. He ended up staying for five years, and worked on a number of big films, including *Mr. Holland's Opus*. Ready to test his wings, he opened Tilted World Music in 1995, and under his own company banner, has supervised a number of independent films, most notably *Still Breathing, Thick As Thieves, Guinevere, Wing Commander, Ring of Fire, Nine Lives,* and *The Jane Austen Book Club*.

CASE STUDY:

JULIE HOULIHAN, MUSIC SUPERVISOR/OWNER, HOULIHAN FILM MUSIC

"I have always been involved in music," says Julie Houlihan. Singing in a choir led her to study voice at Southern Methodist University, followed by short stints with the Dallas Opera, and a touring pop band. Tired of life on the road, she got a job as a morning news producer at a Little Rock radio station for a couple of years. "Although I loved news and felt it was a really important job getting information out to people, it wasn't creative enough for me. I missed music." Leaving radio news behind, she found work at a video production house, learning to write, direct, and produce regional commercials and corporate videos. After another couple of years passed, she felt prepared to take on a bigger challenge. "I decided I would move to L.A., even though I didn't exactly know what I was going to do."

In Los Angeles she discovered that not only was video production a specialized field, in California it was unionized. She found work in a film lab to keep money coming in, while she familiarized herself with the market. In 1994, she got a job as assistant to the vice president of music at New Line Cinema. "I had never been an assistant before, but I knew it was my only way into the industry. I was 28 years old and I had been a vice president of production, and a new producer. I never even considered answering anybody's phones, or typing people's memos, but that is a thing you learn when you get out here [Los Angeles]: the only way to get a job is to be an assistant." Over the next couple of years, she learned supervision from the ground up and slowly began to earn music coordinator film credits. When she was offered a better job at MCA Music Publishing, working with artists and writers and pitching their music for use in film and television, she moved. "They let me do a little music supervision on the side. It takes a while for people in the industry to get to know you and trust you, to build your reputation up so they will trust you with their film project. You're responsible for a lot of money, not to mention the creative ideas."

In 1998, with four years of film work to her credit, she took the plunge into music supervising and, opened Houlihan Film Music. Her first project was *Eve's Bayou* for Trimark, which became the film company's biggest hit to date. Among Houlihan's many subsequent television projects are *Sweet Water* for VH-1, *2+Gether* for MTV, *Roswell* for WB, and *Malcolm in the Middle* for Fox.

BUSINESS AFFAIRS

JOB OVERVIEW

The business affairs office is responsible for obtaining clearances for all music used in film, television, trailers, and other media produced by the company.

PREREQUISITES

A background in publishing or knowledge of music licensing is required. "You have to be able to handle multiple tasks at the same time," say Julie Butchko. "Literally, you're talking on the phone, researching a song, making notes as you're going along, and thinking about what your next step is as far as clearing or finding a song. You have to be organized. You have many different projects at different junctures. You're working on movies that are in post-production and movies that are done, from the initial clearing of songs, to writing up the cue sheets and registering copyrights. You really have to be resourceful, as far as tracking down the owners of songs and the artists that recorded them, and who owns the master rights."

A DAY IN THE LIFE

Julie Butchko beings her day handling incoming faxes. "Normally, there are one or two pieces of business that I'm waiting for an urgent answer on. I like to make my London and New York phone calls in the morning and get those out of the way. I try to touch base with as many people as possible. The rest of the time is spent reading scripts, sending out quote requests, researching music, and doing budget estimates. Guiding the producers and the production staff of television shows, as far as music. How much it's going to cost and how much time we're going to need. What they can and cannot do with a piece of music, and other obligations and costs that they are not necessarily aware of. Throughout the day we get phone calls from our TV shows, from our marketing staff, and from the producers of the films we're working on as far as new music that has come up that they want to get cleared for their projects. We start researching that and I start contacting the publishers and the record labels for clearances, and getting the quotes, clearing the songs for sound track use, and negotiating those deals. Because the world of DVD has opened up, they put a lot of extra bonus materials on them to make them more consumer friendly, so you might have outtakes from the movie, behind the scenes footage, or interviews. This extra programming either isn't cleared because it was not in the film, or it was dropped out of the film, so we didn't pay for those rights. We work with our DVD department and try and clear things at a reasonable rate for them to include all these extra little goodies."

"Getting people checks; getting people paid for their music. Requesting licenses and reviewing licenses that come in. Doing cue sheets for the numerous television shows and films, and different marketing specials is a normal part of the day. Working with our copyright registration people and the score side of our business. Reporting to Todd Homme and Mary L. Jacobs on the music status in the films that I'm working on for them. Licensing the film scores that DreamWorks owns— I don't just spend money, I make it. E-mail is constant."

POINTERS FOR THE JOB SEARCH

"Don't be embarrassed to start out as an assistant. Soak up any possible information, that you can while you're at that desk. When you're an assistant, you hear a lot more about what's going on, about all kinds of different transactions and

> "It's important to be open and honest." It makes it much easier to negotiate a fair deal for a music license if you trust and respect the person on the other end of the phone.
>
> Build relationships with fellow clearance people who you can ask for advice and with whom you can compare deals and pricing.

THE LEAST FAVORITE THING ABOUT THIS JOB:

"All the paperwork that lingers on for months on end, sometimes, after a film is done. I wish things could be wrapped up as quickly as they are started."

THE BEST THING ABOUT THIS JOB:

"I love the feeling you get when you can finally clear a song with an artist or the songwriter. A song that your director really wants and you know it's going to be great for the film, but it's a really hard clearance, or it might be particularly expensive. Just knowing that in the end, you got the approval, and you got it at a price that you thought was fair, and you know that everyone was just waiting for that song to clear because they really wanted it in their movie. It's a really great feeling to know you helped."

pieces of business, that you may not necessarily hear if you're just in one specific position in an office. I think when you're an assistant, you have a good opportunity to be exposed to a lot of different sides of the business. You can learn how things are done and at what stage they're done."

CASE STUDY:

JULIE BUTCHCO, MUSIC CLEARANCE FOR DREAMWORKS

Julie Butchco's introduction to the music business came as a result of her high school student government activities, when she was assigned to hire bands and organize entertainment for school dances. Upon entering the University of California at Santa Barbara, she considered going into entertainment law, but wasn't convinced she wanted to be an attorney. "I just decided to get a job in the industry and see if I liked it." Resumes and interviews failed to produce results, until a cousin was able to get Butchco an interview with the producer of *The Young and the Restless* through a contact with one of the show's writers. The interview was purely informational, as the show had no openings, but did result in a referral to a producer at Columbia Pictures Television. After that interview she was hired as an assistant in the television licensing department.

After a few years in television licensing, Butchco landed an assistant position in film licensing. Not anticipating another move quite so soon, it came as a surprise when a friend called in 1996 to say he had suggested her for a position at newly created DreamWorks, and she was requested to call Todd Homme for an interview.

Many candidates were anxious to work at the prestigious new studio, but Butchco was a perfect fit for the job of clearing music for film and television. Since joining DreamWorks, Butchco has worked on numerous projects, including award winning films: *Saving Private Ryan*, *American Beauty*, *Shrek*, and *Madagascar*.

EXECUTIVE VICE PRESIDENT • OWNER • PRESIDENT • VICE PRESIDENT (MUSIC CLEARANCE AND LICENSING)

JOB OVERVIEW

These executives handle film and television music supervision, clearance and licensing of songs, invoicing and bills payable, and oversee the day-to-day company operations.

PREREQUISITES

To succeed, you should have a broad knowledge of music genres, the ability to negotiate, people skills, and an understanding of music publishing and master licensing.

A DAY IN THE LIFE

When Kathleen Merrill arrives at the office, she boots up her computer and checks e-mail from publishers, societies, record companies, clients, and potential clients who may have found information on the company's web site and need specific questions answered. Then she works through incoming faxes and responds to questions and requests for fee quotes to use specific songs. "We receive all of our requests for quotes in writing. We have a form that we send to clients. Particularly when you're working on a television show, you develop a pattern where the client knows the specific information you need, they fill out the form and fax it to you, and you run with it. You don't

"You have to have a pretty thick skin. You might think some piece of music is a great idea, but your client doesn't like it at all. You can't get offended by that."

"Learn about many genres of music." The more songs you know, the more indispensable you are to your clients.

"You have to learn to deal with both creative and business people, or you will never survive. You have to be a people person."

CAREER TIPS

THE LEAST FAVORITE THING ABOUT THIS JOB:

"When some of the people who own music try to back out of the quote they have given, because they have something better that has come up."

THE BEST THING ABOUT THIS JOB:

"Looking at a tape of a scene. It doesn't matter what it is—a commercial, television show, or film segment—knowing the demographic that my client wants, and coming up with great ideas for music. Then, negotiating and getting the use for the music they want, and having the client just thrilled about it."

really need to talk, you just fax them back the information." Next, Merrill makes phone calls to people with outstanding quotes, asks them to respond, and generally puts out any fires that have arisen. "A lot of times I'll get calls from people who are desperate. They're out of time and they need to get a song cleared." She receives an average of 50 CDs a week and generally listens to two or three songs from each, so throughout the day, she is constantly listening to music. In between, she may offer clients suggestions of music to use, work on budgets, or invoice clients.

POINTERS FOR THE JOB SEARCH

A position as an assistant or intern to an independent music supervisor is a good way to gain a broad understanding of the business, both from a creative and business point of view. Working for the clearance department of a film studio, or a music publisher, is another way to gain experience.

CASE STUDY:

KATHLEEN MERRILL, PARTNER, PARKER MUSIC GROUP

Kathleen Merrill grew up in the San Francisco Bay area and learned the craft of deal making by licensing commercial real estate, before switching to music. "Pieces of music are like any other kind of property. They are intellectual property, and when you want to use them, you have to license them." On a temporary basis, Merrill set aside real estate to handle music licensing for Randy Parker, whose partner had become ill. When the job ended, she went to work in the legal department of Princess Cruise Lines. Later, when Parker formed Parker Music Group, he invited Merrill to join him on a permanent basis. "We enjoyed working together earlier. We complemented each other in our skills and our music knowledge."

Merrill, now a partner in Parker Music Group, has worked on national advertising campaigns for Nissan Motor Company and Fox Television Studios, among others. She has licensed music for numerous television shows, including *X-Files*, *The Simpsons*, *Ally McBeal*, *Law & Order*, *Will & Grace*, and *The Office*, as well as for films, most notably for the *Titanic* sound track. *www.musicclearance.com*

TECHNICAL

MUSIC EDITOR

JOB OVERVIEW

A music editor coordinates the technical aspects of film scoring between the production company and the composer.

PREREQUISITES

To succeed, you should possess musicality, and technical knowledge of, and skill using, music editing equipment; you must be highly motivated, and have the ability to deliver on schedule. "Being diplomatic; able to listen carefully to what people are trying to communicate and then fulfilling their desire without a lot of problems, guesswork, or questions back and forth. It is very important to shut off your mind and listen carefully to what the director is trying to say to you."

A DAY IN THE LIFE

Music editor Jeff Chabonneau's schedule is dictated by where he is in the process of adding music to picture for his current project. On a film spotting day, he meets in the studio with the film producers, director, film editor, and composer. They review scenes to determine where the music should start and end, discuss any stylistic concerns, and address any other issues. If there is a temporary score already in place, they might discuss whether it works in different scenes. They talk about specific songs they want to use and address any synchronization problems, if there is a live performance. The director may discuss a statement he wants to emphasize with music in a particular scene. "Involvement in the spotting session varies from film to film and project to project. Sometimes the composer and the music editor will spot the film on their own, and give their notes or ideas to the producer or the director, although that is very rare. On the series I work on, which is the *X-Files*, I do all the music spotting on my own. I give my notes to the composer and the producers, and they give me feedback. The reason we've done it this way is to streamline the process, because we don't have an enormous amount of time to do the score, and there is a lot of music in the show. They trust me with knowing, or figuring out, where to put the music in, and where to take it out."

"In this business there is always a deadline. A person has to be able to deal with that pressure and accept that responsibility. Know that you're going to have to set aside your own personal life at times in order to fulfill the job. That can be stressful when you've planned a weekend and that gets dumped because the schedule has changed, and you have to get things done by Monday, as opposed to Tuesday or Wednesday. Deadlines are very important. Being punctual is extremely important. These are skills that are necessary."

After the spotting is complete, Chabonneau goes through the film to time the sequences and create timing notes, a breakdown of what is happening in each scene. This is typed out for the composer to see. Within a couple of days, the composer returns with the score, and the music editor and an engineer mix the score. Then, the music editor goes to the re-recording stage and guides the music mixer on how the music should fit into the scene, such as where the music is too loud or too soft, where it should build and fade, and any background source issues. Depending upon the project, the re-recording process can take one to three days, or three to four weeks. "On a television show, we're usually on the stage for about two days." Next, the producers and director may suggest changes, such as adding a sound to a scene, or switching out a particular piece of music.

Those changes are made immediately. The next phase is to document the music. The music editor writes down the timing and order of each piece of music used in the film, adds the author's and publisher's names, and turns over the information to the studio legal department to issue contracts and licenses. The last task is to create a backup of all the materials so they can be placed in the studio vault, and a copy of the score is sent to the Library of Congress for copyright purposes.

THE LEAST FAVORITE THING ABOUT THIS JOB:

"The element I like the least is the egos and personalities involved in the business."

THE BEST THING ABOUT THIS JOB:

"The work itself. I've got the type of brain where I like doing something very creative. I think I have a real aptitude for combining sound and image together in a way that works. I enjoy that aspect. I like the challenge. I view it as a puzzle that I can solve. I like being able to go through and measure music against a picture and make it work."

POINTERS FOR THE JOB SEARCH

"The way I got established was to work on low budget and no budget films to gain some skills and meet people. When those people ended up working on bigger projects, they took me along with them in a lot of cases. This job takes an investment in material costs, too. You have to essentially own a mini recording studio in order to be viable in the present film economy. No one wants to rent equipment for you. They want you to come fully equipped with state-of-the-art equipment and know how to operate it effectively. When they consider hiring you to do a project, the first questions asked are, 'Do you have a ProTools system? Is it transportable? Can you bring it to a stage? How much are you going to charge us to rent it?'"

CASE STUDY:

JEFF CHABONNEAU, MUSIC EDITOR

After playing in rock and roll bands as a teenager, Jeff Chabonneau studied classical guitar at the University of Wisconsin before switching to biology in his junior year. He began his graduate work in anthropology at the University of California at Los Angeles. "About the four-year point of graduate school, I ran out of scholarship and grant money, and decided I really needed a job." Through a friend, he was introduced to another academic who had returned to music as a composer for New York-based Score Productions, writing music for television soap operas, game shows, and sporting events. Impressed with Chabonneau's musical talent, the composer helped him land a job as music supervisor of the soap opera *Capitol*, filmed in Los Angeles. A year later, he was ready for a bigger challenge.

When he heard that the major film studios had jobs for music editors, but not knowing exactly what that entailed, Chabonneau boldly called 20th Century Fox to apply. Told that he needed both experience and union membership to qualify, he left his phone number anyway. Two days later, he got a call to interview for an apprentice music editor position. Hired for his ability to both play and read music, he worked there for two years before the studio closed down the department. For the next three years, Chabonneau worked in television at a small firm in Burbank, frequently with well-known composer, Mike Post.

When Post opened his own music editing company, Chabonneau was one of four editors hired. After two years at Interlock, he returned to film work at MGM, then went out on his own as a freelancer, specializing in temporary music scores for film previews. Chabonneau served as music editor on the highly acclaimed series *The X Files* from 1993 to 2002, when the series ended. He went on to work on another acclaimed series, *24*.

● ● ● ●

13

MEDIA: PRINT, RADIO, AND TELEVISION

The media make the public aware of music by broadcasting it, talking about it, and writing about it. An entire book could be devoted to the diverse jobs available in music journalism, radio, and television. This chapter highlights one job in each category.

JOURNALISM

CRITIC • JOURNALIST • REVIEWER • WRITER

JOB OVERVIEW

Journalists compose reviews, articles, columns, and other text about artists, music, and the music industry.

PREREQUISITES

Verbal and writing skills are essential, and the ability to work with people is important.

POINTERS FOR THE JOB SEARCH

"You have to be willing to be poor. If you can hack that, you've got a shot. You certainly can't be living in an apartment in Manhattan, unless you're squatting or living with mom. There is no money in writing. You're treated as though you're at the absolute bottom of the totem pole. It's something you do because you're driven to do it."

CASE STUDY:

JOHN SWENSON, WRITER, SENIOR EDITOR, JAZZ.COM

"I wanted to be a writer first," says music journalist John Swenson, whose first byline appeared in his high school newspaper. "Growing up during the 1960s in New York, I was drawn to the coffeehouse scene in Greenwich Village—the beatniks, folk music, and blues." He entered Manhattan College in 1968 to study physics ("I was on a full scholarship. If you're smart, you're suppose to study sciences."), but switched to English after his first year. He worked on the college newspaper staff, first writing film reviews, then a record review column, progressing to feature editor and editor-in-chief. "I really learned what it is to be a journalist and I learned a lot about your responsibility to your audience," says Swenson. "It was the best training to learn to be a journalist." After contributing to numerous underground newspapers for two years, he was hired by *Crawdaddy* magazine in 1974 as a feature editor.

"It is really interesting to see the next wave of people coming into Rolling Stone who are Ivy League graduates, who expected journalism to be a fast track to glib success. Virtually none of those people have stayed journalists. They became publicists or talking heads or advertising people."

Write, write, write—for your school newspaper or a local music magazine; write articles to pitch to publications; be working on something all the time.

THE LEAST FAVORITE THING ABOUT THIS JOB:

"Not being able to hire people when my budget freezes."

THE BEST THING ABOUT THIS JOB:

"Working with young writers. First of all, when you edit people, you have an exchange of ideas. More interesting things always happen when people exchange ideas; the faster the exchange, the better. It's like watching a tennis match; you sharpen your skills. I don't know what I'm going to say before I say a sentence and you don't know what I'm going to say. You may have some stock questions you're going to ask me, but the nature of the conversation is a mystery. As it unfolds, we both learn things. That's what happens when you work with people as an editor."

Two years later he was hired by *Rolling Stone* magazine as a freelance writer, and over the years has served as co-editor of the first two *Rolling Stone Record Guide*s, and as editor of the original *Rolling Stone Jazz Guide*. He put in freelance stints with both *Circus* and *High Times* magazines as editor of their record review sections.

In 1984, Swenson slowly went broke writing music biography books until, almost destitute, he took a job in 1986 as a syndicated weekly music columnist with United Press International (UPI). As CNN usurped UPI's position in the news world, he moved to the *New York Post* in 1990 and worked as a horseracing columnist. He was out of work again when a new owner took over in 1993, and fired the entire newspaper staff. Tired of office work, he continued to write about the music scene as a freelance reporter. Swenson's articles are printed in leading industry magazines worldwide, and he serves as senior editor of jazz.com. In 1999, he edited the *Rolling Stone Jazz and Blues Album Guide*. *www.jazz.com*

RADIO

MUSIC DIRECTOR • PROGRAM DIRECTOR • STATION MANAGER

JOB OVERVIEW

The program and/or music director is responsible for selecting the music and formulating a playlist of songs to broadcast on the air. This may sound easy, but it is a studied skill. Songs are selected based on the musical format of the station and the demographics of the target listener, content, and other criteria. The program/music director is also involved in developing contests, promotions, and marketing campaigns for the station. Most program directors are former disc jockeys.

DISK JOCKEY • DEEJAY • JOCK • ON-AIR PERSONALITY

JOB OVERVIEW

The disc jockey, or on-air personality, is responsible for making sure there is no dead air time by filling the time with music and patter. The deejay introduces songs, does commercials, reads news, and is expected to have an engaging personality and voice that keeps listeners tuned in.

PRODUCER (OFTEN THE SIDEKICK TO THE ON-AIR PERSONALITY)

JOB OVERVIEW

In many cases, the radio producers are backup for the on-air personality whose show they produce. They research, write, and assist in advance planning of the show and are available throughout the on-air time to assist the on-air personality.

SPECIAL SKILLS

"Listening and typing," are two skills that have proved extremely important to producer Devon O'Day's success. "You have to type in real time on a computer keyboard so that your host can see it while he's on the air. I type 120 words a minute."

A DAY IN THE LIFE

"My alarm goes off at 3:30 A.M. and I turn on a news channel or CNN and let my subconscious absorb whatever is on," says O'Day. "I get a wake up call at 4:10 A.M. from the person who works overnight, and that's when I know I've got to get up. If I don't get a wake up call and talk to somebody, they [the station staff] have learned I won't wake up. I get to the station at 5:30 A.M. and start going through *USA Today* and *The Tennessean*. Sometimes I'll go through local newspapers too, and make a tip sheet for Gerry [House] with funny stuff he can talk about and questions he can ask. I cut out articles I like, highlight information, and write funny lines at the side. Sometimes he uses what I write and sometimes he uses his own jokes. Every time you open that mike, you've got to have something to say; something new, something funny. It's impossible to do four hours of standup five mornings a week, so he uses the tip sheet. Gerry runs his own board and does all the music, so he has to have someone who can write, listen, and answer the 300 to 400 calls we get each morning. Throughout the morning, he will go to me live; he just hits my microphone button and I'm on. I might be on the phone talking with a listener about their gallbladder

"God puts you in certain places because there is a lesson or a message you're suppose to get. Sometimes you ask, 'Why was I here?' And you realize you weren't there for you, you were there for someone else."

"People would be so much more successful if they would learn to listen."

Intern at a local radio station or get a job at your school radio station and develop an on-air persona, then make a demo recording of your work.

CAREER TIPS

THE LEAST FAVORITE THING ABOUT THIS JOB:

"What I like least is getting up at 3:30 in the morning and having to go to bed early."

THE BEST THING ABOUT THIS JOB:

"I am passionate about the country music format. I love talking to incredibly intelligent listeners. Gerry [House] can ask anything on the radio—'What is the Hebrew word for cracker?'—and a dozen people will call in with the answer. Our listeners are smart and they are also very caring. A lady called in and said, 'I'm adopting a girl from Romania, but I can't afford to fly us there to get her, and back.' She asked if anyone could donate frequent flyer miles. Before we went off the air at 10:00, she had the miles she needed."

and suddenly I'm on the air. I leave the station at 10:00. I answer my phone calls." Because she is also a songwriter, O'Day's morning and early afternoon are often booked with writing appointments or demo recording sessions.

POINTERS FOR THE JOB SEARCH

"In radio, you're going to have to work cheap, and have bad hours in the beginning. Go in as an assistant. Listen to every great radio personality you possibly can and find that person you can best emulate, then develop your own style. I read advertising copy every night of my life before I went to bed. I read books out loud so that my cold reading skills were top notch. I've been doing that for 20 years. Get books you don't even understand and try to make them sound interesting. Get a medical magazine; read the back of a Lysol can. Pretend it's an advertisement. You need to be able to read anything when you're on live radio. You've got to always pay attention to what you're reading, too. In radio, something always breaks down and you've got to be prepared to cover. All of a sudden the CD player doesn't work, and you've got to keep talking. My advice is: listen, read, practice, and hone your craft. Realize that every single person you meet might be the one who is able to unlock the door that gets you an interview or a job."

CASE STUDY:

DEVON O'DAY, PRODUCER, GERRY HOUSE AND THE HOUSE FOUNDATION SYNDICATED MORNING RADIO SHOW, WSIX RADIO

From the age of 17, Louisiana native Devon O'Day worked as a late-night and weekend country music disc jockey on a local radio station. After graduation from University of Louisiana at Monroe, then Northeast Louisiana University, O'Day moved to New York where she did postgraduate work in the writer's program of continuing education at New York University. She became a plus size model for the prestigious Ford Modeling Agency, while trying to break into radio. Despite studying voice with the lead announcer at MTV, she was unable to find radio work in New York. Feeling it was time for a change, and having a longstanding dream of being a singer/songwriter, she flew to Nashville to search for a job. "I had never been to Nashville before. I interviewed for jobs, and although I didn't land one, I just felt like I was supposed to be there." Six days later she was living on Music Row, but couldn't find work in radio.

O'Day got a job as a receptionist at a hair salon. "I heard that the best way to get a job in the music business was to hang out where music business people do. I started frequenting Third Coast." Although she didn't meet anyone to assist her in breaking into radio, she did become acquainted with legendary songwriters Paul Davis and Dean Dillon. Dillon later became a co-writer and helped to further her songwriting career. She left the salon after three months and began working temporary jobs. "I got sent to temp at different law firms. At the salon I had streaked pink through my hair. I would walk in wearing four or five earrings and lots of makeup, and I would be sent home." She continued to drop off demo tapes at radio stations, but was never called back.

Undaunted, O'Day stayed focused on her goal of working in radio, and two important events set the course of her future: she changed her name and got a little help from a stranger. "One day I thought, 'I don't have a catchy enough name.' So I dreamed up the name Devon O'Day." The next round of demo tapes carried the new name and garnered a phone call from WSIX. "They said, 'We've heard of you. We'd like you to come in for an interview.' It was the same tape I'd been leaving the last six times, but when they saw the name Devon O'Day, they called. The person who helped me get in to see [the program director] was a woman I met at the grocery store. She said, 'You have a really good voice. Do you work in radio?' As it turns out, she worked part time at WSIX and offered to make a phone call on my behalf."

Initially hired to work the late night and weekend shifts, she later became the foil for a comic deejay who, she recalls, was "as funny as dirt" on his morning show. When WSIX was bought by a larger corporation that planned to bring in another deejay to pump up morning ratings, O'Day was slated to be let go. Told that she was not cut out for an on-air job, she was offered the chance to produce a new Los

Angeles disc jockey no one else wanted to work with. "There is a professional jealousy in the industry. Rumor was that no one could get along with Gerry. Immediately the Capricorn in me said, 'I've got to work with this man.'" When O'Day first met Gerry House in 1987, the two instantly clicked. Over the next 18 years, O'Day became an integral part of the No. 1 morning show in the United States, *Gerry House and the House Foundation.*

When not working on the drive-time radio show and the syndicated weekend show, O'Day and House began co-writing songs together. Their song "The Big One" was recorded by George Strait in 1995 and went to No. 1 in eight weeks. O'Day-penned songs have also been recorded by Pam Tillis, Hank Williams, Jr., Trace Adkins, and Neal McCoy.

O'Day also applied her writing skills to books. Her first, *My Angels Wear Fur,* was published in 2001. *Goodbye My Friend: Celebrating the Memory of a Pet,* a gift book/CD she co-created with Kim McLean for those grieving the loss of a pet, was released in late 2006.

Earlier in the year, O'Day took on hosting duties for *Country Hitmakers,* heard on 100 radio stations across the country, and launched the weekly gospel/inspirational radio show *Country Spirit* nationally. She also hosts weekend shows on SIRIUS Radio's Spirit Channel. O'Day has narrated specials for Garth Brooks, The Dixie Chicks, John Michael Montgomery, and Trisha Yearwood. *www.devonoday.com*

TELEVISION

DIRECTOR • MANAGER • VICE PRESIDENT OF PUBLIC RELATIONS

JOB OVERVIEW

Oversee the public relations efforts for the firm's network interests.

SPECIAL SKILLS

"I'm very diplomatic," says Judy McDonough. "That has served me well in situations that could have become confrontational. My musical knowledge and writing skills have been a key in making me stand out from the crowd. A lot of skill goes into a well written press release or a pitch letter, and that is crucial to the job."

A DAY IN THE LIFE

"The first thing I do when I come in is check my e-mail," says McDonough. "Because we're dealing with a lot of international people, e-mail is an important part of communication. I'm involved in a lot of meetings. I assist in writing copy that will be used on marketing sheets that are used to help position the channel, so I'm often

"To any employer, there are skills that get you hired, and there are skills that keep you in your job. It's important to be constantly learning and progressing."

"It is crucial for a publicist to look at the big picture and consider how each release affects the overall vision. When I put out a press release that announces a promotion, I look at what it says about our company as a whole. How can I tie in that announcement to foreshadow something that is happening next month?"

"Knowing Spanish or Portuguese would be a tremendous help. Languages are a big plus; that, and studying different cultures."

Written and verbal communications skills are crucial for success. Find a local band and volunteer to write their biography and press releases to practice your writing skills and build a portfolio.

working on that. I might be describing programming that will then be translated into Portuguese and sent to a Brazilian cable guide. On a daily basis, I'm writing copy for one of our programs that's going to be in a cable guide, or a description of one of our networks that is going to be used in a marketing piece. I write press releases to announce the good news and the transitional news. I do a lot of planning to make sure everything I do contributes to the overall vision of the company."

POINTERS FOR THE JOB SEARCH

"Public relations is not a glamorous job. It can seem that way because you're setting up interviews for Garth Brooks, or walking Deana Carter through a press-room and flashbulbs are going off all around you. You have to do this job because

THE BEST AND LEAST FAVORITE THING ABOUT THIS JOB:

"What I love and what I dislike are the same. It's the fact that I never know what my day is going to be like. There is a part of me that wants to be able to control the day and have my agenda. Sometimes I hate that my schedule, and what I want to accomplish in a day, are thrown off by an outside influence. I also love that my job constantly surprises me. It keeps me on my toes; it excites me; it's a blessing and a curse."

you're passionate about being able to communicate your company's message. Walking through a pressroom you may be standing by a star, but you're the person who spent hours setting up those press stories and afterward, you are the person who gets on the phone, and follows through to make sure they got the information they needed. You're the one who has to stop the photographer from taking too many pictures, and the one who is going to have to get in an argument with him if he continues. Often, people don't understand how complicated the job of publicity can be. It's also a thankless job."

CASE STUDY:

JUDY McDONOUGH, DIRECTOR MEDIA AND PUBLIC RELATIONS, CAPITOL RECORDS NASHVILLE

It was watching *The Monkees* television show that first gave Judy McDonough the idea of turning her passion for music into a career. "They worked in music and it was exciting. It gave me a sense of music being a profession." She began to educate herself early for that career, poring over *Rolling Stone* magazine before she was even out of grade school. She attended St. Mary's College, and in her freshman year, served as a disc jockey at the campus radio station, where she was exposed to all kinds of music she had never heard before. After her first year, she transferred to Western University in St. Louis and graduated with a degree in English literature. "English lit proved helpful because it taught me how to think and how to write, which is an invaluable tool."

While attending Western, she got a job at a local record store and later moved up to management. "Working in a record store was a dream job," McDonough recalls. "For the next ten years I managed record stores, and that brought me to North Carolina, where I discovered bluegrass music. That was an epiphany for me. I thought the music was beautiful and the musicianship was astounding." The record store she managed published a free newsletter for their customers, for which she wrote articles. Her love of bluegrass led her to approach the head of Sugar Hill Records about profiling the label. "I thought, 'Man, this is the coolest label in the world.'"

Eventually McDonough thought she would like to work at Sugar Hill, but too shy to call for an interview, she wrote a letter instead. Based upon her writing skills, and the extensive knowledge of music she had gained over time, she was offered a position in public relations. At the label she found mentors in Barry Poss and Bev Paul, and set about learning the business of being a publicist. "I really learned my trade at Sugar Hill. I learned to communicate my love for the music—my passion for it—to journalists and to get them to write about our artists."

Three years later, it was time for a new challenge, which came in the form of an offer from Capitol Records in Nashville. She made the move, found another mentor in Lori Lytle, and learned how to take her skills to the next level through projects with artists like Garth Brooks, Tanya Tucker, and Deana Carter. "I was part of the team that landed Garth Brooks the hosting job on *Saturday Night Live*." During her time at Capitol, McDonough worked with Cindy Williams, then vice president of international for the label. When Williams moved to Gaylord Entertainment to head up Country Music Television (CMT) International, she offered McDonough the chance to expand her publicity capabilities on an international scale. "The international aspect is what sold me on the job," says McDonough, who joined Gaylord Cable Network in 1998 as director of public relations. McDonough rejoined Capitol Records Nashville a few years later, as director of media and public relations, most notably working with superstar Keith Urban. *www.capitolnashville.com*

MUSIC DIRECTOR

JOB OVERVIEW

Music directors are, in basic terms, musical contractors. They are responsible for making the visiting guest artist comfortable, for any re-recorded music, and if there is a theme to be written, they either contract it out, or write it themselves. They are charged with overseeing all source music, walk-on and walk-off music, and the musical segments. "If it is an awards show," says Harry Stinson, "you've got millions of artists on the show that all have musical needs. They may bring their own band, or they may supplement their band with the show band. You hire all the musicians, get all the charts together and rehearse them alone, and then with the artists."

PREREQUISITES

Strong musicianship and the ability to compose music and write charts.

SPECIAL SKILLS

To succeed, you should be able to manage and direct other players, and have a friendly and outgoing personality. "My ear for music and my voice are probably my biggest assets," says Harry Stinson. "Singing teaches you a lot about music. You can tell when a song is too fast if you personally can't sing it, and you write with the right feel if you understand about spitting out the lyrics too fast."

EVENTS, ORGANIZATIONS, SOCIETIES, AND UNIONS

There are numerous organizations, societies, and unions in the music industry (see appendix) that are staffed by interns, volunteers, and full and part-time employees. Each performs a unique service and most sponsor events, seminars, awards programs, magazines, newsletters, and other functions. These offer invaluable opportunities to gain experience, knowledge, and contacts for those trying to break into the industry, through part-time work or volunteering.

EVENTS

SOUTH BY SOUTHWEST ANNUAL MUSIC FESTIVAL

MANAGING DIRECTOR AND PRESIDENT

OTHER POSITIONS

Staff employees and volunteers work on every aspect of the annual event.

"Failure is not necessarily a bad thing—if you learn from it."

"Making it in the music business is one of the hardest things you can do. Most people have to make up their own job. In Austin, there weren't many places that were going to hire me to work in the music business. When you don't have any choices, you're able to do things that you might not have thought you were able to do."

JOB OVERVIEW

Roland Swenson manages and directs the overall marketing and staging of the South by Southwest (SXSW), North by Northeast (NXNE), and North by Northwest (NXNW) annual music festivals.

SPECIAL SKILLS

"Always in demand at SXSW are people skills," says Roland Swenson. "Most of our work is done in a computer program called FileMaker. We use that for just about every aspect of our event, from scheduling to keeping track of all our registrations, volunteers, and bands. Having some strong database background is something we're always looking for, and people that have strong graphic skills and can work in pro-

THE LEAST FAVORITE THING ABOUT THIS JOB:

"As hard as we try, there are always people who are unhappy with what we've done or how things turned out. Whether we've invited them to perform, speak, or use their club. In an event this big, there are people that are unhappy with how it turned out and they complain and we have to deal with that."

THE BEST THING ABOUT THIS JOB:

"The best part of my job is during the ten days of the event. It's stimulating to experience being at the center of this big storm that, upwards of ten thousand people, are involved in during the course of the week. We're all adrenaline junkies. We've worked for a whole year for the event to come to fruition, and the best part is seeing the results."

grams like Quark and PageMaker. A lot of what we do is create documents. It helps to have a background in the music business, whether you've worked at a nightclub, a record store, or maybe a small record company."

POINTERS FOR THE JOB SEARCH

"Most of the people that work for us were initially part of our volunteer core. We have about 900 people volunteer every year for SXSW that work on literally every aspect of the event; doing everything from filing to moving equipment, and answering phones. Working as a volunteer gives you a big leg up in getting a job, because someone on the staff has worked with you and knows your work ethic, your skills, and whether you're effective or not."

CASE STUDY:

ROLAND SWENSON, MANAGING DIRECTOR AND PRESIDENT, SOUTH BY SOUTHWEST, INC.

While Roland Swenson's scholastic endeavors at the University of Texas at Austin floundered, his music career was launched. "I was a history major, a journalism major, and I think I was studying film in the communication school when a friend from high school asked if I would manage his band." Swenson finished out the semester and never returned to school. Over the next five years he added other bands to his roster, worked for a small management firm, an independent record company, and even established his own label. In the mid-1980s, he decided to get out of the music business and go to work for the *Austin Chronicle*. "The *Chronicle* was just three years old and had a very small staff. I would do everything from deliver the paper to the proofreader to write stories, edit, and sell classified ads." Swenson became the newspaper's in-house organizer of benefits, shows, and special events. Through involvement with the city convention bureau, he came up with the idea for an event that would promote Austin as a music capital and tourist destination. After selling the newspaper on the idea, the first South by Southwest event was held in March 1987.

"The first year we figured if we got 150 to come, we'd be a success." Initially showcasing 200 bands, the event attracted 700 attendees. Since that time, SXSW has built a music industry following that has grown to nearly 10,000 registrants. Swenson continued working at the newspaper until 1990, when he began working on the event full time in partnership with the *Austin Chronicle*. The event grew to include a film and interactive media conference in 1994 that split into the South by Southwest Film Festival, and the South by Southwest Interactive Festival, the following year. The film and interactive events bring another 7,000 people to Austin every March. Also in 1995, Swenson and the *Chronicle* spun off their original music event to include North by Northwest in Portland, Oregon and North by Northeast (NXNE) in Toronto, Canada. One of Swenson's original goals for SXSW was to create an event that would bring creative people and companies together to meet and share ideas and to further develop their careers. That continues to be his objective, whether it is through music, film, or the Internet.

ORGANIZATIONS

NATIONAL ASSOCIATION OF RECORDING ARTS & SCIENCES (NARAS)

PUBLICATIONS MANAGER AND MANAGING EDITOR OF *GRAMMY MAGAZINE*

JOB OVERVIEW

The publication manager and managing editor oversees a variety of print projects and publications at NARAS including *Grammy Magazine*, *Grammy Program Book*, and a myriad of in-house publications, as well as the content of the web site.

SPECIAL SKILLS

To succeed, you must have the ability to write; strong verbal and written communication skills; a broad range of knowledge about the music industry, both current and historical; computer skills; drive, and an inquisitive mind.

"Being really driven gets you places. You have to really, really want it." Remember, there is a line of people waiting to take your position.

"I have a good education and I'm very well-rounded, and that makes me a good editor. Every day I read all the trades, I read the newspaper, I watch the news and I read magazines, because it's all relevant to what I do as a copy editor. If there is a problem in an Ice Cube or Blind Boys of Alabama story, or a piece on Internet technology, I need to recognize it."

"Even the best writers need practice. The Internet is a great outlet. Newspapers, magazines—they're always looking for interns. Check that out and see if it's what you want to do."

CAREER TIPS

A DAY IN THE LIFE

The work day differs from day to day, month to month, and season to season for NARAS's Melissa Blazer. In December, January, and February, prior to the annual Grammy Awards show, the thrust is producing the program book. Blazer is involved in the pretelecast program. She oversees print collateral for continuing and special projects, and the live webcast of the awards and web site updates. She is also involved in the advance preparation of the *Grammy Magazine* issue that comes out immediately following the awards. In the summer, the Latin Grammy Awards are the thrust. Other times of the year are spent with continuing projects and events planning, maintaining the web site, and continuing to publish *Grammy Magazine* and other collateral material for NARAS.

POINTERS FOR THE JOB SEARCH

"Get a really good education. Get a really good education. Get a really good education. Intern and volunteer as much as you can. There are some great opportunities that lead to good jobs, but it also gives a young person an opportunity to see if they like something."

CASE STUDY:

MELISSA BLAZER, PUBLICATIONS MANAGER FOR NARAS AND MANAGING EDITOR OF GRAMMY MAGAZINE

When Melissa Blazer says "I don't really have any mercy" on interns and those working under her command, it is because she has been there in the trenches doing the "scud work," and that is what brought about her current success. With an undergraduate degree in English from Rutgers University, Blazer went on to study journalism at the University of Missouri at Columbia. She worked as a news and sports writer at the college radio station, where she first became interested in music. "There was an upperclassman working there and she was really, really cool. She had wild punk hair and she was always smashing records. I was just a geeky newsgirl. I wanted to be like her." While she continued to write and deliver the news, Blazer picked up more and more music shifts as well. Still in college, she landed her first editorial job at an alternative newsweekly in Kansas City. Over the next seven years, she bounced between the city's two weeklies.

"I was an Arts and Entertainment (A&E) editor, doing a lot of managing editor duties, but mostly A&E, and primarily music. I spent a really, really long time honing my skills and being exposed to a tremendous amount of music on all different levels. I started from the bottom. I spent years and years working with the local club promoters and concert promoters, and the local blues and jazz festivals, and the Blues Foundation. It was all volunteer mind you. That's the key word: volunteer! When

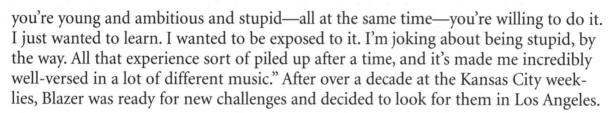

THE LEAST FAVORITE THING ABOUT THE JOB:

"The politics! Also, when you're on the inside of the entertainment business, you understand how it works, and it's hard not to let that spoil things. Sometimes I have a hard time enjoying a movie because I'm into the sound track and I know who did it, or there wasn't something in the credits that I think should have come out."

THE BEST THING ABOUT THIS JOB:

"I'm good at what I do and I'm comfortable doing it. I think very few people find the one thing in life they're really good at, but I found that thing. I like going to work every day. Even if I didn't do all the reading and research for my job, I would do it anyway."

you're young and ambitious and stupid—all at the same time—you're willing to do it. I just wanted to learn. I wanted to be exposed to it. I'm joking about being stupid, by the way. All that experience sort of piled up after a time, and it's made me incredibly well-versed in a lot of different music." After over a decade at the Kansas City weeklies, Blazer was ready for new challenges and decided to look for them in Los Angeles.

"I moved out here [Los Angeles] with no job. I thought I could get a job with my experience. I was a waitress for nine months—it wasn't pretty. I'd always wanted to work and live in Los Angeles, but had I known how scary it was, I would never have done it. Sometimes you just have to close your eyes and just go." With no family or friends to help, Blazer turned to the publicity contacts she'd made while working in Kansas City, and eventually landed freelance work. "I did research on a Priscilla Presley biography and I worked with an author and television producer for awhile. I worked at *Inside Edition* in the editing bay. I tried to pick up writing gigs, but I was working four jobs at once just to pay the rent. I eventually landed an editorial job at the *Album Network*, which is one of the radio trades." After a couple of years at *Album Network*, Blazer made the move to NARAS in the fall of 1999. "It is a fairly small editorial staff. There is an editor above me and there are other editorial staff— I am just one of the many cogs." *www.grammy.com*

COUNTRY MUSIC ASSOCIATION (CMA)

VICE PRESIDENT OR SENIOR DIRECTOR OF INTERNATIONAL AND NEW BUSINESS DEVELOPMENT

JOB OVERVIEW

At CMA, Jeff Green's area of responsibility is twofold: "I help artists and repertoire develop around the world, with particular focus on Australia, Canada, Latin America, and specific markets in Europe. The other half of my job is focused on new and Internet business development. I oversee our web site, webcasts, enhanced CDs and DVDs that we produce, web events, the MINT [Music Industry and New Technology] Conference series and other related educational series, on-line marketing initiatives, venture capitol for startup programs, and legislation issues with respect to rights management, copyrights, new technology, emerging technology, and multimedia."

SPECIAL SKILLS

"Writing skills are very important because of the number of presentations, reports, documents, and analysis you have to formulate and present to people to sell them on an idea. Another is constantly flexing the creative side of your mind as it applies to business. When it comes to building new markets, like international, or relaunching a trade publication in Europe, there are no rules. Being able to rethink how things ought to be and brainstorm without fear of being wrong, is a wonderful point of view to bring to the job."

A DAY IN THE LIFE

"What's on my plate for today is discussions with representatives in London, Cologne, and Australia about an upcoming project," says Jeff Green. "This afternoon I have a meeting with an executive of a company that is interested in webcasting the CMA Awards show, and I'm working on a presentation about the impact of Internet radio for the CMA board of directors. I have a meeting with a company that is involved with multimedia content, that takes live concert footage, and makes it available on line. I'm working on a large proposal for CMA, with respect to our overall Internet strategy and I'm meeting with a German journalist. We're having an MP3 demo session and preparing to teach the staff about that technology. I've got 459 e-mails to go through, and about eight or nine phone calls to talk about how we can make the CMA Awards a multimedia event. I have Yahoo and Yahoo Broadcast coming in to talk about chats with artists and web events." Green is on the road an average of 90 days a year to attend CMA board meetings, and music, Internet, and new technology conferences around the world.

"Don't be afraid to move on to another job when you've gone as far as you can. I've had six or seven jobs in my career. I've stayed employed (knock on wood) every day of my life. I'm very proud of that. Constant growth is important in any career. When you realize that you've done as much as you can, or reached the point of diminishing return in terms of what you are learning from the job, then it's time to reinvent yourself or look for new opportunities."

"The five words I like most to hear from anyone are: 'I'll take care of it.'"

POINTERS FOR THE JOB SEARCH

"The number one thing we [CMA] look for in a new employee is culture fit. If the person fits in terms of attitude, work ethic, team philosophy; then the job skills can be learned."

CASE STUDY:

JEFF GREEN, FORMER SENIOR DIRECTOR OF INTERNATIONAL AND NEW BUSINESS DEVELOPMENT, COUNTRY MUSIC ASSOCIATION (CMA)

"The very first gift I ever got was a record player when I was two years old," says Jeff Green. "I was fascinated with music." He amassed his early record collection from his parents, a disk at a time, as a reward for his achievements. At an early age, he built a radio station in his bedroom, and an even better one for his high school, where he also served as deejay. At age 16 his family moved from Minnesota to San Francisco, where he finished his high school studies and enrolled at San Francisco State College. He majored in radio and television broadcasting, minored in music, and worked at the college radio station. On the side, he played drums in a jazz band and did some

THE LEAST FAVORITE THING ABOUT THIS JOB:

"It's very difficult to stay focused because the demands of time. There is a frustration that I can't do everything that I want to do."

THE BEST THING ABOUT THIS JOB:

"I love the variety and the endless opportunities that come in. The exciting part is that there are so many things to do."

studio session work. Following graduation in 1978, he worked briefly at legendary rock radio station KSAN in San Francisco, and several other stations around the Bay Area, then moved down the coast to Monterey to work for three years at a radio trade publication. He began as adult contemporary (AC) editor, and later was promoted to national music director. When the magazine closed in 1981, he moved to Carmel, California to join former Monkee Mike Nesmith's multimedia company. While there, he worked on *Elephant Parts*, the first video to earn a Grammy Award, and worked on film sound tracks. After eight months, the opportunity arose to join the staff of *Radio and Records (R&R)* in Los Angeles.

After three years as AC editor and three years as managing editor at *R&R*, Green was looking for a better location to raise his children, as well as a way to gain a stronger background in marketing and management. He made the move to Nashville in 1987 to join Film House, where he produced television ad campaigns for radio stations and did music research. After three years, he felt he had learned all he could and was ready for a change. When the opportunity surfaced to move to Amsterdam as editor in chief of *Billboard* magazine's sister publication, *Music and Media*, Green accepted the challenge. He was promoted to associate publisher, but after two years, family needs convinced him it was time to return to the states.

When he left America, Green had not realized that getting a job on his return would be so difficult. After two years away, he felt all but forgotten. He returned to Nashville and Film House late in 1992, but after just eight months, again felt his career development restricted. When he heard about a new department at the Country Music Association (CMA), Green applied, but it was not until spring of the following year that he finally was hired as international director. Charged with launching the newly formed international department, he found himself having to develop a marketing strategy and assemble research and photo archives from scratch. He was promoted to senior director of strategic marketing in 1995. CMA recognized the emerging potential of the Internet and its application to country music and the music business in general, and expanded Green's responsibilities. He now handles issues relating to music on the Internet and develops ways to better serve the music community through online resources. He earned the title of senior director of international and new business development in 1997. A self-described music junky, Green also publishes a reference book called *The Green Book of Songs by Subject*, which classifies songs by subject matter for use by ad agencies, television and film studios, and others.

Green exited his position at the CMA in 2004 to become executive director of the Americana Music Association, a professional trade organization dedicated to building and promoting Americana music. Jim Lauderdale, Lyle Lovett, Kelly Willis, and Marty Stuart are some of the artists that benefit from Green's efforts at AMA. While at AMA, Green received a CMA International Award for his dedication to marketing development of country music outside North America. In October 2007, he departed his post at AMA to pursue other career goals. *www.cmaworld.com* and *www.americanamusic.org*

NASHVILLE SONGWRITERS ASSOCIATION (NSAI)

EXECUTIVE DIRECTOR

JOB OVERVIEW

The executive director of an organization manages the daily operation and oversees the numerous daily events, seminars, concerts, forums, educational programs, and fundraising initiatives staged by the organization. Persons in this position are directly responsible for staying abreast of, and dealing with, legislative matters pertaining to songwriters. They act as spokespersons for the organization.

SPECIAL SKILLS

"My background in finance and political campaign fundraising has been an asset," says Bart Herbison.

A DAY IN THE LIFE

"Every day there is some legislative work," says Herbison. "Today I have to make calls on a Japanese issue and write follow-up letters to Congress members and others in power. (The Japanese have decided that the current copyright limits of life plus 70 years starts when the first writer dies, not the last writer.) I do a lot of that work early in the day; I called Congress from the steps of my house about six this morning because they open their office at seven EST. There is always a mix of administrative work every day, making sure each department is running in sync. We have meetings every day on various events and projects. A part of my day is devoted to fundraising. Every day, even if it's for just ten minutes, I put the phones on hold and listen to music. If a great writer comes in, I shut the door of my office and have a guitar pull."

POINTERS FOR THE JOB SEARCH

"NSAI is a nonprofit organization. I work at the pleasure of the board of 25 songwriters that changes every two years. Because we're a nonprofit organization, there is some degree of turnover in jobs.

"Volunteer. Get involved any way you can." Volunteering provides lots of opportunities for you to rub shoulders with many important executives in the industry and for them to see your work ethic.

CAREER TIPS

THE LEAST FAVORITE THING ABOUT THIS JOB:

"The most frustrating part of my job is telling our story. A songwriter is a unique creature, in that God has given them a gift and that usually equates to some wonderfully blessed idiosyncrasies in their personality. Getting writers indoctrinated into the facts they need to know, and the philosophy and inspiration and passion to fight their own fights, whether it be legislative matters or other issues that affect them, can be hard."

THE BEST THING ABOUT THIS JOB:

"What I like best about my job is the music. There is nobody that gets in their car and loves coming to work every day more than me."

Our mission is broad. I don't care what your skills are, there is probably a job here for you, and the best way to get a job is to volunteer. The last two or three full time staff people I hired, came in as volunteers. I loved their work and they already knew the program."

CASE STUDY:

BART HERBISON, EXECUTIVE DIRECTOR, NSAI

By his own admission, Bart Herbison was not blessed with musical talent. "I learned to play really terrible trumpet, worse drums, and you don't want to hear me sing or pick up a guitar, but I loved it. I love music." Whether his musical ineptitude forced him out of the band, or he discovered his talents were in the business side of music, at age 15 Herbison was managing his buddies' band. The following year, while still in high school, he held down full-time disc jockey positions at three Tennessee radio stations. Over time, his radio work evolved into news reporting which led to a news director job over a group of stations. By 1986 he was working for NBC, and *The Nashville Banner*, as an election campaign reporter. On the campaign trail he became acquainted with Tennessee Governor Edward Porter, who offered Herbison a job in 1987 as his press adviser. After serving 18 months with the governor, he moved to Washington, D.C. to work as administrative assistant to Congressman Bob Clement.

As the congressman from Nashville, Clement's office was the first stop for NSAI lobbyists, and Herbison saw the opportunity to combine his two loves into one. Taking over the responsibility for music related issues, he worked closely with NSAI over the next ten years. When the directorship of the organization was vacated in 1998, Herbison's longstanding relationship and legislative experience made him an ideal candidate. Hired by a committee of 25 members, he serves as executive director of America's largest songwriter's association. *www.nashvillesongwriters.com*

SOCIETIES

AMERICAN SOCIETY OF COMPOSERS, AUTHORS, AND PUBLISHERS (ASCAP)

NATIONAL DIRECTOR OF CREATIVE SERVICES

JOB OVERVIEW

"I try and help people achieve their musical goals; I help anybody who is willing help themselves. I'm like a lawyer for the musical spirit. I'm here to help facilitate and gravitate towards success," says Herky Williams.

SPECIAL SKILLS

Skills that helped Herky Williams become successful are his ability to tell the difference between good and great music. "There are a lot of people walking around with really good songs. The great songs are the ones that have an impact. The difference between good and great is millions of dollars. I have an intuitive instinct that enables me to sit right here and help out."

A DAY IN THE LIFE

"I try to devote time each day to catching up on listening to music," says Williams. "I receive anywhere from 90 to 115 writer or artist packages each week. A lot of times I

"A lot of times when people sit in the chair opposite me, they are looking for a helping hand. I teach them that they have one at the end of their wrist and I show them how to use it."

"You need to have a 'triple H degree.' That's hangin' in, hangin' on, and hangin' out. You've got to hang out and know who the competition is and how high the bar is; see why someone is making lots of money and how you can incorporate what they are doing into what you're doing to make you more successful."

CAREER TIPS

THE LEAST FAVORITE THING ABOUT THIS JOB:

"Dealing with people who are so rigid and so sure they know what they're talking about that they won't take any input or constructive criticism. I don't think I'm the last word, but I think I have a voice."

THE BEST THING ABOUT THIS JOB:

"Knowing I helped facilitate something that was successful. There is a young girl over at EMI Publishing named Nikki Hassman, and I was in the mix in helping her secure a major label deal with Tommy Matolla. I was playing golf with some people and played her music for them. They took it and the rest is history. Those kind of things make me feel successful."

don't have good news for them. People don't realize how high the bar. After listening to music, I have appointments with people I'm working with." On any given day, Williams may attend a writer or artist showcase, or help present an award to a songwriter who has just had a number one hit.

POINTERS FOR THE JOB SEARCH

"I think you've got to really love music and be a student of it if you want to pursue it as a job. The industry takes 100 percent of your involvement to succeed. Whether you're trying to get your songs cut, be a producer, a publisher—whatever— go work in the mail room and learn the business. It's a competitive business on all levels. The people who are persistent and persevere are the ones who succeed. Hangin' in, hangin' on, and hangin' out applies. You've got to know the town and how it ticks. Know who the players are."

CASE STUDY:

HERKY WILLIAMS, ASSISTANT VICE PRESIDENT OF CREATIVE SERVICES, MEMBERSHIP, NASHVILLE, ASCAP

In the 1970s, Herky Williams was an Austin, Texas golf pro with a passion for music and an ear for a good song. Although he made friends with the many music artists he golfed with during their tours through the area, few of them took his interest in the music business seriously. ("I was giving lessons to Willie Nelson, Charlie Daniels, Marshall Tucker, Jerry Jeff Walker.") "I don't write, I don't sing. I don't play an instrument. For years I was trying to get in the music business and they would always introduce me as their golf pro. I had to overcome that. It took a long time to get where I am today. I tell people, 'I slept on more couches than Lassie.'"

He made an unsuccessful attempt to break into the Nashville music community in 1982, and went back two years later after finding songwriter David Lynn Jones, whose work he believed in. Armed with a tape of eight songs, he made the rounds of his contacts, but none of them paid any attention. Back on the golf course in Texas, friend Willie Nelson offered him encouragement and took a copy of the tape when he returned to Nashville to record with Merle Haggard. When Haggard left a session and didn't return, Nelson pulled out the tape and recorded six of the songs. *Living in the Promised Land* became the title of the hit 1985 album, a number one single, and a Nelson classic. On the strength of that success, Williams moved to Nashville to make a place for himself. "I struggled. My wife worked and supported us. I used to tell people 'I'm in the music business, but I can't prove it.'"

After struggling for four years, golf buddy, mentor, and Capitol Records head Jimmy Bowen discovered just how broke Williams was and gave him a job at his publishing company, Great Cumberland Music. "I never asked Bowen for anything," explains Williams. "He thought I was doing great because I could always pay my golf debts—I didn't lose many back then." After his wife gave birth, complications prevented her from returning to work and the family found themselves strained financially. "Scott Simon and James Stroud went to Bowen and said, 'We need to help Herky get a job. He's not doing too good financially.'" Hired as an entry level song plugger, Williams proved he had a gift for discovering and nurturing talent. Among the many artists he found and signed were John Berry in 1990 and Deana Carter in 1991. When the publishing company was sold in 1992, he moved to Capitol Records as head of artist development. Following a major label shake up, he decided to move on, but was unable to find work for 18 months. When Deana Carter's 1994 debut album sold five million copies in the first year, Williams' creative abilities were once again recognized. He settled into a position as director of creative services at ASCAP Nashville, focusing on what he does best: discovering and nurturing musical talent.

In 2001, Williams was promoted to assistant vice president of creative services, membership, Nashville, reporting directly to senior vice president Connie Bradley. His duties include securing publishing and record deals for ASCAP members as well as placing songs with artists, labels, and producers.

Since 2000, Williams has also served on the board of directors for Stereo Vision Entertainment, Inc., a film production company focused exclusively on developing low-cost, high-quality, 3-D films. He is acting secretary-treasurer for the company. *www.ascap.com* and *www.stereovision.com*

UNIONS

AMERICAN FEDERATION OF TELEVISION AND RADIO ARTISTS (AFTRA)

EXECUTIVE DIRECTOR

JOB OVERVIEW

The director manages and directs the day-to-day administration, public relations, and promotional activities, including negotiating contracts, enforcement interpretation, budgets, and staff supervision.

SPECIAL SKILLS

"People skills are the most important above everything else," says Randy Himes, "because we work with the good, the bad, and the ugly. There are people who default on payments, people who are good payers, and people who are irate because they don't like unions. You've got to be able to think quick on your feet and you need strong negotiating skills."

A DAY IN THE LIFE

On one particular day, Himes finished looking over a contract for Jim Owens Productions, researched new technologies to determine what to charge for webcasts of The Opry, and worked on a student film agreement for Watkins Film School. "I always have a lot of phone calls and contract negotiations going on throughout the day. I may be giving someone rates or helping to solve a problem. There is a lot of dictation and follow-up correspondence. There are board and committee meetings. I sometimes have site visits for film and commercial work. I liaison for performers with the governor's and mayor's board for film, and the city film commission; whatever it takes to best represent performers. There are no set hours and no set days. I had a producer roll

CAREER TIPS

"You've got to be able to do whatever it takes to get the job done." Don't be too proud to start as an intern and then hustle and be the best intern anyone has ever seen.

"You've got to be versatile and flexible. With AFTRA and SAG, there are no black and white lines in many areas. You have to be flexible enough to deal with that and not become frustrated."

THE LEAST FAVORITE THING ABOUT THIS JOB:

"What I like the least is the politics that occur in every industry organization."

THE BEST THING ABOUT THIS JOB:

"I like seeing a need and finding a solution. I'm very goal oriented. I like to see results. With a lot of activities we do have closure. You can negotiate a contract, see it through, and then see the performers working under it."

into town to do a commercial and we were up talking until eleven at night, straightening out the employment situation."

POINTERS FOR THE JOB SEARCH

Volunteer to work on a committee or help with an event to learn more about the organization, and for them to become familiar with your work habits and abilities. Previous experience in the music industry is helpful.

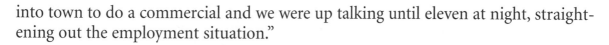

RANDY HIMES, ASSISTANT NATIONAL EXECUTIVE DIRECTOR OF SOUND RECORDINGS, AMERICAN FEDERATION OF TELEVISION AND RADIO ARTISTS (AFTRA)

"I love music," says Randy Himes. "My mother was an organist in the Methodist Church since she was 13 years old and her side of the family is all very musical. I sang in a quartet while growing up in Rockford, [Illinois]." In his youth, Himes learned to play piano, played in rock bands, and devoted eight years to the French horn. He enrolled in the recording industry management program at Middle Tennessee State University with the intention of becoming a recording engineer. After graduating, he sent out resumes and worked at a gas station in Murfreesboro, Tennessee while trying to get a music industry job. A regular customer, who was a local deejay, found out about Himes' interest and recommended him for an interview with the head of the Nashville AFTRA office. Following a marathon three-hour interview to ensure that he did not want to pursue a performing career, Himes was hired in 1978 as a local field representative.

Later promoted to a national representative position, Himes remained stationed in Nashville, but traveled extensively. He found a mentor in an AFTRA attorney who taught him negotiation skills, which proved invaluable as he negotiated contracts at radio and television stations and became involved in troubleshooting operations around the country. When the chapter director left the organization, Himes was appointed to fill the post of executive director in 1986.

During his tenure as executive director, Himes served on the bargaining committees in negotiations for AFTRA's Sound Recordings Code and led organizing campaigns at Disney Orlando, TNN Cable Network, and the Grand Ole Opry. He was named assistant national executive director of sound recordings in 2005. Himes' responsibilities include outreach to sound recording artists, oversight of contract administration, and strategies for protecting performers' rights in the face of new technology and servicing the needs of recording artists. *www.aftra.com*

CHAPTER

15

EDUCATION

Throughout this book many people advise getting a college education from an institution with a music business and internship program. With the rapid advances in new media and technology, the business of music is changing. While not everyone who is successful in the industry has a college education, it has become increasingly important to have the cutting-edge knowledge and tools that an advanced education can provide.

This chapter profiles Pam Browne, the associate dean of the Mike Curb School of Music Business at Belmont University, a school that has earned a reputation for preparing students to become successful leaders in the music industry. It provides basic information about the school's program and Browne's career path.

ASSOCIATE DEAN • ASSOCIATE PROFESSOR • DEAN • INSTRUCTOR • TEACHER • PROFESSOR

JOB OVERVIEW

Educators teach music business, or recording technology courses, at an institute for higher education. As associate dean, Pam Browne is responsible for defining and overseeing the course direction and related programs for the music business program at Belmont University.

PREREQUISITES

To succeed as a music business educator, you should have an undergraduate degree and experience working in the entertainment industry.

"You need to have a dream in front of you. Get the necessary skills, go to college and study music business, and be prepared. You never know who you will meet that may turn into an opportunity. Stay focused on learning and being prepared."

"Network, network, network." Music industry jobs are never advertised. If someone has an opening, they offer it to someone they have worked with or call someone they know for a recommendation.

COURSE OF STUDY OFFERED

Music business students at Belmont University graduate with bachelor degrees in business administration. They take general core classes like accounting, economics, strategic management, and statistics, so they have a firm foundation in business. Then they take music business classes, such as recording technology, music publishing, and intellectual properties. Students then select a specific track, such as artist management, recording company operations, publishing, marketing, productions, and so forth. Internships at music businesses are an important part of the education process. During her tenure at the school, Browne has been instrumental in initiating Belmont West, an extension program based in Los Angeles for undergraduate music business majors, and in offering the first MBA in music business through Belmont's Massey Graduate School.

POINTERS FOR THE JOB SEARCH

"I try to reach out and hire young entertainment attorneys [as instructors]. If you're interested in teaching music business, send your resume to schools with programs. Network and attend music functions and put the word out." For those beginning a career in music, the school's events, programs, and internships are a good way to meet industry leaders and gain practical experience working at a company.

THE LEAST FAVORITE THING ABOUT THIS JOB:

"What I like least is the administrative tasks."

THE BEST THING ABOUT THIS JOB:

"I love working with students. I love helping them achieve their goals, or at least realize what it is they want to do in life, and hopefully give them the tools that they need to go out and be successful."

CASE STUDY:

PAMELA G. BROWNE, ASSOCIATE DEAN, MIKE CURB SCHOOL OF ENTERTAINMENT AND MUSIC BUSINESS, BELMONT UNIVERSITY

Growing up in Nashville, Pamela Browne felt that her interest in pop music precluded entry into the city's country-heavy music business. She graduated from Syracuse University and Vanderbilt University School of Law in the late 1980s. She began her legal career with First American Bank's (now AmSouth Bank) Music Row branch, handling music industry accounts. While there, she met an attorney who represented several top country acts, who advised her that her best chance to get involved with the music business was not through a bank, but by going into private legal practice. She went to work for his firm, and when he sold his practice 18 months later, she opened her own firm to service the many pop and R&B artists who also record in Nashville. "At the time, Nashville had started doing pop projects. Whitney Houston, Aretha Franklin, Vanessa Williams, and others were all coming to Nashville to record. I started representing many of them." When several of her clients were without management, she took on those duties as well and found that she enjoyed that aspect even more. She managed and guided the career of multiplatinum-selling artist Tag Team.

While attending the Leadership Music industry retreat, Browne met an entertainment attorney who also taught in the music business program at Belmont University. Offered the opportunity to teach classes in copyright law, and having previously taught banking classes at a local technical school, Browne felt sure she would enjoy the challenge. In 1994, she joined the faculty of the Mike Curb Music Business Program in 1994 as assistant professor of copyright law and was promoted to associate professor in 1999. She discovered that she loved working with students. Several years later, Browne found herself on the search committee for a new associate dean. After months of not finding a suitable candidate, she accepted the position on an interim basis. Free to try new programs, she instituted a number of innovations, including a sister campus in Los Angeles that offers classes and internships geared to the pop, rock, and R&B markets. Increasingly, it became apparent that Browne herself was the best candidate for the associate dean position, which she finally accepted in 1999. In addition to her duties as associate dean, Browne continues to teach intellectual property law, artist management, legal issues of music industry, and business law. *www.belmont.edu/mb/*

16

EMERGING TECHNOLOGIES AND INTERACTIVE MEDIA

THE INTERNET AND DIGITAL MUSIC

When this book was first published, the iPod had not been invented. The industry was still in the beginning stages of learning how to harness the power of the Internet to promote and distribute music. Today, peer-to-peer (P2P) file sharing over the Internet is the only way many enthusiasts discover and consume their music. This easy accessibility of music has enabled the music industry to flourish.

CAREER TIPS

The music industry is alive and thriving. Thanks to inventors and purveyors of new technology, namely broadband Internet, MP3 players, and file sharing services, music fans can search for songs online, download individual tracks to their laptops, add them to their iPods, and carry their entire music library in the palms of their hands. Music buffs can also download songs and videos to their wafer-thin cell phones. The instant access and easy portability of music has allowed more people to enjoy more music in more areas of their life than ever before.

THE RECORD BUSINESS IS ONLY A PART OF THE MUSIC INDUSTRY

The music industry is booming, but the record business is struggling. Since the advent of digital music, compact disc sales have steadily declined. According to Nielsen SoundScan, in the first quarter of 2006, the record business sold 112 million CDs to U.S. consumers, down from the previous year. During the same quarter in 2007, that number dropped again to only 89 million. Album sales fell 18 percent between 2000 and 2006, after accounting for paid digital downloads from online stores like iTunes. Worldwide sales are down commensurately throughout the rest of the world.

Some attribute the downfall of CD purchases to the digitization of music and the advent of personal computers with CD-recording capability, which led to widespread copying and burning of music tracks on home systems. Others blame the combination of high-speed Internet connections, the advent of MP3 files and players, and P2P file sharing for diminishing sales. But the actual fault may lie with the record companies themselves, who vigorously battled against new technology instead of channeling those resources into discovering ways to make it work for them.

THE RECORD BUSINESS HAS A HISTORY OF CLINGING TO THE PAST WHILE FIGHTING INNOVATION

- Record executives argued the standardization of cassette recorders and tapes in the 1960s, complaining that teenagers taped and swapped their favorite vinyl albums, and advocated for a tax on blank cassettes to make up for lost revenue from bootlegged tape trading. In the 1980s, legislators finally granted music labels a portion of the earnings from every blank tape sold.
- Record labels barely acknowledged the 1982 arrival of MTV—whose staff had to beg record companies for copies of already produced promotional videos to air on the burgeoning music network. Before long, MTV was the most powerful music station on the planet, reaching tens of millions of young music-buying fans. MTV forced record companies to reevaluate how they did business. Artists' looks and potential video appeal became major factors in executives' decisions to sign them to a recording contract. Resources had to be allocated for video production and marketing, sometimes cutting into funds previously allotted for recording. Today, music channels like MTV, VH-1, CMT, BET, and other video outlets have become an integral part of a record label's marketing strategy.
- When the CD entered the marketplace in the early 1980s, the recording industry began a shift from analog to digital recording. Many resisted digitization of music because they felt it lost the warmth and pure organic sound of analog. The release of digitized music on CD opened the door for bootleggers to make infinite numbers of near-perfect copies of recordings. By the early 1990s, per-

sonal computer manufacturers saw the potential of audio applications and began developing affordable consumer machines that included CD-ROM devices and high-quality speakers that could be attached or built right into the computer itself. Soon music fans were swapping tracks and copying and burning their own CDs. The recording business fought back with new legislation. The Audio Home Recording Act of 1992 required manufacturers of digital records to pay a 2 percent royalty rate to copyright holders to compensate for the ease of piracy that digital recording allows and required that recorders contain a device to prohibit serial copying.

• In the late 1990s, instead of embracing MP3 as the new dominant format, record labels banned together and attacked. In 1998, the Recording Industry Association of America (RIAA) filed a lawsuit against Diamond Multimedia, the manufacturer of the Rio MP3 player. That same year they filed the first of many suits against Internet "pirates" for posting audio files online and allowing anyone to download them for free. And then Napster came along.

• Ready or not, the recording industry was forever changed in May 1999 by the unveiling of Napster. The first P2P network, Napster made it possible for users to share and swap music files by remotely accessing each other's hard drives. The major record companies, namely EMI, Sony BMG, Universal, and Warner, felt so threatened by Napster that they joined forces to sue it out of business. Months after its launch, the RIAA filed suit against Napster for alleged copyright infringement. After two years of legal battles, Napster was ordered to remove all copyrighted material from its network, and the service shut down in July 2001 (after filing bankruptcy and selling off assets, Napster re-opened in 2004 as Napster, Inc., a paid subscription service). At the time of its closing, Napster had around 14 million users. Experts in the industry assert that billions of dollars in revenue were lost by suing Napster and trying to thwart P2P file sharing, rather than negotiating a model that would benefit everyone. Seemingly overnight, other P2P file sharing services, such as Grokster, Kazaa, and Morpheus, sprang up. The RIAA filed suit against them in October 2001. Because these networks did not use a centralized server, as Napster did, it was ruled they could not be held liable for illegal activity of file sharing that may take place within their networks. The enormous publicity surrounding the legal scuffles did not scare off users, as the record companies had hoped. The harder they fought against this new distribution channel, the more popular it became.

ARE RECORD COMPANIES AT FAULT FOR THE BROKEN SYSTEM?

Some blamed diminishing CD sales on P2P file sharing; others place the blame with the record labels themselves. Over the last several years, label executives have made a series of botched opportunity decisions. Among their biggest was a failure to address online piracy at the outset and make peace with Napster.

In 2000, the music industry's top executives gathered for secret talks with Napster CEO Hank Berry. Those present included CEOs from Bertelsmann (BMG), Universal, and Sony Corporation. They discussed assessing a monthly subscription fee of around $10 from the estimated 38 million users. Napster publicly offered $1 billion to settle the dispute and to form an agreement to move forward. Labels executives caught cross-fire from retailers who did not want product sold online for less than in-store prices and from artists who feared their promotional deals and sales through Wal-Mart and Best Buy might be jeopardized. In the end, the record labels never completed a deal and instead forced Napster to close in July 2001.

Over the next two years, the labels continued to file lawsuits against unauthorized file sharing sites and failed to offer the public a viable legal alternative. A few labels made unsuccessful attempts at starting their own subscription services: PressPlay, a joint venture between Sony Music Entertainment and Universal Music, carried only those two companies' music, and MusicNet—backed by EMI Recorded Music, BMG Entertainment, Warner Music Group, in partnership with streaming media company RealNetworks—which carried BMG, EMI, and Warner Music titles.

Consumers criticized both services for catalog limitations, their inability to interface with many MP3 players, and restrictions on burning tracks to CDs. Both services failed, while the public demand for and consumption of MP3-delivered music continued to grow.

In the fall of 2003, the RIAA began a full-blown assault on illegal downloading by filing numerous copyright infringement lawsuits. As of 2006, more than 17,000 lawsuits against music fans had been filed. Many were settled or dropped, like that against a 65-year-old Massachusetts grandmother, Sarah Seabury Ward, who was accused of illegally sharing many hip-hop tunes. Ward claimed she knew little about downloading and uploading songs online until a process server pounded on her door late one night.

The RIAA maintained the lawsuits were meant to spread the word that unauthorized file sharing can have consequences. But file sharing did not go away. In 2006, there was a 4.4 percent increase in the number of P2P users, and an estimated 1 billion tracks were downloaded illegally per month, according to research group BigChampagne. Still, record companies were slow to devise a model that would adequately service the online consumer.

In the midst of all the legal wrangling, Steve Jobs and his team at Apple Computers launched iTunes, an online music store, in 2003. Jobs was able to finally lead the recording industry into the digital age by convincing the five major record companies to license their catalogs of songs to Apple for distribution on iTunes. In addition to having a legitimate online music store, Apple also provided users with "rip, mix, burn" tools that made it easy for consumers to make their own CDs. In the first year, iTunes sold 70 million songs at $0.99 per song, earning nearly $70 million in legal Internet music sales. While CD sales diminished, the purchase of downloaded digital music

Are major record companies a thing of the past? That is the question many artists are asking themselves. In the past, major record companies had a monopoly on the creation and distribution of recorded music, but advances in technology and the Internet have changed that.

increased. Music fans bought 582 million digital singles in 2006, up 65 percent from the previous year, and purchased $600 million worth of ringtones. However, these new revenue sources did not make up for the shortfall record companies were still experiencing.

Record executives were not happy to see iTunes/Apple/Steve Jobs making such a healthy profit off their product while their own earnings were shrinking. In late 2007, Universal Music Group announced they would not renew their long-term agreement with Apple. As a temporary solution, and possibly to strengthen their own bargaining power for a higher royalty rate, Universal formed an "at will"—meaning the record company could pull their titles at any time—arrangement with iTunes. This also opened the door for the record company to make deals with other online distributors. According to Nielsen SoundScan data, Universal's titles account for one out of every three new releases in the United States.

TRADITIONAL MAJOR RECORD COMPANIES MAY BE ON THE VERGE OF EXTINCTION

The Internet and emerging technologies have broken their hold on the distribution of recorded music. While some artists find ways to raise funds or barter time in the studio, advances in technology have made it possible for others to purchase hardware and software that enables them to produce quality recordings at home. In the past, once the recordings were finished, artists struggled to get marketing and distribution—national exposure and distribution required the backing of a major record label behind them. Thanks to the Internet, that is no longer the situation.

The advent of social networking sites and web radio have enabled artists to reach potential fans all over the world. Artists can produce their own video and get it played on YouTube, MySpace, Facebook, and other Internet sites and sell their recordings and merchandise over the web. Online exposure can build a fan base that supports live performances, where many acts make the majority of their income.

For some artists, the remaining functions that record labels fulfill, namely artist development, publicity, and radio and retail promotion, no longer (if they ever did) seem to warrant the financial and artistic rights signed away in a traditional recording contract. More and more artists are beginning to question the premium cost of being with a major record company and are instead opting to develop their own game plan.

In the late 1990s, after creative disputes with Warner Brothers, Prince publicly announced he felt like a prisoner to the record label by writing "slave" on his face. After Prince's contractual obligations with Warner were fulfilled and he was "freed" from the major, he turned to the Internet for distribution. Through his web site, Prince released an EP with seven different versions of the song "1999," and a three-CD collection of previously unreleased material.

In 2007, Prince proved he not only was a musical visionary but had marketing ingenuity as well. He gave away his new album *Planet Earth* with the *Daily Mail* in the United Kingdom. The bold move paid off. When Prince announced performances at London's 02 Arena, the 140,000 tickets sold out in 20 minutes, causing the Internet booking site to crash. He added six more shows, making a total of 21 sold out performances.

Paul McCartney, whose young fans were born decades after his Beatles' fame, chose a fresh-thinking partner over his old-school record company for the release of his 2007 album *Memory Almost Full*. He ended his long relationship with EMI Records after discovering they wanted six months to adequately set up and promote his new release. McCartney wanted to get the album out to his fans much sooner, so he partnered with Starbucks to become the first release on their Hear Music label.

To publicize the album release, McCartney made one track available via iTunes and later performed at the iTunes Music Festival in London. He also held free concerts in several cities and kept his fans updated on his MySpace page. However, one of the biggest events the Starbucks alliance made possible was a Global Listening Event to celebrate the album's release. More than 10,000 Starbucks stores in 29 countries and territories worldwide participated by playing the CD in store all day long. An estimated six million people were introduced to McCartney's new album in a single day and they could purchase it while picking up coffee.

Pop superstar Madonna left her long-term relationship with Warner Music to sign a $120 million recording and touring contract with concert promoter Live Nation Inc. Shortly after the 2007 announcement, Madonna stated that she was drawn to the deal with Live Nation because of the changes the music business has undergone in recent years. "The paradigm in the music business has shifted, and as an artist and a business woman, I have to move with that shift. For the first time in my career, the way that my music can reach my fans is unlimited. I've never wanted to think in a limited way and with this new partnership, the possibilities are endless."

VOICES OF EXPERIENCE

In the fall of 2007, industrial rock band Nine Inch Nails left its major record company and made plans to release all future recordings in a manner similar to Radiohead. Nine Inch Nails' Trent Reznor wrote on the band's web site: "I've waited a long time to be able to make the following announcement: as of right now Nine Inch Nails is a totally free agent, free of any recording contract with any label." He went on to say, "I have been under recording contracts for 18 years and have watched the business radically mutate from one thing to something inherently very different and it gives me great pleasure to be able to finally have a direct relationship with the audience as I see fit and appropriate."

Hard-rocker band Radiohead's recording contract with EMI/Capitol Records expired in 2003. The group has since foregone the traditional record label to handle recording, distribution, and marketing as they see fit. For the release of their seventh album *In Rainbows* in late 2007, they allowed online consumers to name their own purchase price. According to *New Music Express*, the average price paid was about $10.

The Eagles also went it alone without major record company support for their 2007 album release *Long Road Out of Eden*. The band formed an exclusive deal with mass merchant Wal-Mart to distribute the disc.

Back in 2005, country superstar Garth Brooks struck an exclusive multiyear deal with Wal-Mart stores for his entire catalog, which he took with him after his Capitol Nashville agreement was mutually terminated.

Established artists are not the only ones choosing to forge their own path, rather than signing on with a traditional major record company. Delbert McClinton and John Hiatt released albums through indie label New West Records. Ani DiFranco, Michelle Shocked, Jonatha Brooke, and Amee Mann have formed their own labels. Mann, her husband Michael Penn, and their manager Michael Hausman even formed United Musicians, an organization that provides support services to indie artists.

Some artists leave or forgo major labels because of creative and financial differences. The expensive overhead at major record companies means that many artists must sell a million records before earning any profits. First, they must recoup costs for recording, marketing, promotional tours—including limo rides and dinner for record executives working on their behalf—and other accumulated expenses. Considering that the artist is recouping these expenses at a rate of about 50 cents to $1 per album, they may never get out of debt to the label. Contrast that with an independent artist who might make $5–8 profit off each disc they sell and have complete creative control.

For the majority of artists, the main source of income is live performances and merchandise. For example, according to the *The Wall Street Journal's* figures, Madonna's four CDs released prior to her split from Warner Music sold 10.4 million copies in the United States, while her last three tours earned $385 million in ticket sales.

RECORD LABELS ARE NOT DEAD YET

The downturn in sales may look bleak; however, the music industry continues to generate profits, and investors remain interested in the business of selling records. For example, an investment group purchased the Warner Music Group in 2004 for $2.6 billion, and EMI was taken over by a British private equity firm for $4.7 billion in 2007. These big financiers would not spend billions of dollars to acquire a company unless they believed the venture would yield strong dividends.

Record companies are attempting to alter their traditional business model and make a concerted effort to develop fresh marketing strategies and create new sources of revenue.

- Perhaps record companies are learning from past mistakes made with Napster. Instead of filing copyright infringement lawsuits against YouTube, they struck a deal. In 2006, the Warner Music Group Corporation, Sony BMG Music Entertainment, and Universal Music Group agreed to license their copyrighted songs and other material to YouTube.
- EMI made a bold step in May of 2007 by allowing iTunes Music Store to sell its catalog without the copy protection that labels had previously insisted upon.
- Also in May 2007, Warner Music Corporation announced the creation of Den of Thieves, to help drive digital music sales as the demand for compact discs declines. The unit develops and produces original programming for network, cable, DVD, broadband, and mobile platforms. Content is distributed in conjunction with artist's releases.
- Some record labels are negotiating deals that encompass music publishing, touring, merchandising, product sponsorships, and other non-recorded music sources of income, to offset the increasing costs of doing business. Some new artists see any deal with a major record company as a necessary step to break through to superstar status.
- After years of legal battles to prevent music fans from listening to music without paying for it, Warner Music Group struck a deal with Lala.com that allows users to stream music from the record label's catalog for free. The hope is that consumers will eventually purchase the songs to download on their iPods and other music-playing devices.

- Record companies have a long history of licensing music for film, television, and advertising communities, but they are increasingly turning to videos games, subscription services, cell phone ringtones, and other avenues to generate revenue.
- Sony BMG Entertainment's strategic marketing guru, Donna Clower, is forming partnerships with big name brands like L'Oreal and Verizon to cross-promote the company's recording artists and their music with other products. For the release of Christina Aguilera's single "Candyman," she aligned with Verizon's LG Chocolate cell phone. The commercial campaign for the Chocolate featured Aguilera's new single and promoted sales for the song's ringtone. The deal included licensing fees and successfully set up the release of Aguilera's album.

WHERE ARE THE JOBS?

It is impossible to predict how rapidly changing technology will affect the music industry in the next decade, or even the next five years. It is increasingly important that those competing for jobs in the music industry have a college education and stay abreast of how new technology is revolutionizing the business.

Fortunately, no matter what problems the record companies and other areas of the business face, music remains a vital industry. There will always be a need for people who can write, record, and produce songs and market and deliver music to fans.

EMERGING TECHNOLOGIES AND INTERACTIVE MEDIA

SENIOR VICE PRESIDENT • VICE PRESIDENT • DIRECTOR (MULTIMEDIA/BUSINESS DEVELOPMENT OR NEW MEDIA TECHNOLOGY)

JOB OVERVIEW

Executives in this department manage and direct marketing efforts of artists and the company on the Internet and through new technology. Camille Hackney directs strategic planning and implementation of marketing campaigns on the Internet. Daily tasks include running the label's web site, maintaining a presence for label signed artists, developing relationships with various Internet companies for cooperative marketing opportunities, and finding other new technology avenues to promote the company and its roster.

PREREQUISITES

To succeed, you must have people skills and a thirst for knowledge. You need to combine creativity with an understanding of new technology, the Internet, and marketing.

A DAY IN THE LIFE

On one particular day, Hackney arrived early to begin work on three different marketing plans—one for Busta Rhymes, one for Phish, and another for Ween—deciding whether to have a music download or a contest promotion. She attended a brainstorming meeting with other marketing executives to solidify plans for a big Busta Rhymes Internet event, then had a meeting outside the office with an Internet company about a Phish cybercast promotion. In the afternoon, she took conference calls regarding new technology, interviewed candidates for an opening in her department, met with the A&R staff about music for the web site, and dealt with a problem with the company that hosts the web site. That evening, she attended a Tracy Chapman concert and met with her afterward to talk about her upcoming AOL chat.

POINTERS FOR THE JOB SEARCH

"Get to know what the music business is all about—that is fundamental. Ask people at all different levels what they do and how they do it. Read about the music business. Do your homework on the Internet, whether it's looking at various music-based sites or reading *Wired* or *Silicon Valley* or *Interactive Age*, any of those journals. Read up on what's going on technology-wise in the music business. Anyone who comes in with a strong knowledge of the music business—how it's traditionally run—and is on top of technology and how it can change the way the business runs, has a pretty powerful information base to walk into any job interview with. You have to pay your dues, though. Most people start as interns."

"There are a lot of people in the music business prepared to do whatever they need to do to get in. Whenever I interview somebody, I like to see that kind of passion. You don't have to have gone to business school. What a lot of people like to see is that you love the music business and everything about it. That will take you far."

"There are new outlets, new .com sites, popping up every day. You really have to, not only keep on top of those, but know how to use those tools to create a new and different marketing plan for artists."

CAREER TIPS

THE LEAST FAVORITE THING ABOUT THIS JOB:

"The music business has been around for decades, but technology has only been combined with music for about five years. Because technology is a new division, it's difficult, sometimes, to get the resources needed. People understand that it's an important part of the music business and it will fundamentally change how we do business in the future, but I struggle to get access to resources, whether that be human resources, monetary resources, or hardware and software. This is one of the things that makes my job difficult."

THE BEST THING ABOUT THIS JOB:

"I love the learning that I get to do in this job. The Internet is changing every day. My challenge is to keep on top of things. I read at least three different newspapers and at least 50 different magazines every week. The magazines range from People *to* Interactive Age *and all points between. I try to keep on top of what's going on marketing-wise, Internet-wise, and technology-wise, so I can apply that to what I do. That's the part I love. In general, I love the energy in the music industry. It is very similar to Wall Street. People work really hard, but they also play really hard. It's never boring. I actually enjoy coming to work."*

CASE STUDY:

CAMILLE HACKNEY, VICE PRESIDENT MULTIMEDIA/BUSINESS DEVELOPMENT, ELEKTRA ENTERTAINMENT

The launch of MTV on her thirteenth birthday proved prophetic for Camille Hackney, who spent her high school and early college years playing bass and guitar in an all-girl band, and dreamed of being a rock star. Not knowing how to get into the music business, or even what jobs existed, she studied economics at Princeton, and after graduation, took a job on Wall Street as a financial analyst for Merrill Lynch. Hackney soon realized that she was in the wrong line of work, and enrolled in business school. While taking classes, she worked in the marketing technology group of HBO cable network, where her varied interests in television, music, and technology converged. "Working at HBO got me into the entertainment field. I sort of started to realize there was a business behind the music."

During her two years at Harvard Business School in Boston, Hackney called everyone she could in the music business. Many of those calls turned into 15-minute informational interviews where she learned about different career opportunities. "I would call people up and say, 'I'm in school, I don't want a job, I just want to find out what you do.' " With a clearer idea of what jobs were available, she got an interview at Elektra Records through a friend of a friend. Hired in 1995 to do business development, her interest in technology led her to explore the potential of the Internet. After two years, she was promoted to vice president of multimedia market development. After label mergers and restructuring, Hackney was promoted to senior vice president brand partnerships and commercial licensing for Atlantic Records.

"No fear," states Marc Geiger as the reason for his success. "A vision and a love for what I'm doing is what drives the passion and the aggression."

It is important to read the major music trade magazines like Billboard *and* Pollstar, *but also read about new developments in technology and trends in the entertainment industry in general.*

ALTERNATIVE MARKETING

COMPANY OVERVIEW

ARTISTdirect Network is a leading on-line music network that provides services, comprehensive information, and a contact community to millions of fans. It is also the leading company that connects artists directly with their fans through their own web sites.

CHIEF OPERATING OFFICER

JOB OVERVIEW

The chief operating officer provides creative vision for the company and directs daily operations.

SPECIAL SKILLS

To succeed, you need determination, commitment, a passion for music, and a creative mind.

A DAY IN THE LIFE

"I get up at seven in the morning, go on line and answer e-mail, read the newspaper on line, make phone calls, and then go to work," says Marc Geiger. "I'm constantly working on a variety of projects and ideas at different stages of completion. I look after personnel matters, strategic initiatives, and helping the management of the company achieve the goals they have set forth; setting new visions as the market changes. I do interviews; I try to do some planning on my own; I meet with artists, evangelizing what the Net means to them. I go home between eight and ten at night."

POINTERS FOR THE JOB SEARCH

"There are three pieces of advice I always give. One is to study before you decide what you want to do and pick a point of entry that has low resistance, because the industry, if you try to enter in New York, Los Angeles, or Nashville, has this whole mail room/assistant hierarchy. If you get into that, my next piece of advice is to be patient. It's like going to med school. Be aggressive while you're there, and be full of ideas, and enthusiastic in trying things. Pick your path so that you can get into a low resistant point and don't be wedded to one job. If you get lucky enough to get in with a label, be willing to do whatever it takes to move up. The other thing is, write down in advance whom you'd want to work for and what companies are the ones that would motivate you the most. Use that list as the starting point and try to enter those companies from the position of 'I love the company.' Study them so you know what they're doing. Then, when you get the opportunity—whether it's a letter or a meeting—show the people that you know everything about the company and that

THE LEAST FAVORITE THING ABOUT THIS JOB:

"The only thing I don't like is the pressure; the pressure of being the top banana and having everybody's livelihood dependent on you."

THE BEST THING ABOUT THIS JOB:

"What I like the most is the feeling that we're involved in changing the world in terms of music. We can actually have a vision and set a course for how we think music is going to work in the future. This gives me a real sense of accomplishment. Second, I love the fact that I work with great people. We now have 210 employees. They are fantastic people that I'm thrilled to be associated with and have as teammates."

you really can make a difference there. Offer to work for free. Be willing to do whatever it takes to prove yourself, because that is the company you want to work for."

CASE STUDY:

MARC GEIGER, VICE CHAIRMAN, ARTISTdirect NETWORK

Marc Geiger chalks up his remarkable success in the music business to two words: "No fear." He grew up in Stamford, Connecticut and managed bands while still in high school. While a first year premed student at the University of California at San Diego, he managed a record store, promoted concerts through the campus events organization, and had an import music show on a local radio station. "After promoting the first few shows, and them going very well, I realized it was a potential career and spent more time on promoting and less at school." The early success of the campus concerts led him to form a fulltime promotion company with a fellow student, and at age 19, he was hired to run the San Diego office of Avalon Attractions and Concerts. In 1982, he opened the seaside music venue, Humphrey's Concerts by the Sea. Hugely successful from the beginning, the enterprise soon attracted the attention of top talent agents who recognized Geiger's ability to do sell-out business with artists who could not fill comparably-sized venues. His reputation as an aggressive talent buyer and promoter earned him job offers from Avalon's Los Angeles office, and from Regency Artists booking agency. He took the latter and became an agent. Regency later merged with a talent agency to become Triad Artists, Inc.

As an agent, Geiger carved out a niche for himself with underground and alternative bands. Among his many successes was the hugely successful Lalapalooza Tour, a concept fashioned after European festivals. After eight years as a booking agent, Geiger wanted a new challenge and found it in the record business. With several offers to choose from, he went to American Recordings as vice president of A&R, marketing, and artist development. Recognizing the potential of the Internet to change everything about the music industry, he bought a site called UBL (Ultimate Band List) and built it into one of the biggest music sites on the Web. With a vision of how artists would connect with their fans in the future, Geiger partnered with friends to launch ARTISTdirect Network in January 1997. The site set the standard for Internet music news and information. Geiger took the company public in 2000. He served as chief operating officer until 2001, when Interscope Records founder Ted Field was brought in as chairman and chief operating manager and Geiger was named vice chairman. In that role, Geiger launched ARTISTdirect's iMusic label.

In 2003, WMA Worldwide head of music Peter Grosslight enticed Geiger to join the firm as senior vice president for the contemporary music department. Grosslight and Geiger had worked together more than a decade earlier at Triad and William Morris. *www.artistdirect.com* and *www.wma.com*

APPENDICES

UNIONS, PERFORMING RIGHTS SOCIETIES, ORGANIZATIONS

The following is a list of major music organizations. Contact them individually or check their web sites to find out about local events, seminars and workshops, membership requirements, and how you can volunteer or become involved in the respective activities.

Academy of Country Music (ACM)
5500 Balboa Boulevard, Suite 200
Encino, CA 91316
tel: (818) 788-8000
fax: (818) 788-0999
e-mail: info@acmcountry.com
web site: *www.acmcountry.com*

The Academy of Interactive Arts & Sciences
23622 Calabasas Road, Suite 220
Calabasas, CA 91302
tel: (818) 876-0826
fax: (818) 876-0850
e-mail: Gabriel@interactive.org
web site: *www.interactive.org*

American Composers Forum (ACF)
332 Minnesota Street, Suite East 145
St. Paul, MN 55101
tel: (651) 228-1407
fax: (651) 291-7978
web site: *www.composersforum.org*

American Federation of Musicians of the United States and Canada (AFM)
AFM has more than 250 local offices throughout the United States and Canada. For additional cities, contact one of the offices below, or check the main web site at *www.afm.org*.

AFM Local 10-208
656 West Randolph, Suite 2W
Chicago, IL 60661
tel: (312) 782-0063
fax: (312) 782-7880
e-mail: local10-208@afm.org
web site: *www.livemusichicago.com*

AFM Local 148–462
551 Dutch Valley Road Northeast
Atlanta, GA 30324
tel: (404) 873-2033
fax: (404) 873-0019
e-mail: local148-462@afm.org
web site: *www.atlantamusicians.com*

AFM Local 47
817 North Vine Street
Hollywood, CA 90038
tel: (323) 462-2161
fax: (323) 461-3090
e-mail: local47@afm.org
web site: *www.promusic47.org*

AFM Local 257
P.O. Box 120399
11 Music Circle North
Nashville, TN 37212
tel: (615) 244-9514
fax: (615) 259-9140
web site: *www.afm.org*

AFM Local 802
322 West 48th Street
New York, NY 10036
tel: (212) 245-4802
fax: (212) 293-0002
web site: *www.local802afm.org*

AFM Local 802—New York Headquarters
1501 Broadway, Suite 600
New York, NY 10036
tel: (212) 869-1330
fax: (212) 764-6134

AFM Local 802—West Coast Office
3550 Wilshire Boulevard, Suite 1900
Los Angeles, CA 90010
tel: (213) 251-4510
fax: (213) 251-4520

AFM Local 802—Legislative Office
910 17th Street NW, Suite 1070
Washington, DC 20006
tel: (202) 463-0772
fax: (202) 463-7441

AFM Local 802—Canadian Office
75 The Donway West, Suite 1010
Don Mills, ON M3C 2E9
tel: (416) 391-5161
fax: (416) 391-5165

American Federation of Television and Radio Artists (AFTRA)
In addition to those listed below, AFTRA has offices in the following cities:
Bethesda/Baltimore, Boston, Buffalo, Chicago, Cleveland, Dallas/Ft. Worth, Denver,
Detroit, Fresno, Honolulu, Houston, Kansas City (Missouri), Miami, New Orleans,
Omaha, Philadelphia, Phoenix, Pittsburgh, Portland (Oregon), Rochester (New York),
Sacramento, San Diego, San Francisco, Schenectady/Albany (New York), Seattle, St.
Louis, Cincinnati, and Minneapolis. Addresses for these cities can be found on the
main web site at *www.aftra.org*, or by contacting any of the listed offices.

AFTRA—Atlanta
455 East Paces Ferry Road, Northeast, Suite 334
Atlanta, GA 30305
tel: (404) 239-0131
fax: (404) 239-0137
e-mail: aftra@aftra.com
web site: *www.aftra.org*

AFTRA—Chicago
One East Erie, Suite 650
Chicago, IL 60611
Eileen Willenborg, Executive Director
tel: (312) 573-8081
fax: (312) 573-0318
e-mail: Chicago@aftra.com
web site: *www.aftra.org*

AFTRA—New York
260 Madison Avenue, 7th Floor
New York, NY 10016

tel: (212) 532-0800
fax: (212) 545-1238
e-mail: aftra@aftra.com
web site: *www.aftra.org*

AFTRA—Los Angeles
5757 Wilshire Boulevard, 9th Floor
Los Angeles, CA 90036
tel: (323) 634-8100
fax: (323) 634-8246
e-mail: aftra@aftra.com
web site: *www.aftra.org*

AFTRA—Nashville
P.O. Box 121087
1108 17th Avenue South
Nashville, TN 37212
tel: (615) 327-2944
fax: (615) 329-2803
e-mail: nashville@aftra.com
web site: *www.aftra.org*

American Society of Composers, Authors and Publishers (ASCAP)

ASCAP—Atlanta
PMB 400
541 10th Street Northwest
Atlanta, GA 30318
tel: (404) 635-1758
fax: (404) 627-2404
e-mail: info@ascap.com
web site: *www.ascap.com*

ASCAP—Chicago
1608 West Belmont Avenue, Suite 200
Chicago, IL 60657
tel: (773) 472-1157
fax: (773) 472-1158
e-mail: info@ascap.com
web site: *www.ascap.com*

ASCAP—Los Angeles
7920 West Sunset Boulevard, Third Floor
Los Angeles, CA 90046
tel: (323) 883-1000
fax: (323) 883-1049

e-mail: info@ascap.com
web site: *www.ascap.com*

ASCAP—Miami
420 Lincoln Road, Suite 385
Miami Beach, FL 33129
tel: (305) 673-3446
fax: (305) 673-2446
e-mail: info@ascap.com
web site: *www.ascap.com*

ASCAP—Nashville
Two Music Square West
Nashville, TN 37203
tel: (615) 742-5000
fax: (615) 742-5020
e-mail: info@ascap.com
web site: *www.ascap.com*

ASCAP—New York
One Lincoln Plaza
New York, NY 10023
tel: (212) 621-6000
fax: (212) 724-9064
e-mail: info@ascap.com
web site: *www.ascap.com*

Association of Independent Music Publishers (AIMP)

AIMP—New York
156 West 56th Street, Suite 1803
New York, NY 10019
tel: (212) 582-7622
fax: (212) 582-8273
e-mail: NYjoin@aimp.org
web site: *www.aimp.org*

AIMP—California
P.O. Box 1561
Burbank, CA 91507
tel: (818) 842-6257
e-mail: LAjoin@aimp.org and info@aimp.org
web site: *www.aimp.org*

Audio Engineering Society, Inc.
International Headquarters
60 East 42nd Street, Room 2520
New York, NY 10165-2520
tel: (212) 661-8528
fax: (212) 682-0477
e-mail: HQ@aes.org
web site: *www.aes.org*

Broadcast Music, Inc. (BMI)

BMI—Atlanta
3340 Peachtree Road, NE, Suite 570
Atlanta, GA 30326
tel: (404) 261-5151

BMI—Los Angeles
8730 Sunset Boulevard, 3rd Floor West
Los Angeles, CA 90069-2211
tel: (310) 659-9109
fax: (310) 657-2850
e-mail: losangeles@bmi.com
web site: *www.bmi.com*

BMI—Miami
5201 Blue Lagoon Drive, Suite 310
Miami, FL 33126
tel: (305) 266-3636
web site: *www.bmi.com*

BMI—Nashville
10 Music Square East
Nashville, TN 37203-4399
tel: (615) 401-2106
fax: (615) 401-2326
e-mail: nashville@bmi.com
web site: *www.bmi.com*

BMI—New York
320 West 57th Street
New York, NY 10019-3790
tel: (212) 586-2000
fax: (212) 246-2163
e-mail: newyork@bmi.com
web site: *www.bmi.com*

Country Music Association (CMA)
One Music Circle South
Nashville, TN 37203-4312
tel: (615) 244-2840
fax: (615) 242-4783
web site: *www.cmaworld.com*

Country Radio Broadcasters, Inc. (CRB)
819 18th Avenue South
Nashville, TN 37203
tel: (615) 327-4487
fax: (615) 329-4492
web site: *www.crb.org*

Film Music Network
Global Media Development Group
23360 Valencia Boulevard, Suite E-12
Valencia, CA 91355
tel: (310) 645-9000 or (800) 774-3700
fax: (310) 388-1367
e-mail: admin@gmdgroup.com
web site: *www.filmmusic.net*

Film Music Society
1516 South Bundy Drive, Suite 305
Los Angeles, CA 90025
tel: (310) 820-1909
fax: (310) 820-1301
e-mail: info@filmmusicsociety.org
web site: *www.filmmusicsociety.org*

Gospel Music Association
1205 Division Street
Nashville, TN 37203
tel: (615) 242-0303
fax: (615) 254-9755
web site: *www.gospelmusic.org*

Harry Fox Agency, Inc. (HFA)
601 West 26th Street
New York, NY 10001
tel: (212) 834-0100
fax: (212) 487-6779
web site: *www.nmpa.org*

International Bluegrass Music Association (IBMA)
2 Music Circle South, Suite 100
Nashville, TN 37203
tel: (615) 256-3222
fax: (615) 256-0450
e-mail: info@ibma.org
web site: *www.ibma.org*

International Entertainment Buyers Association (IEBA)
P.O. Box 128376
Nashville, TN 37212
tel: (615) 251-9000
fax: (615) 251-9001
e-mail: info@ieba.org
web site: *www.ieba.org*

International Fan Club Organization (IFCO)
P.O. Box 40328
Nashville, TN 37204
tel: (615) 371-9596
fax: (615) 371-9597
e-mail: 4info@ifco.org
web site: *www.ifco.org*

International Recording Media Association (IRMA)
182 Nassau Street, Suite 204
Princeton, NJ 08542
tel: (609) 279-1799
fax: (609) 279-1999
e-mail: info@recordingmedia.org
web site: *www.recordingmedia.org*

Music Publishers' Association (MPA)
243 5th Avenue, Suite 236
New York, NY 10016
tel: (212) 327-4044
e-mail: admin@mpa.org
web site: *www.mpa.org*

Nashville Songwriters Association International (NSAI)
1710 Roy Acuff Place
Nashville, TN 37203
tel: (615) 256-3354 or (800) 321-6008
fax: (615) 256-0034
e-mail: nsai@nashvillesongwriters.com
web site: *www.nashvillesongwriters.com*

National Academy of Recording Arts & Sciences (NARAS)

Los Angeles Chapter—Main Office
The Recording Academy
3402 Pico Boulevard
Santa Monica, CA 90405
tel: (310) 392-3777
fax: (310) 399-3090
e-mail: losangeles@grammy.com
web site: *www.grammy.com*

The Grammy Foundation
3402 Pico Boulevard
Santa Monica, CA 90405
tel: (310) 392-3777
fax: (310) 392-2188
e-mail: grammyfoundation@grammy.com
web site: *www.grammy.com*

MusiCares—West Region
3402 Pico Boulevard
Santa Monica, CA 90405
tel: (310) 392-3777 or (800) 687-4227
fax: (310) 392-2187
web site: *www.grammy.com*

NARAS—Atlanta Chapter
3290 Northside Parkway, Suite 280
Atlanta, GA 30327
tel: (404) 816-1380
fax: (404) 816-1390
e-mail: Atlanta@grammy.com
web site: *www.grammy.com*

NARAS—Chicago Chapter
224 South Michigan Avenue, Suite 250
Chicago, IL 60604
tel: (312) 786-1121
fax: (312) 786-1934
e-mail: chicago@grammy.com
web site: *www.grammy.com*

NARAS—Florida Chapter
311 Lincoln Road, Suite 301
Miami Beach, FL 33139
tel: (305) 672-4060

fax: (305) 672-2076
e-mail: florida@grammy.com
web site: *www.grammy.com*

NARAS—Memphis Chapter

493 South Main Street, Suite 101
Memphis, TN 38103
tel: (901) 525-1340
fax: (901) 521-6553
e-mail: memphis@grammy.com
web site: *www.grammy.com*

NARAS—Nashville Chapter

1904 Wedgewood Avenue
Nashville, TN 37212
tel: (615) 327-8030
fax: (615) 321-3101
e-mail: nashville@grammy.com
web site: *www.grammy.com*

NARAS—New York Chapter

156 West 56th Street, 17th Floor
New York, NY 10019
tel: (212) 245-5440
fax: (212) 489-0394
e-mail: newyork@grammy.com
web site: *www.grammy.com*

NARAS—Pacific Northwest Branch

159 Western Avenue West, Suite 485
Seattle, WA 98119
tel: (206) 834-1000
fax: (206) 834-1005
e-mail: pacificnw@grammy.com
web site: *www.grammy.com*

NARAS—Philadelphia Chapter

One Liberty Place
1650 Market Street
36th floor, Suite 3640
Philadelphia, PA 19103
tel: (215) 985-5411
e-mail: philadelphia@grammy.com
web site: *www.grammy.com*

NARAS—San Francisco Chapter
1702 Union Street
San Francisco, CA 94123
tel: (415) 749-0779
fax: (415) 749-1780
e-mail: sanfrancisco@grammy.com
web site: *www.grammy.com*

NARAS—Texas Chapter
3601 South Congress Avenue, G-500
Austin, TX 78704
tel: (512) 328-7997
fax: (512) 328-7998
e-mail: texas@grammy.com
web site: *www.grammy.com*

NARAS—Washington, D.C. Branch
529 14th Street, NW, Suite 840
Washington, DC 20045
tel: (202) 662-1341
fax: (202) 662-1342
e-mail: washingtondc@grammy.com
web site: *www.grammy.com*

National Association of Campus Activities (NACA)
13 Harbison Way
Columbia, SC 29212-3401
tel: (803) 732-6222
fax: (803) 749-1047
web site: *www.naca.org*

National Association of Composers
P.O. Box 49256
Barrington Station
Los Angeles, CA 90049
tel: (818) 274-6048
web site: *www.music-usa.org/nacusa*

National Association of Music Merchants (NAMM)
International Music Products Association
5790 Armada Drive
Carlsbad, CA 92008
tel: (760) 438-8001
fax: (760) 438-7327
e-mail: info@namm.com
web site: *www.namm.com*

National Association of Record Merchandisers (NARM)
9 Eves Drive, Suite 120
Marlton, NJ 08053
tel: (856) 596-2221
fax: (856) 596-3268
web site: *www.narm.com*

National Music Publishers' Association, Inc. (NMPA)—Main Office
101 Constitution Avenue NW, Suite 705 East
Washington, DC 20001
tel: (202) 742-4375
fax: (202) 742-4377
web site: *www.nmpa.org*

Recording Industry Association of America (RIAA)
1025 F Street NW, 10th Floor
Washington, DC 20004
tel: (202) 775-0101
web site: *www.riaa.com*

SESAC—Nashville (Headquarters)
55 Music Square, East
Nashville, TN 37203-4324
tel: (615) 320-0055
fax: (615) 329-9627
web site: *www.sesac.com*

SESAC—New York
152 West 57th Street, 57th Floor
New York, NY 10019
tel: (212) 586-3450
fax: (212) 489-5699
web site: *www.sesac.com*

SESAC—Los Angeles
501 Santa Monica Boulevard, Suite 450
Santa Monica, CA 90401
tel: (310) 393-9671
fax: (310) 393-6497
web site: *www.sesac.com*

SESAC—Atlanta
981 Joseph E Lowery Boulevard Northwest, Suite 111
Atlanta, GA 30318
tel: (404) 897-1330
web site: *www.sesac.com*

SESAC—Miami
420 Lincoln Road, Suite 502
Miami, FL 33139
tel: (305) 534-7500
web site: *www.sesac.com*

Songwriters Guild of America (SGA)

SGA West Coast (Los Angeles)
6430 Sunset Boulevard, Suite 705
Hollywood, CA 90028
tel: (323) 462-1108
fax: (323) 462-5430
e-mail: la@songwritersguild.com
web site: *www.songwritersguild.com*

SGA Central (Nashville)
209 10th Avenue South, Suite 321
Nashville, TN 37203
tel: (615) 742-9945
fax: (615) 742-9948
e-mail: nash@songwritersguild.com
web site: *www.songwritersguild.com*

SGA East Coast (New York)
1560 Broadway, Suite 408
New York, NY 10036
tel: (212) 768-7902
e-mail: ny@songwritersguild.com
web site: *www.songwritersguild.com*

SGA Administration (Nashville)
209 10th Avenue South, Suite 321
Nashville, TN 37203
tel: (615) 742-9945
fax: (615) 742-9948
e-mail: corporate@songwritersguild.com
web site: *www.songwritersguild.com*

South By Southwest (SXSW)
P.O. Box 4999
Austin, TX 78765
tel: (512) 467-7979
fax: (512) 451-0754
e-mail: sxsw@sxsw.com
web site: *http://www.sxsw.com/contact.shtml*

Women in Music National Network
1450 Oddstad Drive
Redwood City, CA 94063
tel: (866) 305-7963
fax: (510) 234-7272
e-mail: info@womeninmusic.com
web site: *www.womeninmusic.com*

DIRECTORIES AND MAGAZINES

What follows is a selection of important industry magazines and directories of who's who in the music business.

All Music Guide
All Media Guide
1168 Oak Valley Drive
Ann Arbor, MI 48108
web site: *www.allmusic.com* and *www.allmediaguide.com*
(Database of recorded music.)

ARTISTdirect, Inc.
17835 Ventura Boulevard
Encino, CA 91316
tel: (818) 748-8700
web site: *www.artistdirect.com*
(Online music magazine, resource, and store.)

ASCAP Playback
ASCAP Building
One Lincoln Plaza, 6th Floor
New York, NY 10023
tel: (212) 621-6000
fax: (212) 632-7328
e-mail: info@ascap.com
web site: *www.ascap.com*

American Songwriter
1009 17th Avenue South
Nashville, TN 37212
tel: (615) 321-6096
fax: (615) 244-6065
e-mail: asongmag@aol.com
web site: *www.americansongwriter.com*

Billboard Magazine
770 Broadway
New York, NY 10003
tel: (646) 654-4400
fax: (646) 654-4681
web site: *www.billboard.com*
(In addition to the weekly magazine, *Billboard* publishes a variety of music industry guides including *Billboard International Talent & Touring Directory*; *Billboard International Buyer's Guide*; *Billboard Record Retailing Directory*; *International Tape/Disc Directory*; *The Radio Power Book*; *Billboard International Latin Music*

Buyer's Guide; *Nashville 615/Country Music Sourcebook*; *Music & Media/Billboard EuroFile*; and *Musicians Guide to Touring and Promotion*.)

Close-Up
Country Music Association
1 Music Circle South
Nashville, TN 37203
tel: (615) 244-2840
web site: *www.cmaworld.com*

The CMJ Network
151 West 25th Street, 12th Floor
New York, NY 10001
tel: (917) 606-1908
fax: (917) 606-1914
web site: *www.cmj.com*
(Resource for new music industry professionals and fans.)

CMJ New Music Monthly
151 West 25th Street, 12th Floor
New York, NY 10001
tel: (917) 606-1908
fax: (917) 606-1914
web site: *www.cmj.com*
(Monthly magazine.)

Daily Variety
Los Angeles Office
5700 Wilshire Boulevard, Suite 120
Los Angeles, CA 90036
tel: (323) 857-6600
fax: (323) 857-0494
web site: *www.variety.com*

Film Music Magazine
1146 N Central Avenue, Suite 103
Glendale, CA 91202
tel: 888-678-6158
fax: (888) 507-4944
e-mail: *info@filmmusicmag.com*
(Monthly trade publication for film and television music professionals with articles on performing rights, legal issues, audio engineering, technology, studios, and more.)

Guitar World
4000 Shoreline Court, Suite 400
South San Francisco, CA 94080

tel: (650) 872-1642
fax: (650) 872-1643
web site: *www.guitarworld.com*
(Monthly magazine with product reviews, interviews, and studio chatter.)

Film Score Monthly
5455 Wilshire Boulevard, Suite 1500
Los Angeles, CA 90036-4204
e-mail: lukas@filmscoremonthly.com
web site: *www.filmscoremonthly.com*
(Monthly magazine)

Gavin Report
140 Second Street
San Francisco, CA 94105
tel: (415) 495-1990
fax: (415) 495-2580
web site: *www.gavin.com*
(Weekly magazine)

Gig Magazine
460 Park Avenue South, 9th Floor
New York, NY 10016
tel: (212) 378-0400
fax: (212) 378-2160
e-mail: gigeditor@uemedia.com
web site: *www.gigmag.com*
(Monthly magazine)

Film & Television Music Guide
7510 Sunset Boulevard, Suite 1041
Los Angeles, CA 90046
tel: (818) 769-2722
fax: (818) 769-9818
web site: *www.musicregistry.com*
(Guide to publishers, composers, studios, music supervisors, and others in the film
and television music industry.)

Hits Magazine
14958 Ventura Boulevard
Sherman Oaks, CA 91403
tel: (818) 501 7900
fax: (818) 789-0259
web site: *www.hitsdailydouble.com*
(Reports on chartmakers and hits in contemporary pop music, with general industry
news and information.)

Hollywood Reporter
5055 Wilshire Boulevard
Los Angeles, CA 90036
tel: (323) 525-2000
fax: (323) 525-2377
web site: *www.hollywoodreporter.com*
(Weekly magazine)

Lone Eagle Publishing Inc.
Hollywood Creative Directory
5055 Wilshire Boulevard
Los Angeles, CA 90036
tel: (323) 525-2369
fax: (323) 525-2348
e-mail: info@loneeagle.com
web site: *www.loneeagle.com*

Mix Magazine
6400 Hollis Street, Suite 350
Emeryville, CA 94608
tel: (510) 653-3307
(Publishes this monthly magazine and *Electronic Musician*, *Mix Books*, *Recording Industry Sourcebook*, and *Mix Master Directory*.)

Music Business International
1 Penn Plaza, 11th Floor
New York, NY 10119
tel: (212) 615-2785
fax: (212) 279-3969
web site: *www.dotmusic.com*
(International magazine)

Music Connection, Inc.
16130 Ventura Boulevard, Suite 540
Encino, CA 91436
tel: (818) 995-0101
fax: (818) 995-9235
web site: *www.musicconnection.com*
(Published every other Thursday)

Music Row Publications, Inc.
P.O. Box 158542
Nashville, TN 37215
tel: (615) 321-3617
fax: (615) 329-0852
e-mail: news@musicrow.com

web site: *www.musicrow.com*
(Weekly magazine and annual *In Charge* guide that profiles Nashville music executives.)

Music Supervisors 411
SES Publishing
8441 Sunset Boulevard, #1771
Los Angeles, CA 90069
(Databases for TV and film music.)

Performing Songwriter
33 Music Square West
Nashville, TN 37203
tel: (615) 256-4708
e-mail: editorsps@performingsongwriter.com
web site: *www.performingsongwriter.com*
(Monthly magazine.)

Pollstar
4697 West Jacquelyn Avenue
Fresno, CA 93722
tel: (559) 271-7900
fax: (559) 271-7979
e-mail: info@pollstar.com
web site: *www.pollstar.com*
(Weekly magazine that publishes several directories including *Agency Rosters*, *Concert Support Services Directory*, *Concert Venue Directory*, *ConneXions*, *Record Company Rosters* (including distribution and publishing companies), and *Talent Buyer Directory*.)

Radio & Records, Inc. (R&R)
10100 Santa Monica Boulevard, Fifth Floor
Los Angeles, CA 90067-4004
tel: (310) 553-4330
fax: (310) 203-9763
e-mail: radioandrecords@espcomp.com
web site: *www.radioandrecords.com*
(Produces a variety of music directories—many of which are on-line—and a weekly magazine.)

Rolling Stone
1290 Avenue of the Americas
New York, NY 10104
tel: (212) 484-1616
web site: *www.rollingstone.com*
(Monthly magazine.)

Spin
205 Lexington Avenue
New York, NY 10016
tel: (212) 633-8200
fax: (212) 633-9041
web site: *www.spin.com*
(Monthly magazine.)

FOUR-YEAR SCHOOLS OFFERING DEGREES IN MUSIC BUSINESS MANAGEMENT

The following is a list of four-year schools offering degrees related to music business management. They are grouped by state. A web address or e-mail address has been provided for each school. Check the most recent edition of Barron's *Profiles of American Colleges* for schools offering other music-related degrees.

ALABAMA
Oakwood College
Huntsville, AL 35896
www.oakwood.edu

CALIFORNIA
Biola University
La Mirada, CA 90639-0001
www.admission@calbaptist.edu

Point Loma Nazarene University
San Diego, CA 92106-2899
e-mail: *discover@ptloma.edu*

University of Southern California
Los Angeles, CA 90089
www.usc.edu

University of the Pacific
Stockton, CA 95211-0197
www.uop.edu

CONNECTICUT
University of Hartford
West Hartford, CT 06117
e-mail: *admissions@uhavax.hartford.edu*

University of New Haven
West Haven, CT 06516
www.newhaven.edu

DISTRICT OF COLUMBIA
Howard University
Washington, D.C. 20059
www.howard.edu

FLORIDA
Jacksonville University
Jacksonville, FL 32211
www.ju.edu

University of Miami
Coral Gables, FL 33124
www.miami.edu

GEORGIA
Shorter College
Rome, GA 30165-4298
www.shorter.edu

ILLINOIS
Blackburn College
Carlinville, IL 62626
www.blackburn.edu

Columbia College Chicago
Chicago, IL 60605
e-mail: *admissions@popmail.colum.edu*

DePaul University
Chicago, IL 60604
e-mail: *admitdpu@wppost.depaul.edu*

Elmhurst College
Elmhurst, IL 60126-3296
www.elmhurst.edu

Quincy University
Quincy, IL 62301-2699
www.quincy.edu/

Roosevelt University
Chicago, IL 60605
www.roosevelt.edu

INDIANA
Anderson University
Anderson, IN 46012
www.anderson.edu

Butler University
Indianapolis, IN 46208
www.butler.edu

DePauw University
Greencastle, IN 46135
www.depauw.edu

University of Evansville
Evansville, IN 47722-0329
www.evansville.edu

IOWA
Drake University
Des Moines, IA 50311
www.drake.edu

MASSACHUSETTS
Berklee College of Music
Boston, MA 02215-3693
www.berklee.edu

MICHIGAN
Wayne State University
Detroit, MI 48202
www.wayne.edu

MINNESOTA
St. Mary's University of Minnesota
Winona, MN 55987-1399
www.smumn.edu

University of Saint Thomas
St. Paul, MN 55105
www.stthomas.edu

NEBRASKA
Peru State College
Peru, NE 68421-0010
www.peru.edu

NEW JERSEY
Monmouth University
West Long Branch, NJ 07764-1898
www.monmouth.edu

NEW YORK
Five Towns College
Dix Hills, NY 11746
e-mail: *admissions@ftc.edu*

New York University
New York, NY 10011
www.nyu.edu/ugadmissions/

State University of New York at
Oneonta
Oneonta, NY 13820-4015
www.oneonta.edu

State University of New York at
Potsdam
Potsdam, NY 13676
e-mail: *admissions@potsdam.edu*

Syracuse University
Syracuse, NY 13244
www.syracuse.edu

NORTH CAROLINA
Johnson C. Smith University
Charlotte, NC 28216
www.jcsu.edu/

Methodist College
Fayetteville, NC 28311-1420
www.methodist.edu

Montreat College
Montreat, NC 28757
www.montreat.edu

Saint Augustine's College
Raleigh, NC 27610-2298
www.st-aug.edu

Wingate University
Wingate, NC 28174
e-mail: *admit@wingate.edu*

Winston-Salem State University
Winston-Salem, NC 27110
www.wssu.edu

OHIO
Baldwin-Wallace College
Berea, OH 44017-2088
e-mail: *jbaker@rs6000baldwinw.edu*

Ohio Northern University
Ada, OH 45810
www.onu.edu

OREGON
Southern Oregon University
Ashland, OR 97520-5005
www.sou.edu

PENNSYLVANIA
Geneva College
Beaver Falls, PA 15010
www.geneva.edu

Grove City College
Grove City, PA 16127-2104
www.gcc.edu

Mansfield University
Mansfield, PA 16933
www.mnsfld.edu

SOUTH CAROLINA
Erskine College
Due West, SC 29639
www.erskine.edu

South Carolina State University
Orangeburg, SC 29117
e-mail: *admissions@scsu.edu*

SOUTH DAKOTA
South Dakota State University
Brookings, SD 57007
www.sdstate.edu

TENNESSEE
Belmont University
Nashville, TN 31212-3757
e-mail: *buadmission@belmont.edu*

Middle Tennessee State University
Murfreesboro, TN 37132
www.mtsu.edu

Trevecca Nazarene University
Nashville, TN 37210-2877
www.trevecca.edu

University of Memphis
Memphis, TN 38152
www.memphis.edu/

TEXAS
University of the Incarnate Word
San Antonio, TX 78209-6397
www.uiw.edu

VERMONT
Johnson State College
Johnson, VT 05656
www.jsc.vsc.edu

WEST VIRGINIA
University of Charleston
Charleston, WV 25304
www.uchaswv.edu

WISCONSIN
Marian College of Fond du Lac
Fond du Lac, WI 54935
www.mariancollege.edu

GLOSSARY

A&R Artist and Repertoire. The department within a record company assigned to scout talent and songs, develop artists, match artists with record producers, and oversee record production.

AC Adult Contemporary. A radio format that broadcasts material drawn from soft rock contemporary artists.

accounting statement A statement of royalties earned by an artist from either a publisher or a record company, usually issued quarterly.

ACM Academy of Country Music. Los Angeles-based country music industry organization.

acoustic Musical instruments that are not electronically amplified.

add A record added to a radio station or video channel playlist.

administration deal A publishing contract in which a music publisher issues licenses, and collects mechanical royalties on behalf of an artist, in return for a percentage of receipts, but does not control the copyrights and is not obligated to exploit the artist's material.

advance A prepayment of royalties or other earnings that will later be recouped from sales.

affiliate *See* network.

AFM American Federation of Musicians. A musicians' union.

AFTRA American Federation of Television and Radio Artists. A broadcast talent union.

airplay The broadcast of a recording or music video on radio or television.

AMC American Music Conference. An organization that promotes music education.

amplitude Volume. *See* dynamic range.

AMVB Association of Music Video Broadcasters. A video industry organization.

analog A recording and playback method where the speed and loudness of sound waves are reflected in a similar fashion onto magnetic tape or a phonograph record.

ancillary income Concert revenues derived from parking, food and beverage service, and so on, which are not subject to artist or promoter commissions.

AOR Album-Oriented Rock. A radio format that broadcasts material drawn from rock albums, rather than from singles.

ARB *See* Arbitron.

Arbitron The American Research Bureau (ARB) radio rating service.

arrangement A written or mental musical score specifying instrumental parts, vocal harmonies, and overall form of a composition.

artist concessions Concert revenues derived from the sale of the artist's own merchandise, which may be subject to venue commissions.

ASCAP American Society of Composers, Authors, and Publishers. A royalty collection and performance rights organization.

audio engineer A person who designs or operates sound recording and reproduction equipment.

author The creator of a copyrightable work.

automation Radio or television broadcast of prerecorded material by electronically programmed machinery.

bar code The series of black and white stripes assigned by the Universal Product Code (UPC) to encode product information.

BDS Broadcast Data Service. The company that uses computers to monitor radio airplay.

BET Black Entertainment Television. A cable television broadcaster whose programming is geared toward the African-American market.

blanket license Permission to use a recording, or group of recordings, for unlimited play for a set fee, rather than on an individual per-use basis.

BMI Broadcast Music, Inc. A royalty collection and performance rights organization.

book Management terminology for selling a performance date to a promoter or venue.

bootleg An unauthorized recording manufactured and sold without payment of royalties.

branch distributor A regional distributorship owned and operated by one of six conglomerates.

break To gain sufficient airplay or exposure to generate a significant sales increase.

break-even point The dollar amount at which income equals expenses.

breakage allowance A percentage deducted by the label from artist royalties to cover product damage.

broadcast The electrical transmission of sound or image through waves that can be reconstituted by a receiver mechanism.

budget line A record label product line that sells for less than new releases by established artists.

bump Also called an "escalation"; this is a provision in a recording contract that increases an artist's percentage points if a certain number of records are sold. *See* point.

burnout Radio industry terminology for when the public grows tired of a particular record.

buy-back An agreement that a given promoter will promote an artist's show the next time the artist is in the promoter's area of influence.

© Symbol signifying that a particular work has been copyrighted.

call-out Market research based upon a radio station calling the public within its listening area to solicit opinions on programming.

CARP Copyright Arbitration Royalty Panel. A panel appointed to arbitrate a specific copyright or royalty dispute.

catalog The song copyrights owned by a publishing company, or the master recordings owned by a record company.

catalog album The previously released recordings owned by a record company, but that are no longer being promoted.

census The logging by a performance rights organization of every single recorded performance played by a broadcaster. *See* sample.

chain A group of retail outlets owned by the same parent company.

channel A specific electronic path for broadcast or recording signals.

chart Industry ranking of records according to rate of sales and/or broadcast.

CHR Contemporary Hit Radio. A radio format that broadcasts material drawn primarily from the 20 most popular records of each week.

clearance Permission granted to reproduce a copyrightable work.

clip A film segment of a performance.

CMA Country Music Association. Nashville-based country music industry organization.

collective work Individual works assembled into a copyrightable whole. An anthology.

commercial spot A prerecorded radio or television advertisement.

commercially acceptable The minimum level of artistic and technical merit necessary for a recording master to warrant manufacture and distribution by a record label.

commission A percentage of an artist's income paid for agent or management services.

common-law copyright Copyright protection applied to works not fixed in a tangible form.

compression Reducing the range between the highest and lowest frequencies of audio signals, particularly during mastering of phonograph records.

compulsory license Permission personally granted by the artist to reproduce a copyrightable work.

concept video A music video that tells a story beyond the simple recording of an artist performing a song.

configuration The media format on which a recording is fixed, such as cassette or CD.

container charge A percentage deduction from artist royalties to cover the cost of product manufacturing and packaging.

contemporary Music and broadcasting terminology for current popular music.

contributory infringer One who receives benefit from copyright infringement.

controlled composition A song or master, partially or wholly owned by an artist, which his record label wants to acquire at a reduced rate.

co-op advertising Money paid by a record label to distributors or retailers to locally advertise the label's product.

co-publishing An arrangement whereby two or more publishing companies, one of which usually belongs to the songwriter, share copyrights and royalties to a single song.

copy Advertising and public relations terminology for written advertising or press releases.

copyright Ownership or licensed control over artistic or intellectual property.

copyright administration The registration of artistic works with the Copyright Office and the licensing of those works for reproduction.

corporate A derogatory term for music specifically created to fill a market niche, rather than as an artistic expression.

counterfeit recording A "pirate" recording that is duplicated and sold with the intent to defraud the legitimate owner of royalties.

cover A performance of a song by an artist other than the one who originally recorded it.

creative controls Authority granted to control various creative aspects of a recording.

cross-collateralization A provision within a recording contract that allows the label to recover losses on one recording from the sales of the artist's future earnings.

crossover When a record gains sales or is broadcast in more than a single market format.

crosstalk The leaking of sound from one track to another on audiotape.

cutout A recording deleted from a record label's catalog, with remaining stock sold at a discount.

dB Decibel. The standard unit of measure for audio loudness.

dbx A patented noise reduction system that compresses sound and encodes it onto tape or disc for recording and playback.

defaulter Union terminology for an individual who refuses to pay singers or musicians for a live or recorded performance.

delay The electronic analog or digital close repetition of a sound signal during recording.

demo Demonstration recording of a song or performance.

derivative work A copyrightable work that draws heavily on other pre-existing works.

development deal A short-term contract and fee supplied to an artist not sufficiently developed to warrant a true contract, giving a record label or publishing company the option to sign the artist during a specified time period.

digital A recording system where sound is sampled and converted by computer into a high-speed binary pulse code for storage on magnetic tape or compact disc.

digital sampling Sound transformed and stored as a numerical sequence, which can then be reproduced in such a way as to be indistinguishable from the original sound.

disc mastering Cutting a master acetate disc from which vinyl phonograph records will be pressed.

distortion The variation in tone from the original source that occurs during recording or playback.

distributor A person or company that distributes products to retailers.

Dolby/Dolby Stereo A patented high-frequency noise reduction system for audio recordings and film sound tracks.

door The revenue from admission fees to a small venue. *See* gate.

draw A monetary payment against future sales or receipts. *See* advance.

drum machine The piece of electronic equipment that reproduces the sound and rhythmic patterns of drums.

dub (1) To blend several recorded sources into a single sound track. (2) To make a copy of recorded material. (3) A copy of recorded material.

dues Monthly or annual fee to maintain membership in an industry association or union.

dynamic range The range between the softest and loudest sound possible on any recording or playback system.

echo The controlled reverberation of recorded sound.

editing Assembling recorded material into the order it will appear on the finished album or video project.

end cap The portion of a retail display at the end of a fixture, facing the main aisle.

engineer The technician who operates the sound board during the recording process.

equalization (EQ) Electronically adjusting the frequency levels of individual audio tracks during the recording process or mixing.

established artist An artist with a proven marketability.

evergreen A song that maintains a consistent popularity over many years. A standard.

exclusive artist An artist contractually obligated to record for a single record label.

exclusive contract The contractual obligation that binds an exclusive artist.

exclusive license Copyright permission granted to a single user and none other.

exclusive songwriter A songwriter contractually obligated to write for a single publisher.

fair use A provision that permits limited use of copyrighted works without payment of royalties.

FCC Federal Communications Commission. The government agency that regulates all broadcasting and telephone transmissions.

filter The electronic suppression of specific pre-chosen audio frequencies.

first sale doctrine A provision that allows the lawful owner of a reproduction of a copyrighted work limited rights to sell, rent, lease, or give away that reproduction.

flat A full-size album front cover reproduction used for display purposes.

flutter *See* wow and flutter.

folio A songbook containing multiple song scores, as opposed to individual sheet music.

45 A 45 RPM vinyl phonograph record with one song recorded on each side.

four walls A deal where a concert promoter rents a venue with no other services provided beyond use of the building itself.

free goods A recording contract provision that provides a distributor or retailer free copies of a record, usually 15 percent of the total quantity ordered, for which the artist receives no royalties. *See* promotional copies.

frequency The speed of sound wave vibration that produces any given sound. *See* Hz.

front line A record label's most recent releases from its top artists.

gate The revenue from admission fees to a concert venue. *See* door.

GATT General Agreement on Tariffs and Trade. International treaty that sanctions World Trade Organization member nations for failing to protect copyrights.

glass master Sometimes called the "mutha," it is the CD master used for duplication.

gold The RIAA designation for records that sell 500,000 wholesale copies, or videos that sell 50,000 wholesale copies. *See* platinum.

good ears Industry terminology for a person who can choose songs or artists that will be successful.

Grammy Awards Annual recording industry achievement recognition awarded by NARAS.

grand rights Permission granted to perform a copyrighted dramatic musical work, such as an opera.

gross income Total income before expenses, taxes, and so on are deducted.

guarantee The fixed amount an artist will be paid to perform, regardless of ticket sales.

hard tickets Admission tickets preprinted and distributed before going on sale. *See* soft tickets.

harmonics The use of complementary full and half tones to create a composite tone.

Harry Fox Agency A royalty collection and licensing agency organized by NMPA.

hiss The high-frequency background noise picked up during recording with analog tape. *See* dbx and Dolby.

hold A verbal agreement to reserve a song for a specific artist, or a venue date for a specific promoter.

hype Exaggerated claims of worth or value. Short for "hyperbole."

Hz Hertz. The standard unit of measurement of audio pitch, communicated in cycles (vibrations) per second.

IATSE International Association of Theater and Stage Employees; a union for backstage technicians who work at theater and concert events.

in-house promotion A performance promoted by the venue itself, without an outside promoter.

independent distributor A wholesaler of product from independent record labels.

independent label A record label not affiliated with any of the six music conglomerates.

independent record store A record store not part of a chain.

indie Short for "independent."

infringement The act of violating the rights of a copyright owner.

initiation fee A one-time fee to join an industry association or union. *See* dues.

jingle A short song used in radio and television product advertising.

joint work A work created by two or more people that is copyrightable as a whole.

key-man clause A recording, publishing, or management contract provision that allows an artist to terminate the contract if a specific person, who is integral to that artist's career, leaves the company.

label An individual record company, or one of several product names under which a record company releases its recordings.

lacquer (1) Industry slang for a master disc. (2) The compound from which blank master discs are made.

lacquer master *See* lacquer and master.

Librarian of Congress The appointed officer of the Copyright Office, charged with distributing royalties collected by the office and convening arbitration panels. *See* CARP.

license Permission granted to reproduce a copyrighted work.

liquidate reserves When a record label must pay out any funds reserved beyond the actual dollar value of product returns.

listening station A record store outpost for "test driving" selected recordings.

local Union terminology for the regional union office.

logging *See* census.

long form A music video that is longer than five minutes, or is made up of several songs.

loss leader A product sold below cost to attract customers into a store.

major label One of six music conglomerates owning its own distribution system.

MAP Minimum Advertised Price. The price a record company sets to discourage a retailer from selling product below cost.

margin The difference between the cost of a product and its selling price.

mass merchandiser A retail outlet selling a wide variety of products, like a department store.

master The final, multitrack mix of a recording, either on tape or cut into a lacquer master disc, from which copies will be manufactured.

MBS Mutual Broadcasting System. A radio network.

mechanical license Permission granted to manufacture and distribute copies of a copyrighted sound recording.

mechanical royalty Fee paid by a record label to a music publisher in exchange for a mechanical license.

merchandising Any product that utilizes an artist's image, name, or likeness to promote that artist.

MIDI Musical Instrumental Digital Interface. The standard connection of digital electronic musical instruments to each other, computers, and software.

mid-line A record label's product priced between its front line and budget line.

mix/final mix The combination of multiple audio tracks into one or two tracks/the combination of multiple audio tracks into the final, two-track tape from which a master will be made.

mom and pop store *See* independent record store.

MOR Middle of the Road. A radio format that broadcasts material drawn from various sources termed as "easy listening" for an older adult market.

MSRP Manufacturer's Suggested Retail Price. The basis for computing recording artist royalties.

multitrack A recording system that allows from four to twenty-four separate audio tracks to be simultaneously recorded onto a single tape.

musicology A branch of scholarship that focuses primarily on music history.

NAB National Association of Broadcasters. A broadcast industry organization.

NAIRD National Association of Independent Record Distributors. An industry trade organization for independent record labels and distributors.

NAMM National Association of Music Merchants. An industry trade organization for music store owners.

NARAS National Academy of Recording Arts and Sciences. A recording industry organization. *See* Grammy Awards.

net income The remaining income after expenses, taxes, and so on, are deducted.

network A group of radio or television stations (affiliates) that broadcast programming supplied by one of the major broadcasting systems like ABC, CBS, or NBC.

niche marketing Specialized advertising aimed at specialized product consumers.

NMPA National Music Publisher's Association. An industry trade organization.

nonexclusive license Permission granted to reproduce a copyrighted work that may also be granted to other users at the same time. Performance and mechanical licenses are nonexclusive.

nonreturnable A prepayment of royalties or other earnings that will not be recouped from sales, or returned to the provider.

notice The copyright notice printed on published reproductions of copyrighted works.

NPR National Public Radio.

O Symbol signifying that the particular phonorecording has been copyrighted.

one-nighter A performance booked into a venue for a single night.

one-stop A distributor who sells all records from all labels to retailers.

option A provision that allows a contract to be extended for a specified amount of time beyond the original termination date.

out-of-the-box Radio terminology for adding a record to the playlist immediately upon receipt.

overdub To add new audio tracks to the tape of a music performance that was previously recorded.

overlay Overdubbing as applied to film sound tracks.

P&D deal Pressing and Distribution deal. An agreement between an independent record label and a distributor/manufacturer to make and distribute copies of recordings.

parallel imports Copies of records legitimately manufactured outside the country of origin for foreign distribution, but imported back into the country of origin for sale alongside copies that were manufactured for sale within the country of origin.

pay-for-play The practice of artists paying to perform at a popular nightclub as a way to gain recording industry attention.

pay-or-play A recording contract clause that allows a label to pay an artist scale wages for a recording session in lieu of actually having the artist play on the session, as a way of fulfilling the label's contractual obligation to the artist.

payola The illegal practice of a record label paying a disc jockey to play its records.

per-use license Permission to use a single recording on a one-time basis.

performance clause A publishing contract provision that reverts copyright ownership back to the songwriter if the publisher fails to exploit the writer's work in a specified manner.

performance right The right to publicly perform a copyrighted work.

performance royalty Fees paid to songwriters and music publishers in exchange for performance rights.

personality folio A songbook of compositions written or recorded by a particular artist.

piracy The unauthorized duplication and sale of sound recordings.

pitch (1) The relative location of a given musical sound within the range of audible frequencies. (2) The attempt to interest an artist in recording a particular song.

platinum The RIAA designation for records that sell one million wholesale copies or videos that sell ten thousand wholesale copies.

playlist A radio station's weekly programming list of songs to be played. *See* rotation.

PMCD Pre-mastered compact disc.

P-O-P Point of Purchase. Advertising and display materials supplied by a record label to record stores.

point Each point is equal to a percentage, usually 1 percent, of an artist's royalty rate.

point of sale The cash register where the sale of a product is actually recorded.

power of attorney The assigned right to act in a legally binding manner on behalf of another person.

pre-echo/post-echo A faint echo distortion on a taped recording caused by the "bleeding" of sound from an adjacent wrap of tape.

print rights Permission granted to reproduce printed sheet music of a copyrighted work.

progressive A radio format that broadcasts material drawn from artists and albums not usually receiving Top Forty airplay.

project studio A recording studio owned by an artist or producer for the sole use of the owner.

promotion The label department or outside agency whose job it is to get radio airplay for the label's records.

promotional copies Copies of recordings given to radio stations and record stores for airplay or giveaways.

public domain Works whose copyrights have expired or were not eligible for copyright, and are available for public use without licensing.

publishing administration A sub-licensing agreement where a large music publisher issues licenses and collects royalties on behalf of a smaller company, in exchange for a percentage of income.

rack jobber A distributor who services the record department of a mass merchandiser.

rack location A store with a record department serviced by a rack jobber.

rating The percentage of listeners a radio station attracts within its listening area.

recording fund Money advanced by the label to pay the costs of a master recording.

Recording Trust Fund A small percentage of a record's list price paid to the AFM by the label to fund free public concerts.

recoupable Advance money repaid to the label through deductions from the artist's royalties.

recurrent Radio terminology for a recent hit record still popular enough to warrant fairly regular airplay, but that is neither a current hit nor an "oldie."

release A recording available to the public for purchase.

release date The actual day a recording is first available to the public for purchase.

renegotiate The practice of an artist using his success to obtain more favorable contract terms.

reserve A percentage of royalties due an artist that are withheld by the label until sales are confirmed.

reserve for returns The amount of artist royalties withheld by the label to cover the estimated royalties lost through the return of unsold recordings.

returns Defective and overstock recordings sent back by a retailer to the label.

reverb An electronically produced echo effect with a depth of sound.

reverberation The acoustic echo characteristics of a room.

reversion The point at which a song's copyright returns to the songwriter.

RIAA Recording Industry Association of America. Industry trade association for record labels and manufacturers. Certifies gold and platinum sales status.

rider An attachment to a performance contract that lists specific needs, such as lighting, catering, technical requirements, and so on.

right to work A statute in some states releasing employers from hiring only union labor.

rotation The number of times a given song is played during the course of a radio station's daily or weekly playlist.

royalty A fee paid to writers and performers based upon the sale or licensing of their copyrighted work.

RPM Revolutions Per Minute. The standard measure of speed for disc recordings.

sampling The digital capture of a recorded sound for manipulation and integration into a new recording. *See* digital sampling.

scale wages The minimum payment set by a union for its members' services.

score The orchestration of a musical work broken down into individual parts for specific musical instruments.

self-contained An artist who writes his own material, or a band who does not require additional musicians to perform.

SESAC Society of European Stage Authors and Composers. The smallest of the three royalty collection and performance rights organizations.

share The percentage of the listening public actually listening to a particular radio station within that station's listening area.

shed An outdoor amphitheater.

shelf price The standard price a recording sells at within a given store, as opposed to the sale price.

short form A music video containing a single song.

shortfall Label-supplied tour support that makes up the difference between an artist's per-performance price, and what the artist actually earned per performance.

showcase A short performance where an artist "auditions" for invited industry and label representatives for recording contract consideration.

shrinkage Inventory lost through theft, damage, or other problems.

side A recording of one song. To "cut a side" is to record one song.

signal The electrical pattern representing sound waves.

signal to noise ratio (S/N) The comparison of relative levels of signal (sound waves) to noise (interference) within a sound system.

single A record released with one song recorded on each side.

small rights The right to perform a musical work licensed through a performance rights organization like ASCAP, BMI, or SESAC.

SMPTE Society of Motion Picture and Television Engineers. An industry organization for audio engineers.

soft tickets Admission tickets printed at the time of sale. *See* hard tickets.

sound-alike A new recording made to closely mimic the original recording.

sound recording A recorded audio performance that is captured in a tangible medium, considered an artistic work, and qualifies for copyright protection. *See* phonogram and phonorecord.

SoundScan The company that determines recording sales patterns through collection of UPC information at the point of sale.

sound track (1) the audio portion of a film. (2) A record album containing the musical portions of a film.

source music Music in a film produced by artists pictured onscreen, as in a nightclub scene.

SPARS Society of Professional Recording Services. An industry organization for recording studio owners.

special payments fund A small percentage of a record's list price paid to the AFM by the label. It is distributed annually to recording session musicians based upon the number of sessions each musician played on that year.

sponsored tour A performance tour whose costs are underwritten in full, or in part, by a corporation, in return for advertising consideration.

spot *See* commercial spot.

SRDS Standard Rate and Data Service. Publications that list media outlet information.

SRLP Suggested Retail List Price. *See* MSRP.

staff writer A songwriter exclusively signed to a publishing company.

statutory rate The standard royalty rates set by CARP.

stereo/stereophonic sound Sound recorded on two or more tape tracks and requiring an equal number of speakers to reproduce.

stiff Radio terminology for a record that receives little or no airplay.

stylus/cutting stylus The needle used to play a phonograph record/the needle used to cut the grooves into a lacquer master.

sweetener An overdubbed audio track used to enhance a multitrack tape recording.

sync right Synchronization right. The owner of a copyrighted musical work has the right to apply that work to moving images, such as film or television.

syndication Prepackaged radio or television programming distributed for local broadcast.

synthesizer A keyboard controlled electronic instrument that reproduces a wide variety of sounds and effects.

take A complete version or incomplete attempt of a recorded performance.

technically acceptable The minimum level of technical merit necessary for a recording master to warrant release. Artistically inferior to "commercially acceptable."

tempo The speed of music, expressed in beats per minute.

term The time period that a contract is in force.

termination right The right of an author to regain ownership of transferred copyrights after a specified amount of time.

Top Forty A radio format that broadcasts material drawn primarily from the forty most popular records of each week.

tour support The recoupable label-supplied financial assistance. It allows artists to tour who would otherwise be unable to sell performances at a cost to cover their expenses.

track A recorded single voice or instrument that will ultimately be meshed with others to form a complete orchestration.

tracking The process of recording individual tracks.

trades Publications devoted to industry information, such as *Billboard* and *Pollstar*.

traffic The scheduling and reporting of radio commercial spots for billing purposes.

transcription license Permission granted to reproduce a copyrighted work for a purpose that does not involve sale to the public.

turntable hit A record whose airplay success fails to translate into record sales.

UPC *See* bar code.

venue The location where a live performance is held.

video An electronic medium, combining audio and visual elements, that is stored on videotape or videodisc, broadcast via airwaves, and viewed on television or a monitor.

video jockey A television announcer/host who plays music videos as part of his show.

videodisc Video programming recorded onto disc and played via laser illumination.

videogram A video recording of a visual work made for consumer purchase.

VJ *See* video jockey.

wholesale price The price at which a manufacturer sells a product to a retailer.

work made for hire A work produced by an employee as part of his job duties that is owned and copyrightable by his employer.

wow and flutter Distortion in the speed of recorded sound. Wow is a slow undulation; flutter is a rapid fluctuation.

WTO World Trade Organization. An international trade organization charged with the protection of copyright laws, among other things.

● ● ● ●

ADDITIONAL RESOURCES

Avalon, Moses. *Confessions of a Record Producer: How to Survive the Scams and Shams of the Music Business*. San Francisco: Miller Freeman Books, 1998.

Baskerville, David, Ph.D. *Music Business Handbook & Career Guide*. 6th ed. Thousand Oaks, CA: Sage Publications, 1995.

Berry, Ann Marie Seward. *Visual Intelligence: Perception, Image & Manipulation in Visual Communication*. Albany, NY: State University of New York Press, 1997.

Borwick, John, ed. *Sound Recording Practice*. 4th ed. New York: Oxford University Press, 1994.

Boswell, William R. *Life on the Road, A Beginner's Guide to the Stage Production Touring Industry*. New York: Ginn Press, 1991.

Bowen, Jimmy, and Jim Jerome. *Rough Mix, An Unapologetic Look at the Music Business and How It Got That Way, A Lifetime in the World of Rock, Pop, and Country*. New York: Simon & Schuster, 1997.

Brabec, Jeffrey, and Todd Brabec. *Music, Money and Success*. New York: Schirmer Books, 1994.

Burgess, Richard James. *The Art of Record Production*. New York: Omnibus Press, 1998.

Burlingame, Jon. *Sound & Vision, 60 Years of Motion Picture Soundtracks*. New York: Billboard Books, an imprint of Watson-Guptill Publications, 2000.

Chadbourne, Eugene. *I Hate the Man Who Runs This Bar! The Survival Guide for Real Musicians*. Emeryville, CA: Mix Bookshelf/Mix Books, 1998.

Cusic, Don. *Music in the Market*. Bowling Green, OH: Bowling Green State University Popular Press, 1996.

Dannen, Fredric. *Hit Men*. New York: Vintage Books, 1991.

Davis, Clive. *Clive: Inside the Record Business*. New York: William Morrow & Co., 1975.

Davis, Richard. *Complete Guide to Film Scoring: The Art and Business of Writing Music for Movies and TV*. Boston: Berklee Press, 2000.

Denisoff, Serge R. *Inside MTV*. New Brunswick, NJ: Transaction Publishers, 1990.

Fink, Michael. *Inside the Music Business: Music in Contemporary Life*. New York: Schirmer Books, Macmillan, Inc., 1989.

Fox, Ted. In the Groove: *The People Behind the Music*. New York: St. Martin's Press, 1986.

Frascogna, Xavier M., Jr., H. Lee Hetherington (Contributor). *This Business of Artist Management*. 3rd ed. New York: Watson-Guptill Publishers, 1997.

Frascogna, Xavier M., Jr., and H. Lee Hetherington. *Successful Artist Management, Strategies for Career Development in the Music Business.* New York: Billboard Books, an imprint of Watson-Guptill Publications, 1990.

Gibson, David. *The Art of Mixing: A Visual Guide to Recording, Engineering, and Production.* George Petersen, ed. Emeryville, CA: Mix Bookshelf/Mix Books, 1997.

Glatt, John. *Rage & Roll: Bill Graham and the Selling of Rock.* Secaucus, NJ: A Birch Lane Press Book published by Carol Publishing Group 1993.

Graham, Bill. *Bill Graham Presents: My Life Inside Rock and Out.* New York: Doubleday, 1992.

Hall, Charles W., and Frederic J. Taylor. *Marketing in the Music Industry.* New York: Simon & Schuster Custom Publishing, 1996.

Halloran, Mark, Esq., comp. and ed. *The Musician's Business & Legal Guide.* 2nd ed. A Presentation of the Beverly Hills Bar Association Committee for the Arts. Upper Saddle River, NJ: Prentice-Hall, Inc., Simon & Schuster, 1996.

Heil, Bob. *Practical Guide for Concert Sound.* Everyville, CA: Mix Bookshelf/Mix Books, 1999.

Huber, David Miles. *Modern Recording Techniques.* 4th ed. Woburn, MA: Focal Press, an imprint of Butterworth-Heinemann, 1997.

Hustwit, Gary. *Releasing An Independent Record, How to Successfully Start & Run Your Own Record Label in the 1990s.* 5th ed. San Diego: Rockpress Publishing, Co., 1995.

Kimpel, Dan. *Networking in the Music Business.* Emeryville, CA: Mix Books, 2000.

King, Tom, and Thomas R. King. *The Operator: David Geffen Builds, Buys, and Sells the New Hollywood.* New York: Random House, 2000.

Kohn, Al, and Bob Kohn. *The Art of Music Licensing.* 2nd ed. Upper Saddle River, NJ: Prentice Hall Law and Business, 1996.

Koller, Fred. *How to Pitch & Promote Your Songs.* New York: Allworth Press, 1996.

Krasilovsky, M. William, and Sidney Shemel. *This Business of Music, A Practical Guide to the Music Industry for Publishers, Writers, Record Companies, Producers, Artists, Agents.* 7th ed. New York: Billboard Books, an imprint of Watson-Guptill Publications, 1995.

Krasilovsky, M. William, Sidney Shemel, and John Gross. *This Business of Music: The Definitive Guide to the Music Industry.* 8th ed. New York: Billboard Books, an imprint of Watson-Guptill Publications, 2000.

Krasilovsky, M. William, and Sidney Shemel. *More About This Business of Music.* Lee Zhito, ed. New York: Billboard Books, an imprint of Watson-Guptill Publications, 1994.

Lathrop, Tad, and Jim Pettigrew, Jr. *This Business of Music Marketing and Promotion.*

New York: Billboard Books, an imprint of Watson-Guptill Publications, 1999.

Mandell, Jim. *The Studio Business Book, A Guide to Professional Recording Studios, Business & Management*. Emeryville, CA: Mix Books, 1995.

Mansfield, Richard. Studio Basics, *What You Should Know Before Entering the Recording Studio*. New York: Billboard Books, an imprint of Watson-Guptill Publications, 1998.

Martin, George, ed. *Making Music, The Guide to Writing, Performing & Recording*. New York: William Morrow & Company, 1983.

Massey, Howard. *Behind the Glass: Top Record Producers Tell How They Craft the Hits*. San Francisco: Miller Freeman Books, 2000.

McDonald, Jack. *Handbook of Radio Publicity & Promotion*. New York: McGraw-Hill, 1990.

McLeish, Robert. *The Technique of Radio Promotion*. 2nd ed. Woburn, MA: Focal Press, an imprint of Butterworth-Heinemann, 1988.

Miller, Lisa Anne, and Mark Northam. *Film and Television Composer's Resource Guide: The Complete Guide to Organizing and Building Your Business*. Milwaukee: Hal Leonard Publishing Corporation, 1998.

Monaco, James. *The Dictionary of New Media, The New Digital World of Video, Audio, and Print*. New York: Harbor Electronic Publishing, 1999.

Moody, James L. *Concert Lighting Techniques, Art & Business*. Woburn, MA: Focal Press, an imprint of Butterworth-Heinemann, 1989.

Morgan, Bradley. *Radio & Television Career Directory: A Practical One Stop Guide to Getting a Job in Public Relations*. Newton, MA: Gale Research, 1993.

Olim, Jason, Matthew Olim, and Peter Kent. *The CDNow Story: Rags to Riches on the Internet*. Lakewood, CO: Top Floor Publishing, 1999.

Olsen, Eric, Paula Verna, and Carlo Wolff. *The Encyclopedia of Record Producers*. New York: Billboard Books, an imprint of Watson-Guptill Publications, 1999.

Owens, Joe. *Welcome to the Jungle, A Practical Guide to Music Business*. New York: Harper Perennial, Harper Collins Publishers, 1992.

Passman, Donald S. *All You Need to Know About the Music Business*. rev. ed.: New York: Simon & Schuster, 2000.

Pettigrew, Jim. *The Billboard Guide to Music Publishing*. New York: Billboard Books, an imprint of Watson-Guptill Publications, 1997.

Pinskey, Raleigh. *The Zen of Hype: An Insider's Guide to the Publicity Game*. Secaucus, NJ: Carol Publishing Group, 1991.

Poe, Randy. *Music Publishing: A Songwriter's Guide*. Cincinnati: Writer's Digest Books, 1997.

Rachlin, Harvey. *The Encyclopedia of Music Business*. New York: Harper & Row Publishing, 1981.

Robertson, Michael and Ron Simpson. *The Official MP3.com Guide to MP3*. San Diego: MP3.com Publishing, 1999.

Schultz, Barbara. ed. *Music Producers, Conversations with Today's Top Hitmakers*. Emeryville, CA: Mix Books, 2000.

Shagan, Rena. *Booking & Tour Management for the Performing Arts*. New York: Allworth Press, 1996.

Singular, Stephen. *The Rise and Rise of David Geffen*. Secaucus, NJ: Carol Publishing Group, 1997.

Soifer, Rosanne. *Music in Video Production*. White Plains, NY: Knowledge Industry Publications, Inc., 1991.

Stone, Al. *Jingles, How to Write, Produce & Sell Commercial Music*. Cincinnati: Writer's Digest Books, 1990.

Summers, Jodi. *Moving Up in the Music Business*. New York: Allworth Press, 2000.

Underhill, Rod. *Complete Idiot's Guide to Music on the Internet with Mp3: Music on the Internet*. Indianapolis: Que, A Macmillan USA Imprint, 2000.

Vasey, John. *Concert Sound and Lighting Systems*. Woburn, MA: Focal Press, an imprint of Butterworth-Heinemann, 1989.

Vasey, John. *Concert Tour Production Management: How to Take Your Show on the Road*. Woburn, MA: Focal Press, an imprint of Butterworth-Heinemann, 1997.

Wilson, Lee. *Making It in the Music Business: A Business & Legal Guide for Songwriters & Performers*. New York: Allworth Press, 1999.

Wadhams, Wayne. *Dictionary of Music Production & Engineering Terminology*. New York: Schirmer Books, 1987.

Wadhams, Wayne. *Sound Advice, The Musician's Guide to the Recording Industry*. New York: Schirmer Books, 1990.

● ● ● ●

ACKNOWLEDGMENTS

I am honored and privileged to have heard and shared the stories of the individuals profiled in this book.

Thank you to those who have influenced my career in music: Rick Shipp for being the best boss I ever worked for and who I grew to appreciate more long after I was working elsewhere; Evelyn Shriver for helping me get the job as Randy's agent at Lib Hatcher Agency that enabled me to move to Nashville; Alex Cooley for the gift of $200 on my first trip to Nashville; and Bill Bachand, Barbara Hubbard, and Jon Stoll for kindness and plane tickets when I was an agent wannabe; Pat Higdon for teaching me about publishing and introducing me to Shawn Camp; Shawn Camp and Bob Romeo for the opportunity to manage; Barklie Griggs and Art Ford for encouragement and sharing of knowledge that helped me place songs in film and television; Vince Gill, Jann Browne, Foster & Lloyd, McBride & The Ride, and Restless Heart, who I worked for as an agent and spent time with on the road; songwriters Matt Barnes, Jann Browne, Robert Hart, Tommy Lee James, and Wil Nance, who I worked with and signed to publishing deals. To Barbara Orbison for the five wonderful years I worked for you that enabled me to meet many of the people profiled in this book, afforded me the opportunity to travel around the world, expanded my knowledge of the industry, and allowed me to work on extraordinary projects of which I will be forever proud.

Thanks to Pat Hilliard, publisher of *Nashville Woman* magazine, who allowed me to write "It All Begins With the Song," an article that profiled Renee Bell, Stephanie Cox, and Stephanie Smith (whom I also thank for their stories), which became the springboard for this book. Thanks to my assistant Debbie Gurney who typed my transcriptions, the Brentwood Library, Center for Popular Music at MTSU.

Special thanks to my agent and friend Deidre Knight of the Knight Agency, who poked and prodded me to write a book about the music industry, and for her continued support and creativity. (You are a gift from God and I treasure you in my life.) Thanks to my editor at Barron's Educational Series, Wendy Sleppin, for her guidance and encouragement in writing this book. Thanks to Darrell Buono, my editor on the second edition. Thanks to Steve Matteo, Barron's Publicity Manager, for his energy and excitement.

Thank you to my family for their love and support: Charles and Luana Peck, Jim and Linda Peck, Dustin Peck, Stacy Peck Norton, Bob and Earlene Crouch, Jody and Stephen Williams, Rob and Georgia Crouch, Julie and David Ashby, Kevin, Dani, Bryan, and Cami Crouch. My son, Cory Crouch, whom I love and am so proud of. I could not have completed this book without my husband, best friend, and love, Kevin, who is a gifted writer and editor, and my first line of defense. Above all, I am grateful for my Heavenly Father and Savior Jesus Christ for making all things possible.

INDEX